ROOF OF AFRICA

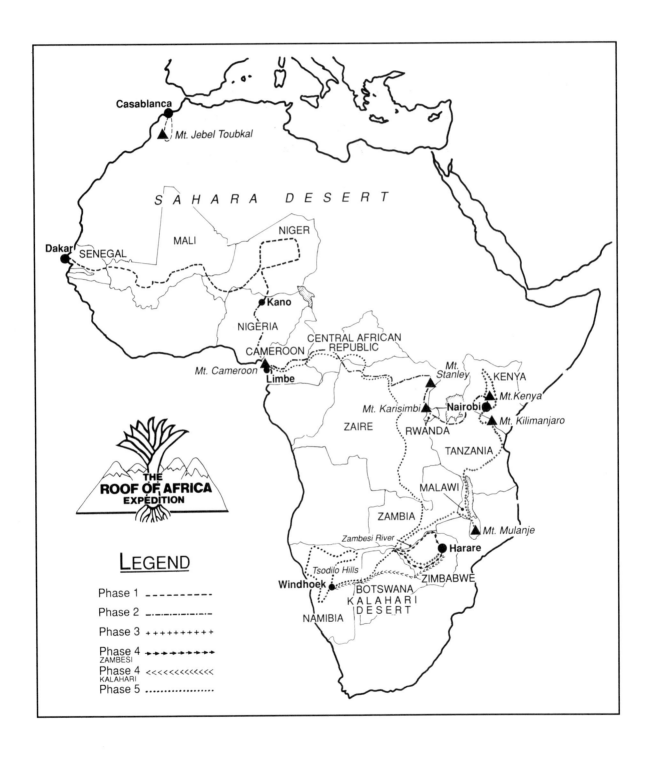

ROOF OF AFRICA

JOHN WARBURTON-LEE

SWAN·HILL
PRESS

DEDICATION
To the patients and staff of The Midlands Centre for Spinal Injuries

Copyright © 1992 by John Warburton-Lee

First published in the UK in 1992 by Swan Hill Press
an imprint of Airlife Publishing Ltd.

British Library Cataloguing in Publication Data
A catalogue record for this book is available from the British Library

   ISBN 1 85310 330 6

Printed by Livesey Ltd., Shrewsbury.

Swan Hill Press
An imprint of Airlife Publishing Ltd.
101 Longden Road, Shrewsbury SY3 9EB, England

Contents

KENSINGTON PALACE

When I heard that one of the young officers in my Regiment had been seriously injured as a result of a mountaineering accident I sent him my commiserations and a bottle of whisky. I did not anticipate at the time that, two and a half years later, the same officer would be leading a team of Welsh Guardsmen into the wilds of Africa on a 40,000 mile expedition.

I had the chance of meeting the team during their journey through Cameroon in 1990 and found them indefatigable, infectiously enthusiastic and relishing the challenges that lay ahead.

It is hard to believe that teams of novices, relying more on determination, common sense and a good measure of soldier's humour than on technical expertise, emerged unscathed from such a catalogue of hair-raising escapades. Their journey through desert and jungle provides a fascinating glimpse of the full spectrum of African life far removed from our everyday experience of first world civilisation.

It is the pursuit of adventures such as these in peace time which helps to make our young servicemen the effective force on which we all rely in war. I warmly congratulate the teams on the success of their adventure.

Acknowledgements

There are so many individuals and organisations without whom this expedition would never have come about that it is hard to know where to start.

First of all I should like to thank the army, the Welsh Guards and in particular all of the Commanding Officers under whom I have served for supporting, in some cases bravely, my various schemes.

Secondly, I extend the most grateful thanks of all of the team to the governments of Morocco, Senegal, Mali, Niger, Nigeria, Cameroon, Central African Republic, Zaire, Rwanda, Tanzania, Kenya, Malawi, Zambia, Zimbabwe, Botswana, and Namibia for allowing us to visit their countries and derive the tremendous benefits and pleasures of exploring, adventuring and observing in such fantastic environments.

Thirdly, again on behalf of the team, I should like to thank all of our sponsors for their incredibly generous support: Land Rover Ltd, ICI Pharmaceuticals, UKWAL Shipping, Church of England Services Trust, Fraser Trust, Dunhill Trust, Nuffield Trust, Nikon UK, Joe's Basement, Abercrombie and Kent, British American Tobacco, Lonrho, Artix Ltd, Sportlite Leisure Ltd, W L Gore & Associates UK Ltd, Sprayway, Haymarket Publishing, Thomas R Miller & Sons Insurance, ML Holdings, Robert Lewis Partnership, Broadland Properties, David Evers Ltd, Foster Homes Ltd, Fenchurch Group Services, Ferranti, Oxford Underwriting Agency Ltd, Pyrhana Mouldings, Avon Inflatables Ltd, Western Estates Ltd, McGraw Hill Information Services Ltd, Haverhill Generators, Intraphoto Ltd, Biro Bic Ltd, Casio Electronics, Ilford, BCB International Ltd, Russell Reynolds & Associates Ltd, Printique, Mountain Equipment Ltd, Dymac Systems, DanAir, Mona Safety Products, Cotswold Camping, Asolo, Zenith Data Systems, Francis Barker & Son, John Bartholomew & Son Ltd, Smith, Kline and French, Bull HN Information Services Ltd, David Holman & Co, Mountain Range, Belzona Ltd, UTA French Airlines, May and Baker Pharmaceuticals, Sony UK, Siebe Plc, Filfit Sports, Randle Cooke & Associates, Sir Carol Mather, BP Cameroon, Cooper Motors (Kenya) Ltd, Tusker Breweries (Kenya), GEC Plessey (Kenya), House of Mangi (Kenya), Minet ICDC Insurance Brokers (Kenya), International Distillers (Kenya) Ltd, ICI Malawi Ltd, Malawi Distillers Ltd, Cadbury Schweppes (Zambia) Ltd, Shearwater Safaris (Zimbabwe) Ltd, Kingdom Safaris Zimbabwe, Fothergill Island Safaris Zimbabwe, AWD Bedford Zimbabwe, Leyland Zimbabwe Ltd, Castle Printers London Ltd.

On a personal note I would like to extend my sincere gratitude to all of those many individuals who provided support, advice, help, encouragement or just a reviving glass of whisky at any stage during the planning or execution of the expedition. In particular:

In Britain: Dr El Masri, Bob Lewis, Lieutenant General Sir Charles Guthrie, Major General Simon Cooper, Brigadier Christopher Drewry, Colonel Paul Belcher, Lieutenant Colonel Reddy Watt, Major Tony Davies, Major Tony Bowen, Major Ray Evans, Captain Chris Klein, Colonel Frank Essen, Lieutenant Colonel John Wyatt, Major Frances Canham, Mrs Cathy Davenport, Brigadier Richard Ohlenschlarger, Major Ken Mullins and the staff of RAOC Thatcham, Major Jeremy Turner-Bridger, Jill Parkin, Simon Weston, Richard Jarman and all of the team at Weston Spirit, Roger Embley, Bob Gibson and the driving instructors from Land Rover Ltd, Colonel Sir John Miller, Martin Thompson, Nigel Massey, Don Neighbour, Jane Davis, Amber Hall and all at Sloane Hospital Travel, David Mason, Oliver Shepard, Anthony Cazalet, Huw Bartle-Jones, Gypsy Joe and all at Joe's Basement, Les Baynham, Malcolm Fowler, Nancy Fouts, Mike Slater and the editing team at HTV, Tim Wakefield.

In Africa: Jean Michel and the staffs of USIMA throughout West Africa, Hamma Akano, Lieutenant Colonel Peter and Diana Cable, the staff of the British Consulate Kaduna, Lieutenant Colonel Simon and Suzy Fordham, Dick and Diana Howe, Jonathon and Vicky Dunlop, the staff of BASTOS Cameroon, the managers of the many BAT depots across Zaire, François Senneque, Patrick Ingles, Colonel Henry Hugh-Smith, Lieutenant Colonel Norman West and all the staff BATLSK, David and Richard Markham, Bongo Woodley, Chris and Fran Moore, Tony Hicks, the members of the Mulanje Club, Major Ted Ricketts, Paddy Fleming, Sir Nicholas and Lady Dee Powell, Simon Rhodes and all at Abercrombie and Kent Zimbabwe, BMATT Zimbabwe, Paul Connolly and all of the Shearwater guides, Rob and Dee Shattock, Liz and Bud Whittaker, BMATT Namibia, Laurie Davis.

Top marks for perseverance in the face of insuperable odds go to Caroline Dewergifosse and Caroline Hill Trevor for typing up my scribbled diaries, my sister Louisa Lawson for typing this manuscript, Christopher Woodhead my agent for frequent reassurance and advice during the writing and John Beaton and Swan Hill Press for believing in it.

Finally a very special thank you to Captain Richard Gaffney, Captain Matthew Roberts, Company Sergeant Major Allen Bennett, Tetta Nicholls and Captain Alasdair Johnstone for seeing it through and making it all work.

To all those above and everyone else who gave their time, effort and energy to make this expedition a success thank you and I hope that you will be there the next time.

Beginnings

In front I could see the metal pyramid that marked the summit, perched on a spur to the right of the main ridge. In between us and this, the highest point in North Africa was a knife-edge ridge, lightly corniced, with a spectacular drop, on our right, 3,000 feet down to the valley floor. I looked around the rest of the team to see how they were getting on. Several were suffering the effects of altitude; pounding headaches and nausea. Others looked concerned by the exposure of our situation; that sensation of vulnerability so often experienced by climbers high on remote mountain faces. On the whole the team was coping well particularly as it almost exclusively consisted of novices.

Twelve of us had left England on 14 January and flown to Casablanca. Surrendering ourselves to the mercies of the Moroccan public transport system we had taken a bus into the city and then caught a night train bound for Marrakech. For most of the five-hour, 150-mile journey everyone had tried to grab what sleep they could, huddled into their duvet jackets. Arriving at 5.30am we stiffly shouldered our packs and walked through the largely deserted streets towards the bus station. We passed the occasional Berber street cleaner or tradesman clad in distinctive long woollen robes with large pointed hoods raised against the morning chill. After a two-hour wait and endless cups of strong black coffee we boarded a local bus for Asni. We passed through flat dusty wastelands where the only cultivation was supported by a lattice-work of irrigation ditches. As the sun rose we caught our first glimpse of the High Atlas mountains laid out before us. Thirty miles distant through the haze the lofty peaks appeared sugar-coated under their mantle of snow. Having arrived in Asni I went to find a vehicle to carry us the last 6 miles to the road head at Imlil whilst the others were besieged by vendors each claiming to sell the Mahdi's original sword. After some protracted haggling, with all of the usual offer, counter-offer and exaggerated theatricals that accompany any purchase or financial arrangement in Africa we piled into the back of a small pick-up truck. Despite traces of ice on the puddles it was warm enough to wear just a T-shirt as we bumped our way along the road to the valley base.

Imlil is a loose collection of small mud-built houses and stores, the latter offering only the barest of essentials, set around meandering dusty alleys through which barefooted children, donkeys and a variety of poultry roamed at will. We were deposited with all of our kit in the centre of the village. The headman approached us offering accommodation for the night and when he saw that we were intent on setting off up the mountain he tried to rent donkeys for us to carry our loads. Ever mindful that we had set out considerably short of our expedition budget and not wanting to set a precedent for always taking the easy option, I refused. Little did I realise how far in the opposite direction we were about to go. We shouldered our packs, having clipped day sacks, helmets, boots and ropes to the outside and set out laden like refugees, to the amazed expressions of the locals. We had become the focal point of attention and as we set off we were accompanied by a retinue of Berber tribesmen riding donkeys. The first stage of the walk ascended steeply following a winding trail up through deciduous woodland. We sweated profusely under the unfamiliar weight of our packs. Laden with technical climbing equipment, ropes, camping equipment, spare clothing and ten days' rations, each man's pack weighed eighty to ninety pounds. Struggling along under the watchful gaze of the Berbers with their frequent offers of help did nothing for morale. However, aside of a few soldierly oaths which, if translated would have done nothing to foster British-Berber relations, everyone settled in to their own pace.

As the path levelled out along the valley I was able to look around and take in the scenery. The land was terraced and partitioned by low drystone walls. Women and children were tilling the earth by hand. They had curiously Mongolian features with slightly slanted eyes, round faces and straight, dark hair. We passed a couple of hill villages, closely packed mazes of flat-roofed mud buildings clinging like beehives to the steep valley walls. After several miles we stopped beside a stream for the night. Reluctant stoves were urged into action and we sampled the dubious delights of our first meal of freeze-dried rations. As the sun went down the temperature dropped sharply so we clambered into our new sleeping bags and bivvi bags for the long night.

In the morning, after a breakfast of instant porridge and hot chocolate we continued on our way. It took some time for our legs to loosen off from the first day's stiffness and our progress was slow. The further we went the harder the track became as it twisted its way up the valley. After two hours we reached the last village, Chamharouch, which consisted of ten to fifteen brick buildings nestling into a small boulder-strewn bowl. A tiny mosque had been carved out of the centre of the largest of these boulders. Beyond the village the track wended its way up the valley for mile after mile. Shortly we reached the snow line and trudged on through ever deeper snow. As the straps of our rucksacks bit into our shoulders we began to feel the weight of our loads. In my mind, I started questioning whether I really wanted to be doing this when I could be comfortably ensconced with a glass of whisky in front of the television in the warmth of my flat in London but thinking back the start of every trip was like this. It was only once all of those generally unused muscles had been found and tightened up that you could enjoy the great feeling of confidence engendered by physical fitness.

I began to get concerned that we should reach the hut before dark. The prospect of a bivouac on the snow-covered rocks was fairly unappealing. The path was icy and treacherous so we were using our ice axes as an aid. On and on we went, each in our own misery, until just at dusk we spotted the hut in the distance. I increased the pace worried that if the front runners didn't reach the hut before nightfall we would miss it in the dark. Ridge followed ridge but the hut didn't seem to get any closer. I was aware that everyone was tired, some nearing their physical limits, but I felt that the benefits of reaching a comfortable base justified pressing on. I was also aware that we hadn't been drinking enough and that dehydration was contributing to the exhaustion. The front group forged on, becoming smaller as individuals couldn't keep up. We stopped more and more frequently, bent over to take the weight off our shoulders and rest our legs. I was vaguely worried by Dr El Masri's parting shot: 'John, try not to carry heavy weights more often than you need to. It may not hurt you now but it will catch up with you later in life.' By the end it was pitch dark. We stumbled and slipped on the icy patches. The final slope seemed to go on forever. I must have stopped three or four times on the last hundred yards.

Inside the hut was warm. I stood blinking in the light of the storm lamp and threw off my pack. I tore into a ration pack and stuffed myself with biscuits, jam and chocolate whilst waiting for the water to boil on the gas stove. The first brew made the whole walk worthwhile. We took it in turns to stand outside waving a torch to guide the others home whilst the other first arrivals prepared copious hot drinks and food. I felt desperately sorry for those who were still outside battling their way on. At the back, far behind everyone else a small group were helping LSgt Rowlands. He had pulled a muscle in his back early in the day and had been suffering ever since. Added to that he was the oldest man in the group by a full ten years. A few of us went back down the last slope to meet them. As I suspected they had been struggling. LSgt Rowlands had collapsed and they had had to take his pack off him and carry it on top of their own — a tremendous achievement and a great example of the way that soldiers help each other in the face of adversity. LSgt Rowlands was clearly in pain and exhausted. As he reached the hut he threw up with the effort. Once inside he took some time to settle but plenty of hot sweet tea revived him. It had been a tough initiation for a group of complete novices and so far we were still only at the base of our objective.

Over the next few days we made forays up the valley, wading through deep, fresh snow to explore some of the cols, ridges and side valleys. The recent fall of snow, laid like a thick carpet, deadened any sound and heightened the virginal feel and tranquillity of the mountains. In contrast the sharp ridges and high peaks towering above us seemed to shout a challenge. Bob Finch and I were the only two members of the group with any mountaineering experience so we started instructing the basic principles of winter mountaineering. People had to be shown how to strap on their crampons and then walk in them without snagging the sharp points into their other leg or foot. We practised the use of ice axes as a walking aid, to cut steps, to climb and to act as a brake during a fall. We set up rope-belays and different forms of snow-anchor. We dug emergency snow caves so that, should we ever get caught out, we could quickly burrow into the snow and create a safe shelter from a storm. After a hesitant beginning the soldiers threw themselves at it and were soon hurling themselves down sheer slopes, yodelling as they went, to practise their newly learnt ice-axe arrests. They revelled in the physical exertion and as always it was accompanied by a liberal measure of bawdy humour. In the evenings we returned to the spartan hut. There we would force down meals of rehydrated beef and vegetable hotpot or shepherd's pie followed by indescribably sweet custard and banana or strawberry and apple mush. After supper people would read, write their diaries or chat. The hut had the insulation qualities of a deep freeze. It was never long before we all surrendered to the draw of our sleeping bags.

One day Bob took 2Lt Harry Lloyd, LCpl Williams and Guardsman Paul, who had shown themselves to be the strongest amongst the group, to attempt the second summit in the range, Ouanoukrim. They set off early taking advantage of the crisp morning conditions to make quick headway up the valley. Having reached the col at the top they turned right onto a sharply rising ridge. Immediately they were exposed to freezing winds that buffeted them forcefully. I followed up the valley with the remainder of the team later on and met them coming down. They had had to turn back before making the summit. The conditions had become appalling with ferocious winds and cold so intense that they had lost feeling in their hands and feet. LCpl Williams hadn't fully acclimatised to the altitude and had become giddy and disorientated. As a result Bob had wisely decided to put him on a rope and lead him down. They all looked shocked by their experience. Back at the hut Matthew examined each of them. Harry's big toe had cracked in the cold and Guardsman Paul had frostnip on one of his. LCpl Williams was still suffering mild altitude sickness which was affecting his breathing.

When the day of our summit attempt dawned it was cold but clear. This was what we had come to climb: the first of our seven mountain objectives around Africa and the only one for this group. We got up, lit the stoves, had breakfast and prepared our flasks. We then packed harnesses, ropes, ice axes and crampons, and spare clothing into our packs and set off. An imposingly steep snow slope rose behind the hut. We made our way slowly up, zig-zagging all the while. Our breath froze in the icy morning air. The angle of ascent was relentless. Our calves and thighs burned with the effort. After two hours we crested the rise. The hut lay far below us. We were at the front of a gently rising hanging valley with ridges in a horseshoe all around. To attain the summit ridge we had to make our way to the head of the valley hugging the right-hand side to keep out of the now intense sun. At the far end another steep snow slope with patches of icy scree led up to the summit ridge running right to left across us. A number of the men were feeling the altitude; we were now over 12,000 feet and some were complaining of headaches and nausea. LSgt Rowlands and Cpl Scholes, in particular, seemed to be struggling. I felt strong having started slowly and now with our first goal within reach I seemed to be bubbling with energy.

I could see the weather beginning to close in on us. Towers of cumulus were joining up and advancing in ranks like some hostile army. I longed to race ahead and grab some photographs from the summit of the surrounding High Atlas Range but then we hit a huge patch of bare ice. LSgt Rowlands had no crampons — somehow they had got lost. The angle was intimidating and at the bottom there was no safe run out should anyone fall. Bob cut steps for those who were still not confident in their crampons. LSgt Rowlands clearly wasn't going to make it past this barrier so I climbed above, set up a belay, and then brought him up on a tight rope. He looked exhausted as his boots scrabbled to gain hold on the ice. He was unhappy with the exposure so I kept him on a short rope as we climbed up to the sensational knife-edge ridge leading to the summit. We edged our way across and then there, in front, was the small snow-covered spur and a hundred yards further on the metal pyramid that marked the summit. LSgt Rowlands was given the honour of reaching the summit first. Not a bad effort for a forty-one-year-old novice who was now over four times higher than Snowdon — his previous high point.

As the others scrambled around taking the ritual summit photos I sat looking over the High Atlas Range and beyond through the haze into the Sahara. It was a strange feeling to be sitting in the snow, huddled into my duvet jacket, yet gazing at one of the hottest wastes on earth. I thought back to the summer of 1987, lying in the Spinal Injuries' Unit of The Robert Jones and Agnes Hunt Orthopaedic Hospital near Oswestry. I had fallen 150 feet whilst rock climbing in Snowdonia. On rejoining contact with the earth I had smashed two vertebrae in my spine, broken a collar bone and some ribs and both of my lungs had collapsed. The present had been desperate and the future had looked bleak. My morale hit rock bottom when my mother, in an attempt to reassure me, said, 'It's all right darling, you are going to walk again.' I had never considered that I wouldn't walk. I wasn't interested in walking; I wanted to run, climb, canoe, parachute and all the other crazy things that I enjoyed. My entire way of life as a soldier in the Welsh Guards depended on physical fitness. Undeniably I was lucky not to have been killed or paralysed by the fall. It must have seemed terribly self-indulgent to all those around me, as I wallowed in a slough of self-pity and despair, when most of them were faced with never being able to walk again.

And then there was a ray of hope. A friend of mine from the regiment, Rupert Cockcroft, came to visit me. We chatted about regimental news and mutual friends and then he dropped a bombshell into the conversation. There was talk in the Mess of the principle of a large expedition in 1990 to celebrate the regiment's Seventy-Fifth Anniversary. However no one had, as yet, come up with any ideas. I didn't take in anything else that he said to me. Here was a straw to cling to. For days after he had gone I lay in bed turning the idea over and over in my mind. Unable to do anything but lie flat and let nature take its healing course I had plenty of time to think and I certainly wasn't short of ideas. It became a release — a way of escaping from the tedium of lying for day after day unable to sit up for any reason, avoiding the harsh question of what I was going to do with my life when I got out of hospital.

The Spinal Injuries' Unit was a place of great bravery in the face of, at times, almost overwhelming personal despair. The staff were brilliant and the patients got by on guts and black humour. The majority of patients left after six months when they were capable of looking after themselves. By this stage they were heartily bored of the ward and would roar around using the new found mobility provided by their wheelchairs to amuse themselves by causing general havoc. Thus it was that when I left, tottering rather unsteadily under the weight of a plaster cast that bound me rigid from my waist to my shoulders, and supported by a nurse on either side, I did so with the Superman logo emblazoned across my chest courtesy of the wheelchair chapter of the Hell's Angels.

After a couple of months I had learned to cope with life in my unwelcome suit of armour including putting on my socks using a mechanical claw on the end of a long stick. I returned to the regiment in

Germany on sedentary duties. There seemed no time like the present so I asked for an interview with the Commanding Officer to reveal my plan. I had joined the army, rather arrogantly telling my selectors that I wanted to live a life of adventure and expeditions having never done anything particularly adventurous to justify these claims. I had had a lucky break shortly after being commissioned and was posted to the Infantry Junior Leaders Battalion as an adventure training instructor. There, I spent a year trying to conceal from the junior soldiers, whom I taught, that as far as heights were concerned I was just as afraid as they were. Slowly I gained in confidence and competence, fortunately avoiding any serious mishap. By the end of this period the adventure training bug had bitten deep. Since then I had led or been on a variety of small expeditions: trekking in Norway, Alpine mountaineering in Switzerland and Austria and canoeing and climbing in the Canadian Rockies. At the time of my accident I was planning another small expedition to climb Mont Blanc.

I enjoyed my climbing as an enthusiastic amateur, preferring the travel, variety and isolation offered by general mountaineering to clinging onto bleak rock faces by my finger-nails amidst hordes of Lycra-tights-clad human flies who were inclined to make my bravest leads look tiresomely simple.

At the time of my fall I had reached a crossroads. With time and experience my standard had improved and I was looking for greater challenges. I had recently applied for a position as a novice climber on a large expedition to climb Shishapangma in the Himalayas, one of the fourteen peaks in the world above 26,000 feet. Despite this I rather baulked at the idea of serving a long apprenticeship on large scale expeditions run in true military style by a plethora of colonels and brigadiers. To me adventure training was about getting away from the rigid rules governing service life and having the freedom to think, plan and do as I pleased. I now saw 1990 as the long awaited opportunity to set up a major expedition on my own terms. I wanted the expedition to be open to the average man in the regiment, regardless of rank, who wouldn't necessarily have done any significant amount of adventure training before. I wanted to involve as many people as possible and intended to do this by changing teams over. This had the two-fold advantages of giving me the time to undertake a broad variety of challenges and also having longer on expedition. Thus the aims had to be suitable for novice expeditioners; challenging, demanding and potentially dangerous but not requiring vast amounts of technical expertise or experience. In short I was looking for an adventure. I juggled many different ideas from trekking in the Himalayas, or climbing peaks along the length of the Rockies to the rather ambitious concept of climbing the highest peak of every country in the Commonwealth. However, I finally settled on Africa: specifically to go to any country in Africa with a mountain over 10,000 feet and climb the highest peak in each of those countries. To my eyes it had everything: jungles, deserts, mountains and plains, abundant wildlife and fascinating tribes. When I had left school, I had spent a year travelling around Africa with a rucksack on my back. As for so many people before me the sights, sounds and smells of the Dark Continent left a lasting impression.

To my Commanding Officer the prospect was slightly different. He was clearly confronted by a lunatic who, whilst still trussed in a suit of plaster of Paris, was propounding that he should be allowed to formulate a plan of Machiavellian proportions to imperil platoons of innocent Welsh Guardsmen, all in the name of adventure. To his eternal credit he neither burst out laughing nor had me arrested on grounds of insanity. Instead he took the rather more sanguine view that, as I was most likely to be invalided out of the army, by allowing me to continue with my scheming he would be keeping me occupied and out of further mischief. I left the interview fully aware that I had a lot to prove before either I, as a soldier, or my plan would be taken seriously. In addition the grandiose nature of the plan had led to considerable and obvious suspicion from the Commanding Officer.

At the beginning of 1988 I returned to England to begin a series of visits to RAF Headley Court, the Services' residential physiotherapy and rehabilitation centre near Epsom. I was allocated to a group with the unprepossessing name of Early Spines. After a week of light mobility exercises, and still not strong enough to do even a single press-up, I was sent on leave for a month to give me more time to develop my strength. I had a blissful holiday out in Zimbabwe with my girlfriend. She had to leave early so to fill in time I went on a canoe safari on the lower Zambesi. I had no business to be canoeing and the doctors would have been horrified had they known. However I fell in love with the Zambesi valley and resolved to come back and canoe more of it in the future.

Back in England I returned to Headley Court for another fortnight of gentle exercises, physiotherapy, radiotherapy, sessions in the soporific hydro pool and short walks around the ornamental gardens. I was sent back to the regiment for a couple of months and then returned at the beginning of the summer for a four-month spell. My treatment now started in earnest. Headley Court, like the Oswestry Hospital, had a special atmosphere best typified by an incident that occurred early during my time there: I arrived one morning just before the normal opening session of aerobics which all the patients, regardless of their injury or state of fitness, did together. In the gym a large group had gathered in a circle, in the centre of which were a Ghurka and a British soldier having a mock boxing match. The other patients were laughing and shouting encouragement as they shadow boxed their way through their own championship bout with one and a half arms between them. With an atmosphere like that, particularly set by junior ranks, you couldn't give anything but your best effort. At times, following day after day of repetitive exercises it seemed as if I was getting nowhere but all of the time I knew why I wanted to get better; the expedition had become the focal point of my recovery. I was determined to make it work.

All the while in my spare time I was continuing to research and plan the expedition. This began with visits to the libraries of the Royal Geographical Society and Alpine Club and then a meeting with Major Frances Canham, the major domo of the hugely overworked and understaffed department of the Ministry of Defence responsible for the clearance and overseeing of all army expeditions. Frances was to become an enthusiastic supporter of the project but at this initial meeting she appeared most disapproving. After I had carpeted her office with an enormous map covered in various hieroglyphics and expounded my plan she regarded me with deep suspicion. She was quite used to young officers cluttering up her office with wild-assed ideas which were frequently doomed to failure. She fired questions back — Did I have any idea of the implications of trying to set up an expedition on this scale? Did I understand the problems associated with obtaining political clearance for a British Military expedition to visit all of these African countries? Hadn't I heard of the instability of the governments in many of the regions that I wished to transit? What did I think it was all going to cost? I shudder at the memory of answering sagely that, yes, I quite understood that it would be difficult but I knew what I was letting myself in for and proffering the figure of £20,000 as the first stab at a budget (a true fantasy if ever there was one).

I left with her words of caution ringing in my ears and the suggestion that if I was to get a Royal Patron then it just might work. With that last statement she thought that she had thrown down a challenge which I wouldn't be able to meet and thereby put an end to this crazy project which could surely only cause a great deal of work and embarrassment when it failed.

Royal Patrons were rather out of my league but I managed to persuade the Commanding Officer to write to His Royal Highness The Prince of Wales, who is also Colonel of the Regiment, to ask whether he would be prepared to be Patron of the expedition. Whilst I waited what felt like forever for the reply, life at Headley Court continued. I progressed slowly initially but having narrowly avoided being given a medical discharge by an overly pessimistic RAF doctor, I went on to the 'lates' group. There we were no longer treated for our specific injuries but concentrated on building up physical fitness. After lazy periods relaxing in the hydro pool or receiving electrical massage the new regime of circuit training and runs came as a rude awakening. However the training worked and by the time that I left I could comfortably run for three miles with a rucksack full of medicine balls through the fields behind the Chessington Adventure Park. I returned to the regiment reasonably fit, although unable to lift very heavy weights or stand still for long periods without suffering sharp pains up my back. Although I had been passed 'fit for duty' I felt considerable trepidation as to whether I would really be able to cope with the rigours of a normal army life.

Planning for the expedition continued. My original estimate for the budget had been reviewed to £60,000 but I was at a loss as to how to set about raising this sum. I received an urgent telephone call from the Adjutant: there was a man called Bob Lewis coming down to Pirbright, our new posting now that the regiment had returned from Germany, to take some promotional photos. I was to meet him at all costs and explain the problem. Bob turned out to be a short, rather overweight, TR7-driving PR-type in his forties. I launched into my by-now-familiar explanation of the expedition and my plans but wasn't too sure why. He replied by saying that he knew nothing about expeditions and abhorred any undue physical exercise but he understood PR and marketing and had many connections within the Defence Sector and would be prepared to guide me in the right direction towards winning sponsorship. As I was totally ignorant of these fields and longed for someone to help I was all too delighted. Neither of us thought that it would be all that difficult and felt that sponsors would fall in swiftly to such a worthwhile event. We couldn't have been more misguided in our optimism. Our confidence was further bolstered when shortly afterwards we heard that His Royal Highness The Prince of Wales had agreed to be our Patron. I was elated.

For a short while this new-found boost to our status cleared a number of stumbling blocks. Lorries were procured from a reluctant Army pool, a department which had been on the attack about illicit approaches by service personnel to defence contractors ('Does Lieutenant Warburton-Lee realise that this is not allowed under Section . . .?') backed off and the Ministry of Defence, now inspired by the idea of an expedition that would involve a large number of novice expeditioners rather than a limited number of semi-professional mountaineers who regularly went on expeditions, lent its enthusiastic support.

Over the following months Bob became my guide and mentor. We started in the summer of 1988 with a visit to the British Army Equipment

Exhibition where we trailed around trade stand after trade stand chatting up potential sponsors and collecting business cards, contacts and mounds of promotional literature. The Camping and Outdoor Leisure Exhibition, Farnborough Air Show and Covert Operations Exhibition all followed in similar vein. It would be hard to assemble a larger collection of would-be spooks, dodgy arms dealers and general proponents of incredible personal protection gimmicks than I encountered at the latter. The results were dissected in infinite detail and having identified any possible sponsors we sent them a copy of our so-simple first brochure, proudly bearing the expedition logo and a statement of support from our Patron. The only instantly positive response amidst the sea of refusals was from Haverhill Generators who promised the loan of a portable generator. We might be poor but we had power! If only we could have fuelled the expedition on all of the regrets and best wishes that we received. For each refusal we sent out another approach; aside from companies with obvious connections with the services of expeditioning, we tried a broad trawl across commerce and industry; all of the clearing banks, retired officers in senior positions in business; Welsh businesses, or anyone with whom we could find a connection however small or spurious. With each new idea we were sure that we had found the winning solution but whilst the file for refusals grew quickly our list of sponsors remained painfully short.

The paper warfare associated with all of this was beginning to take on epic proportions and I was gradually losing control. I had tried to get a clerk from the army only to find that there weren't any available. On a general advice-seeking visit to Col John Blashford Snell I put this problem to him. He replied that this was always a difficulty whilst starting up expeditions but that his solution was to find a widow, mother with young children at home, student or anyone who had spare time on their hands. One didn't have any funds to pay them but they worked on the basis that in receipt of their services, they would come on all, part or just a visit to the expedition for free. I was a bit short of contacts in the first two of those categories and so put the word around that I was in the market for people with secretarial skills, time on their hands and an adventurous spirit. Having interviewed a variety of Sloanettes, each of whom proved more unsuitable than the last, a friend suggested that I ring a girl called Henrietta Nicholls. Tetta was twenty-six, an ex-Cambridge graduate and currently worked as a signing teacher of deaf children at Hounslow. At our first meeting Tetta came over as confident, self-assured and vivacious and was clearly excited by the project. She finished teaching at 3.30pm every day and so had the time to offer but didn't have any secretarial skills. We both decided that these couldn't be all that hard to develop. Our relationship didn't remain purely professional and before long we combined work with pleasure and started going out with each other.

In the autumn and winter of 1988 the expedition planning began to meet a series of major problems. Obtaining clearance for a military expedition to visit each of the countries that we wanted to go to, many of which were politically sensitive, was always going to be difficult. The clearance procedure occurs on two levels, with at the higher level the Foreign and Commonwealth Officers in London applying foreign policy on behalf of the British government and at the lower level Embassy and High Commission Staffs advising on local relationships of safety of potential visitors and approaching the host nations government for permission to visit.

Of the countries that were due to be visited under the original aim 'to visit any country in Africa with a mountain over 10,000 ft and climb the highest peak in each', I left out Libya and South Africa as politically impossible and then submitted a plan to FCO London. This was rejected because the mountains in Chad, Sudan and Ethiopia were within war zones. They also objected to several of the countries that I wanted to transit. I submitted a second plan taking into account their objections.

At times I found the process immensely frustrating particularly when I was being encouraged to visit by the FCO representatives in the host country and yet was in some cases still facing what appeared to be stonewall opposition in London. The negotiations weren't made any easier by virtue of my having to follow a chain of command which denied me direct access to those making the decisions and at the same time, due to the sensitivity of those decisions, I was not cleared to be told the reasoning behind them. It was a system designed quite correctly for the protection of the British Government and in many ways built in a large measure of protection for us but it was one that was to provide many headaches throughout the expedition and it was only through prolonged negotiation, much massaging and the professional goodwill of the FCO staff at all levels that we managed to ease the plan through the machinery of political bureaucracy.

On the sponsorship side, equipment sponsors continued to trickle in along with a variety of small donations but we received no major cash injections. As so often happens many of those who had lauded the concept of the expedition began to fall by the wayside when time, effort and commitment were needed. To add to the frustration I felt a very strong personal commitment to raising funds for the Spinal Injuries Unit and wanted to do so on the back of the expedition. However, this went against services' guidelines which prohibited open, active support for charities on the grounds that if the services were to promote one particular charity they would be plagued by requests for support from others and public funds could be misinterpreted as being redirected to registered charities.

We spent countless evenings brainstorming new ideas in Bob's office but it seemed that each time our hopes grew with a 'dead cert' they were dashed again. Bob remained throughout a great source of support and encouragement and even at the bleakest moment would generally take the view that it would all fall into place soon. Meantime as far as he was concerned the only reasonable course of action was to retire to a nearby wine bar and sink the odd bottle.

In search of further inspiration I arranged to go and see David Mason. David was a former Welsh Guard who had the reputation of being a fairly hard man with a penchant for the more unconventional side of soldiering. Having completed a tour commanding native troops in Oman, he had left the army to go and work for Sir Ranulph Fiennes on the organisation and backup of his Trans Globe Expedition. It was for this reason that I went to see him. I wanted to pick his brain about sponsorship opportunities and fund-raising techniques and half hoped to persuade him to come and help me. As I poured out my tale of woes, David looked markedly unimpressed and then, fixing me with a rather steely glare, said that he had a number of questions to ask me. 'Did I take my army career seriously? Was I afraid to rock the boat? Did I mind going around or over the heads of senior officers? In short did I baulk at chatting up, cajoling, flattering, telling half truths, placating, persuading, exploiting, insisting, badgering or even, in the last instance, threatening to get my own way?' If the answer to any of these questions was 'yes' then I had better give up the whole project now before I got my fingers burnt. If not then I should shut up, stop whingeing and get on with it. He gave me many useful hints and ideas. Over lunch, I brought the conversation round to the mundaneness of life in the country and asked whether he wouldn't like to get back to the excitement of an expedition. He replied that I was as bad as Fiennes for trying to inveigle people into helping and that whilst he would like to take part he was too busy with business commitments. I left with his main message going round in my head, rather ashamed of having been so wet and with considerably strengthened resolve to 'get on with it'.

The first three months of 1989 were a rush of activity to try and get as much done as possible. In April the battalion was due to leave for a six-month tour of Belize with a rather reluctant Regimental Signals Officer, myself, in tow. I continued to plague the executives of potential sponsors with endless letters and telephone calls. Our list of confirmed sponsors grew with the addition of Nikon UK, Abercrombie and Kent and

EBS Francis Barker and Son but we still lacked a major part of the funding. Some of the difficulties over political clearance were cleared up, I submitted a redrafted route for approval and we prepared our first press release. Alongside of this I made frequent forays to The Tower of London as Officer of the Guard, a week on exercise on Salisbury Plain and another week in Scotland trying to recover my nerve for mountaineering.

Belize is a sleepy Central American backwater. Whilst it has lots of character it is not the ideal location from which to organise a major expedition due to its limited communications. Thus Tetta was left holding the fort. She would rush to Pirbright after school every day to pick up the mail, reply to letters, and to try to decipher the machinations of the army system. She would then keep me posted on any progress or problems. Out in Belize I was in the frustrating position of feeling the planning lose momentum and yet being unable to do much about it. I flew back to England on two quick visits. We set up an outside broadcast with Sky TV at Land Rover Ltd's driving training track at Solihull. This was intended to demonstrate to potential sponsors a level of media interest to try and jog some of them including Land Rover Ltd, into confirming their support.

We had begun the process of trying to organise documentary film coverage of the expedition. Having sent our proposal to all of the major television networks, most advised us to try an independent company. On one of my flits back to England I raced up to the Mountaineering Film Festival to trawl for interest. The response was heartening. Several people were excited by the idea and could see the photographic potential with the variety of challenges set against a huge range of African backdrops from desert to jungle.

Belize produced its own adventures aside from our main soldiering tasks. I made one trip in a car inner tube along a river that disappeared into a cave system for several miles. On another I was asked to investigate a remote series of sink holes that had been spotted by pilots flying over the jungle. At the end of the Belize tour I had planned two three-week-long expeditions to climb Mexico's highest volcanoes. These were intended to train and select a core of mountaineers for the main expedition the next year. I led the first of these. It was great fun, physically hard work and not without some drama including a mountain rescue of one of the team by stretcher throughout the night. We made our main objective Orizaba at 18,701 feet and I finished confident that I could now cope with carrying a heavy rucksack in the mountains.

The Commanding Officer had kindly agreed to let me go back to England early from Belize to work full time on the expedition. With six months to go there was still much to be done. Land Rover Ltd had now joined our growing list of sponsors having offered the loan of two vehicles — another major headache dealt with. However, as before, we were still critically short of funds. Tetta and I ploughed on. We received approval at last for a charitable involvement. In addition to the Spinal Injuries Unit it seemed that we were in a position to help Weston Spirit. This charity had been set up, by ex-Welsh Guardsman and Falklands casualty Simon Weston, to take young people from inner cities and motivate them to be more effective members of their communities. Following a meeting with Simon I offered to take one young person from the charity on each phase of the expedition. We also decided to run a charity ball in Cardiff at Christmas to raise funds for both of the charities and the expedition.

From the office we put the complicated flight changeover plan out to tender, looked at ways of extracting funds from a variety of service sources and continued to put as many irons in the sponsorship fire as possible. August and September were difficult months with most executives away on their summer holidays. The film company that we had been talking to dropped the documentary on the rather curious grounds that despite having over eighty team members they didn't think that the expedition was going to have enough characters. Another company who had come on very strong and talked about sponsoring us to the tune of £100,000 opted to spend £1 million sponsoring a football series instead.

With the return of the regiment in September Captain Richard Gaffney and Colour Sergeant. Alan Bennett came to join the team. Richard was to be the expedition Second-in-Command. Although we were in the same regiment we had never served together for any length of time and didn't know each other well. Richard came on the Mexican expedition and I found him good company, easy going and physically very determined. Back in Pirbright he showed himself undismayed by the mountain of information and size of workload that he had to take on. Colour Sergeant Bennett is a larger than life Liverpudlian, a great bear of a man with limitless enthusiasm and a reputation for being fairly wild. He was to be responsible for the equipment management, camp routine and minor discipline on the expedition. The fifth and final member of the central team was Captain Matthew Roberts, an army doctor currently serving with the Parachute Regiment. Matthew was a fit looking guy with a definite twinkle in his eye. He was to provide emergency and routine medical cover through the year and conduct a medical research project which he chose to do on the subject of Malarial Prophylaxis. With Richard and CSgt Bennett working on the project full time we could triple the work output. However time was running out.

In October we were due to hold a two-week training and selection camp in Snowdonia for potential expedition members. Office life was close to frantic but physical signs of progress began to appear. When the Land Rovers first arrived I couldn't stop myself from continually walking out to look at and touch them just to reassure myself that they were really there. Kit was now pouring in from service ordnance depots and civilian sponsors; however, trouble struck from an unexpected direction.

The day before we were due to go to North Wales on the training camp I received a telephone call from Regimental Headquarters saying that the regiment had been looking at our accounts and that as we were clearly still far short of our budget they were seriously considering cancelling the expedition to prevent any embarrassment. I was to present my case to the Regimental Lieutenant Colonel, Brigadier Johnny Rickett on my return from Wales. We were now into full crisis management.

Whilst CSgt Bennett and I went to run the camp in Wales, I had no alternative but to leave Richard behind with the almost impossible brief of making a significant inroad into our cash deficit by the time we returned. We had made applications for grants to a number of charitable trusts which I hoped might arrive in time. One of our major costs was the freighting of vehicles and equipment out to Africa so he set about trying to find a sponsor for that.

In Wales we had rain such as I had never seen before. The climbers found themselves trying to scale rock faces swept by torrents of water, the canoeists had a rather stiffer introduction to white water kayaking than they had anticipated on heavily swollen rivers, the vehicle recovery became a mud slide and the campsites on Llanberis Pass were washed out. All in all it provided excellent conditions to sort out who was up to the challenge ahead and who wasn't. The basic criteria for team members were physical fitness, determination to succeed, a sense of humour and the ability to get on with others. I fitted in as much instruction as I could around taking press and local television to film the activities. Every evening I rang Richard to see how he was getting on. By the end of the first week he had made no real progress and my heart sank knowing that I had set him an unattainable goal. Surely all the hard work hadn't been for nothing?

Then we had a breakthrough. UKWAL Shipping rang Richard in reply to an earlier cold call to say that they would sponsor the freight carriage, two of the charitable trusts came up trumps with grants and ICI Pharmaceuticals said that they would sponsor us for £10,000 in return for copies of the Malarial Prophylaxis report. We were back in with a chance.

I returned to Pirbright clutching video copies of the television items and together with these and our rather healthier accounts Richard and I managed to flannel our way through the meeting with Brigadier Johnny. The expedition was allowed to continue with the proviso that if we ran out of money we would have to cut it short and come home.

From that moment on the pace became more and more frantic as we neared our departure date. At last, with sponsors beginning to fall in I started to think that, maybe, we could do it. Richard dealt with the visas, documentation and finances. CSgt Bennett sorted out all of the kit and I was left to carry on with the sponsorship and PR. On top of all the expedition arrangements we were organising a Charity Ball for four hundred people at Cardiff City Hall to raise money for both of our associated charities and the expedition. In addition we were raffling a top of the range three-week safari for two courtesy of Abercrombie and Kent. Anyone who came within range of the office was pounced on to buy raffle tickets, expedition T-shirts and stickers. We became a very commercial organisation.

Christmas 1989 was, for me, a charge between homes saying goodbye to all of my family and trying to get some rest. I had returned on Christmas Eve utterly shattered and barely capable of holding a coherent conversation. I went to the Spinal Injuries Unit for a last check-up and received Dr El Masri's well-meaning warning to try and avoid carrying very heavy weights and let others do the donkey work if I didn't want to suffer the consequences later in life. During one quiet moment my father approached me with a concerned look in his eye. 'John, are there any grown-ups going along on this trip of yours?' A greater vote of no-confidence has any man received.

The New Year saw Richard, CSgt Bennett and me at Middle Wallop airfield where we were to receive a brief course on the usage of our recently sponsored paragliding chutes. The weather was appalling. We only got one flight in each but left under the firm impression that there was more to this game than met the eye. We definitely needed to return the next weekend for more training if we weren't to kill ourselves in the desert.

The next ten days until the vehicles sailed are a blur in my memory. Transport was dispatched all around the country to pick up kit from sponsors and ordnance depots. We were still getting 'Dues Out' notices on vital items of equipment and had begun begging or borrowing from any military unit that held the items which were required. Sponsors were almost unanimously failing to make deadlines whilst everyone on the team kept coming up with ideas for more items of kit that we needed. The telephone lines were burning. We got more sponsorship of small items of kit in the last few weeks than in the entire preceding two and a half years. Many firms were superb and pulled out all the stops to meet these last minute requests but others tried to renege on their previous offers of sponsorship. I was furious and felt that they had just taken advantage of all of the publicity that we had worked so hard to obtain for them.

The weekend before the vehicles left was a mad scramble to get everything done in time. We were in the office until 1am on Saturday morning and then drove down to Middle Wallop for a fruitless day with more bad weather and no flying. That night I raced up to London to pack some gear to go on the vehicles and start trying to tie up my personal affairs which had hitherto been sadly neglected. Richard and I went back to Middle Wallop leaving CSgt Bennett in an office knee-deep in clothing, climbing hardware and tools to continue packing. We had a much better day. By the end we both had several flights and acted as launch marshals, wing tippers and drivers and tested the whole system from our own vehicles. I had nearly wiped myself out by doing flat spins too near the ground and only just pulled out in time to land. We left confident that we knew the basics but with a lot of respect for the dangers. That night was another 2am finish as we piled all that was available of the equipment onto the vehicles. The weight of the food and vehicle spares was staggering.

The vehicles left for the docks the next day. Last minute items of kit were dispatched to Tilbury to catch the ship before it sailed. Meanwhile I began to plan for our reception for sponsors and press launch on Wednesday. As seemed to have become the pattern this was another rush to get everything done on time. The reception was held in the Guards Museum. Photographic boards were erected, maps of our route displayed, food and drink laid on and all of the Phase 1 team present in freshly ironed expedition T-shirts. Just as we were beginning to get organised Mike Slater arrived with his HTV film crew wanting interviews. As always this took far longer than anticipated so by the time I got downstairs into the museum the press were beginning to arrive. Robert Fox, defence correspondent for the *Daily Telegraph* led the field with representatives from the *Daily Mail*, Press Association, BBC World Service and a variety of regional press. By 12.30pm I didn't think that any of the sponsors were going to turn up and then suddenly they all began to arrive. At that point it began to fall into place that we were really going and the rest of the day became rather unreal. ICI, Land Rover, UKWAL, Pyrhana, Sportlite, Nikon, Haverhill Generators, Cotswold Camping, Joe's Basement were all represented. Out of the helpers there was Bob Lewis, Roddy Malone, Cathy Davenport, Jill Parkin, Don Neighbour, Nigel Massey amongst a sea of other faces. From the army, Major-General Simon Cooper, Brigadier Johnny Rickett, Lieutenant Colonel John Wyatt, my Commanding Officer Lieutenant Colonel Reddy Watt and others. I eventually called the gathering to order and launched into a totally unprepared speech. I don't recall what I said but I remember recognising various faces out of the crowd and receiving encouraging smiles. As I neared the end a large lump rose in my throat and it was all that I could do to utter my final thank-you. The rest of the afternoon was a series of interviews followed by an attempt to get around as many of the sponsors as possible to say a personal thank-you.

The next couple of days were rather an anti-climax. With the vehicles gone and the reception over there was not the same feeling of urgency. I began to get used to the idea that it was all happening. On the Friday I picked up my travellers' cheques and then went home to my flat. I had a small farewell drinks party that night. It still seemed unreal to be saying goodbye to all my friends for a year. Everyone was wishing me luck but somehow I felt removed from the gathering. I found it hard to talk to people; I was leaving their world for the time being and going out into another. I knew that the majority of them could not comprehend what I was trying to do — sometimes I wondered whether I could myself.

On Saturday I pottered off shopping after my first lie-in for weeks. I had no idea when the next might be. I drifted around buying mundane necessities such as supplies of toothpaste, sun barrier cream and mosquito repellent. In the evening Tetta and I went to another farewell party given by some friends. Sunday 14 January dawned a clear, crisp day. We both awoke with hangovers from the previous night's excesses. We got up and loaded the remainder of my belongings from the flat into her car. As I took a last look round and locked the door I had tears in my eyes. The first part of the journey was spent in silence as I tried to control my emotions. Neither of us dared look at the other. Over the past few months Tetta had experienced a period of deep soul-searching, questioning her own ability to cope with the conditions of life on the expedition. Despite my constant reassurance she was still beset by grave self-doubts.

The silence was dramatically shattered as I let out a groan, clapped my hand to my head and shrieked. I had left all the money for the first part of the expedition under my pillow at the flat and had left, as instructed, having locked my keys inside. There wasn't time to turn back and anyhow I didn't have a spare key. In desperation I rang my sister, Jenny, who had the only spare key. Although I had woken her up, she agreed at once to go and get the money and bring it to Pirbright.

Once at Pirbright we unloaded all the contents of my flat into my room and then I hurriedly began to pack my kit for Morocco. It was a measure of how busy we had been that at this final hour I was to be found scrabbling around the darkest recesses of my room for clothes and climbing gear. I felt desperately ill at ease and panicky. What kit did I need? What had I forgotten? How would it ever fit into my rucksack? All of my usual confidence deserted me. By the time I had got my kit together I could barely lift my rucksack and all of the men were waiting for me to leave for Heathrow airport.

Tetta and Alasdair Johnstone, who was to run the rear party in the U.K. came with me to the airport. I couldn't seem to get my brain in order and, hard as I tried, I couldn't brief Alastair coherently. My mind swam with all that had passed before. Now that all the hype of the past few months was gone I had to get down to the basic realities of the expedition: Where was the next meal coming from? Where could we refuel? Where were we to camp for the night? I felt not so much that I was just beginning but that I had finished. I had been unable to look beyond mounting the expedition and now that had been achieved it was strange to be faced with these new issues.

I said a quick goodbye to Tetta who was to fly straight to Dakar with the Admin Party. She barely managed a brave smile and exhorted me to calm down. As I followed the rest of the team through customs I could see the aeroplane waiting to take us to Africa, to deserts and jungles, mountains and rivers. The adventure had begun.

Chapter One
Desert Tracks

Phase 1

Captain John Warburton-Lee, Welsh Guards, Expedition leader

Captain Richard Gaffney, Welsh Guards, Expedition Second in Command

Captain Matthew Roberts, Royal Army Medical Corps, Expedition doctor

Colour Sergeant Alan Bennett, Welsh Guards, Senior Non Commissioned Officer and camp manager

Miss Tetta Nicholls, Expedition secretary

Sub Lieutenant Bob Finch, Royal Navy

Second Lieutenant Harry Lloyd, Welsh Guards

Lance Sergeant Ken Rowlands, Welsh Guards

Lance Sergeant Dave Jenkins, Welsh Guards

Corporal Andy Goodier, Royal Electrical and Mechanical Engineers, Mechanic

Corporal Adie Chesterfield, Royal Air Force, Mechanic

Lance Corporal John Prestidge, Welsh Guards

Lance Corporal Darren Williams, Welsh Guards

Lance Corporal Lee Scholes, Welsh Guards

Guardsman Paul Newman, Welsh Guards

Guardsman Mike Paul, Welsh Guards

Guardsman Pete Hughes, Welsh Guards

Guardsman 'Rosie' Watkins, Welsh Guards

Craftsman Steve Heath, Royal Electrical and Mechanical Engineers, Mechanic

Miss Leslie Watson, Weston Spirit

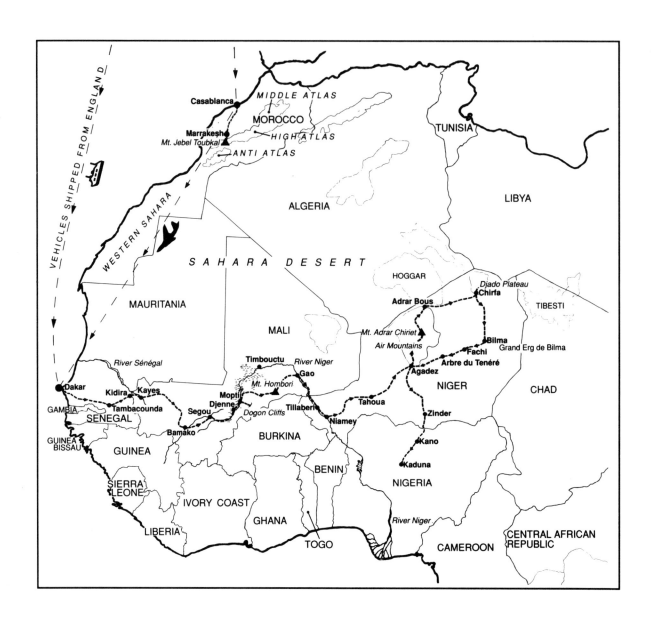

The flight to Dakar was unremarkable. I was longing to see Richard and CSgt Bennett to hear how they had got on. Unable to affect matters from Morocco I had fretted over all sorts of unpleasant possibilities: Had any vital customs clearance forms been forgotten? Would they have been allowed into the country? Would they have had problems due to all the camera equipment and film that they were carrying? Would they have got the vehicles off the ships? Had they found anywhere to stay?

My delight at seeing their beaming faces leaning over the passenger arrivals railing was short-lived when I heard their news. CSgt Bennett had flown out ahead of the main admin. party. He had arrived to find the city packed for the arrival of the Paris-Dakar Rally. Every hotel bed in the city was taken with the exception of a room in the Independence Hotel, Dakar's smartest and most expensive hotel. After one night, with his money allowance for the week already used up he had had to check out. He tried to find a bed everywhere until finally a receptionist, at the Independence, Ahmadou, had taken pity on him and asked him to stay.

Ahmadou's family lived in a shanty town fifteen miles from the city centre. Despite their incredibly spartan living conditions, bare concrete rooms, no electricity or heating, no furniture and toilet facilities that he shared with six other families in his compound, Ahmadou and his family showed great hospitality and shared the little that they had. CSgt Bennett then hit his next problem — Senegalese bureaucracy. Every day for a week he travelled into the city either hitching or taking the bus. There he was sent from one government office to another until finally with the aid of USIMA, our shipping company's representative in Senegal, he was able to get the Carnets de Passage signed and the vehicles released from customs. He was now joined by Richard, Tetta and the remainder of the admin. team including the mechanics. When they finally went to collect the vehicles we had been dealt the cruellest blow: all four vehicles had been broken into. In the back of the Bedfords the sight that greeted them brought tears to CSgt Bennett's eyes. Thieves had ripped off the locker doors and broken into every box and case taking whatever they wanted, scattering the remnants everywhere. Ropes, tools, vehicle spares, sleeping bags, food and personal clothing were all missing in addition to his own highly cherished fishing rods. Months of work and a career's worth of returned favours lay in tatters before him. True to form he had set about sorting out the mess, identifying the items that were missing and scouting the open air markets and back street shops to try and replace whatever possible.

Our first task on arrival was to go to the USIMA freight compound where the others were camped amidst the containers, and look through all of the items remaining to identify that which was ours. It was a pitiful sight as items as mundane as pairs of socks, underpants and shampoo were held up to be claimed. Despite initial anger and disappointment the majority of the team took it surprisingly well. The worst affected, Cpl Goodier, had lost all but a pair of shorts and one shoe. He had met us at the airport clad in a long African cloak secured at the waist by a webbing strap, a pair of flip-flops and sporting a broad grin.

Dakar was a depressing place. Poverty screamed out from every angle. In the centre the old colonial buildings were now dilapidated. Pickpockets roamed the streets as several of the team found to their cost. Outside, corrugated iron shanty towns stretched away as far as the eye could see. Even in the compound we were camped under the oppressive gaze of the African workforce. Their eyes followed each move we made and seemed to be mentally valuing every piece of equipment we handled.

We left the next day with considerable relief. The tarmac highway rapidly deteriorated to narrow dirt roads blocked by horses and donkey carts. Ducas selling everything from galvanised buckets to packing foam lined the road. As we left the outskirts mile after mile of baobab trees stretched into the distance. Their enormously wide trunks tapered upwards towards strangely root-like branch systems making them look as if they had been planted upside down. We made good progress covering 200 miles before pulling off the road into a small disused quarry to set up camp for the first time in the bush. The red soil emanated the earthy smell of Africa. Camp was a simple affair. Each Land Rover paired off with a Bedford. We stretched a canvas tarpaulin between them and then arranged the camp beds and mosquito nets in two tight lines underneath — privacy wasn't a feature. Cpl Andy Goodier and LSgt Dave Jenkins had volunteered to cook for the phase. As they fired up the large petrol cooker others set up the kitchen under Cpl Goodier's direction. He quickly established himself as a Major Domo figure and his cheerful face was generally found to be streaked with soot, beaming over some indeterminate culinary concoction.

As we continued eastwards into the Sahel, the countryside changed to thorn scrubland. The thick carpet of red dust that lay over the roads billowed up in each vehicle's wake obscuring the vision of those behind. For the guys in the back of the trucks it was most unpleasant. It was stiflingly hot and on top of that the all-encompassing dust made breathing difficult. Whenever we stopped they emerged blinking and coughing, their hair, starched in crazy angles, solid with dust. It became so bad that a couple of people showed signs of developing tonsillitis.

On the third day we reached our first border crossing — from Senegal to Mali. The negotiations were long and slow but at the cost of a few medicines and being asked to carry a rather unattractive pony-tailed

French hitch-hiker we were allowed to proceed. We drove on with the hitch-hiker on the roof of one of the lorries. CSgt Bennett muttered darkly about 'fucking yetis' making his vehicles look untidy — a guardsman to the last. This plan all went horribly wrong when the first Malian police post that we came to tried to fine us heavily for contravening traffic regulations for carrying 'the yeti' on the roof. Traffic regulations in Africa have about as much relevance as an altar in a brothel but there was no doubting the policeman's resolve. Fortunately the propitious offer of some headache pills got us through. We dumped 'the yeti' once we had rounded the next corner, much to CSgt Bennett's glee.

The Malian customs post at Kayes was shut so we drove back into No Man's Land to camp. In the morning we returned to the police station. We started once again the long procedure of entering all the details into their log. Meanwhile other policemen and various locals were coming in and out of the dirty office. All the time money kept changing hands which did little to reassure my confidence in the incorruptibility of the Malian police. The police sergeant kept giving us dirty looks and refused to smile or be drawn into conversation. Presently he stood up and then issued a stream of orders which sent two others out to search our vehicles. Fortunately they weren't very enthusiastic in their task. I was concerned lest they found the trunk full of film and started demanding import duty. I felt distinctly uncomfortable. I was sure that the sergeant was looking for a way to fleece us.

Having entered all of the passport details in their log and charged us a 'fee' they then wanted to see everyone in turn with their passports. This was going fairly well until suddenly there was an uproar. The sergeant stormed up to me. He was clearly furious. Apparently one of the men had had a crap in their shower. They were after blood. A very indignant Cpl Chesterfield came forward saying that he had known it was a shower but he had been led in there by one of the policemen and told to use it. For a while the situation looked nasty, but in the end we cleared up the mess, completed the formalities and got out as fast as possible. Whilst I breathed a large sigh of relief at having got out of a potentially difficult spot the men hooted with laughter at Cpl Chesterfield's embarrassment and pulled his leg remorselessly.

We continued on the main route east through open bush land and decided to turn off at Sandare, avoiding Nioro du Sahel, and take a short cut to Diema. The ninety-mile minor road clearly marked on our Michelin map apparently saved us some thirty-eight miles. Short in distance but certainly not on time, our chosen route led us along narrow tracks which at every turn splintered into half a dozen even smaller passages. Soon we were feeling our way along trails that were little more than footpaths. There was no central route so we headed east using this network of tracks to force our way through the bush. The going was painfully slow due to the rough, rocky nature of the ground and the closeness of the bush. At times we had to retrace our steps to find a wider passage for the Bedfords. The sun was fierce and relentless. All around the bush was tinder dry. On occasion we startled flocks of guinea fowl. We came across trees and bushes groaning under the weight of locusts which whirred away as we approached, to settle in a great devouring horde on the next bush. One found its way down Richard's shirt as he was driving, evoking shrieks of alarm from him, cackles of mirth from the rest of the vehicle crew and nearly causing the first accident of the expedition.

Aside from a feeling of isolation and exploration the greatest joy was arriving in the villages. These remote outposts, consisting of thatched mud rondavels with beaten earth courtyards and small penned stockades burst into instant life. Hundreds of people would surround us, laughing at this unexpected diversion in their lives. The women wore clothes of the brightest colours and often had intricate patterns and jewellery woven into their hair. Many had tribal markings; series of long scars and lines of blue dye running down their faces. They were wonderfully open and friendly. Children would engagingly slip their hands into ours and lead us around the village, meanwhile surreptitiously feeling in our pockets for sweets.

After three days of bouncing our way along these meandering tracks, having covered not more than twelve miles per hour the whole way we emerged back onto the road to Bamako. We passed through the Malian capital stopping briefly to post letters and ring Pirbright. We gave them a brief report on our progress and asked for a new generator to be sent out as ours had blown up in a great electronic débâcle. Although it was necessary to stop in the cities to complete formalities and sort out our logistics I loathed doing so. The Africans of the cities were different from the open, welcoming bush tribespeople. They were aggressive and avaricious.

Further east again we passed San and Segou. Here, we noticed a shift in the style of buildings. The rondavels gave way to flat-roofed dwellings with straight, even walls bordering neat courtyards. The people showed their Muslim faith through their dress and behaviour. Every village had a mosque; some no more than tiny, single-roomed mud and wood constructions with low, cramped doorways.

We were now following the ancient camel caravan route linking dark Africa with the Mediterranean coastal ports to the north. For hundreds of years the Malian kingdoms had grown rich by exacting a customs levy on traders carrying their cargoes of copper, gold, spices and slaves north and porcelain, silk and cotton south. Now, with the caravans long since ceased and harsh droughts preventing the farming of any significant produce many of the cities were decrepit shadows of their former glory.

A narrow, raised causeway took us across the flood plain towards the fourteenth-century city of Djenne, power base of one of the finest of these Songhai Empire fiefdoms. The flood plain was dry save for the occasional pool of water in which paddled white storks and cattle egrets. The sun painted the sky a gradually fading pink as it settled behind the minarets of a nearby village mosque. There was open grumbling amongst the team that night. Some of the men were fed up with the long hours of travelling and the uncomfortable conditions. I was disappointed that the junior non-commissioned officers didn't set a better example and weren't able to rise above the discomforts and take an interest in the fascinating world around them. I went to bed tired and rather depressed.

Our first problem in the morning was to cross a branch of the Niger river. Whilst the others collapsed camp Cpl Goodier, Sgt Jenkins and I walked down to the river to recce a crossing site. We waded out into the cool water. Already a couple of local fishermen were casting nets from their pirogue. The water didn't come up above the tops of our thighs so we decided to ford the river with all four vehicles. We walked back to collect the others to find on our return that CSgt Bennett was not well. His eyes were all puffed up and he looked weak. He had obviously had a bad night but I assumed that he just had a bad case of diarrhoea and vomiting.

We took the vehicles down to the river but before crossing we had to help a horse and cart that was stranded in the middle. The cart driver was beating the poor animal mercilessly about the head and flank. We attached one of our electric winch cables to the cart and quickly freed it. We then transferred all of the equipment to the Bedfords and fitted wading plugs to the Land Rovers. The Bedfords crossed with no problem but the Land Rovers were rather more dramatic. The water rushed up to the windscreen, the forward motion creating a huge bow wave. LSgt Jenkins rode on the bonnet shouting directions to the driver. I took lots of photographs standing in the river. CSgt Bennett should have been videoing but I found him sitting slumped on the river bank, camera in his lap, head down, eyes shut and looking desperate. We put him into his Bedford cab where he went straight to sleep.

As soon as we reached the far side we were approached by two officials who announced themselves as representatives of SMERT. Suppressing the temptation to laugh I learnt that SMERT stood not for the long term adversaries of M, Q and James Bond 007 as I suspected but '*Société Malien pour l'Exploitation de la Resource Tourisme*'. From the visitor's point of view they were similarly unscrupulous. Having bargained down the fee for a mandatory SMERT guide we set off to explore the twisting alleys and compact squares of Djenne. The houses were tall and multi-storeyed but at the same time ramshackle with small bare rooms and cramped doorways. There was a general air of mustiness and dilapidation. Built exclusively of mud, the city appeared curiously monochromatic in the harsh morning glare. Even the people were dressed dowdily. The only decoration was provided by ornately carved wooden doors and shutters covered with a smattering of brass studs and handles.

The city centred around the large market square. Towering above, tall and imposing, was the mosque — a great expanse of red mud walls, towers, buttresses and crenellations. We were guided by the Chef de Ville who doubled as religious leader; a distinguished rather severe looking man who stood head and shoulders above most of his congregation. He was clad in a long black robe and adorned by a white scarf, skullcap and matching goatee beard. He spoke solemnly of better times when the city was wealthy and not in the grip of droughts. He spoke, also, of the harsh Muslim rules by which they conducted their lives; prayers five times per day, readings from the Koran and strict social and sexual mores.

Inside, the mosque was cool and tranquil. Based around the square courtyard each room was segregated by dozens of pillars between which the faithful prayed. Fine nets were strung above to catch the bats that flew around. The walls were bare save for an old wooden clock and a wall chart of clock faces showing the times for prayer. He led us up a steep stairway onto the roof where we were greeted by a fabulous view over the whole city and away into the haze of the flood plain. The roof was literally baking in the sun. Blinking because of the glare, we had to dance a rather undignified jig to prevent the soles of our soft European feet from burning. Rows of low ventilation shafts, each fitted with a small brass cap were lined along the roof. The Chef de Ville assured us that these would be removed in summer when it became hot! As we left, the city reverberated with the calls of the muezzin beckoning the faithful to prayer.

We drove on for an hour and camped not far from Mopti. CSgt Bennett's condition had deteriorated throughout the day. He was by now delirious and totally unaware of anything going on around him. He was running a high temperature and suffering, at the least, from advanced heat exhaustion. Matthew set up a saline drip and ran two pints of fluid into him to replace that which he had lost.

The next day we left Matthew looking after a recumbent CSgt Bennett in the shade of a Bedford awning whilst the rest of us went to explore the old city of Mopti. Lying on the southern bank of the Niger river, Mopti has the feel of an African version of Mississippi. Two aged river steamers complete with tiered decks, wrought iron railings and striped sun awnings were reminiscent of the *Mississippi Belle*. There was a crescent-shaped harbour across which long, slim pirogues glided, seemingly effortlessly, at their poler's behest. Elsewhere heavily overladen motorised boats chugged precariously low in the water under their cargo of people, animals, bicycles and sacks of produce. The waterfront reaching back into the town was one teeming mass of humanity ablaze with colour and rich in sights, sounds and smells. It was Thursday: market day. People thronged around the stalls. There were four different markets within the city each specialising in its own merchandise. Within each of these markets, stalls selling similar items were grouped together. On the beach, mountains of calabashes competed for space with onions, exotic fruit and nuts were all laid out in brightly coloured carpets of produce. Great stinking, fly-ridden heaps of blackened, dried fish tainted the air.

Other markets offered vegetables, goats and myriad items of archaic ironmongery. We left clutching our purchases, hot, hassled and somewhat shell-shocked from this bombardment of our senses. We returned to camp to find CSgt Bennett not much improved but deemed fit to travel a short distance so we packed up and made our way towards Bandiagara and the Dogon escarpment. On the way we stopped at a roadside stall which was, to our amazement, stacked high with tins of corned beef. The answer to this unexpected booty lay in large lettering on each tin 'GIFT OF THE GOVERNMENT OF DENMARK'.

At Bandiagara we engaged a guide to show us the Dogon escarpment and then bumped our way along another twelve miles of uneven dirt road to Djiguibombo, an amazing collection of over a hundred tightly packed, tiny square mud buildings. Each was capped with a steeply pointed grass thatch roof which jutted up into the evening sky. Crammed in the middle was an equally tiny mud church crowned with a simple wooden cross. There wasn't a single straight line in the village and the whole place gave the impression of having been dropped in an ancient game of spillikins.

The track leading the final two miles to the crest of the escarpment had deteriorated to such an extent that at times it was indistinguishable from the surrounding boulder-strewn scrubland. The lorries bounced and lurched their way along trying to avoid the worst of the bumps.

After a peaceful night's camp under a wonderfully starry sky we set off on foot in the early morning cool. Our guide led us for a half-mile through the bush to a broad plateau of rich reddish brown rock which looked as if it had solidified from a flowing molten mass. We were halted by sheer cliffs that dropped several hundred feet. Looking out over the vast plains, speckled with short spiky trees that stretched away as far as the eye could see until they disappeared into the haze, there was a feeling of immense space

We contoured around to a gully where we scrambled down the easiest line. All around the cliffs were mostly vertical or overhanging and there was much evidence of rockfall. We passed in front of the village of Kani Kombole and then turned east along the base of the cliffs to Teli. This sprawling village nestled up against the side of the cliff with the highest buildings some three hundred feet above the main bulk of the houses. As we approached we could see two large groups of people; the first comprised women and children pounding millet, the second was their menfolk who were busy constructing a deep well.

In the village the buildings were simple but carefully crafted. The houses were low, mud-built and single-roomed with small wooden stoppers to fill the windows and doors. Around each a low mud wall bordered a courtyard typically containing round storage bins, ovens and a pestle and mortar for their millet. Chickens ran around loose with the children, many of whom were naked. There were many signs of malnutrition; distended stomachs and gross, protruding tummy buttons. Several of the children tried to sell us simple carved wooden whistles which made a surprisingly tuneful sound.

As we climbed up a system of convoluted paths and ladders to the top of the village we entered the world of their predecessors, ancestors and spiritual life. Pygmies had inhabited the cliffs before the Dogons drove them out. Their dwellings were unbelievably small, some no more than three feet long with microscopic doors and windows. Now this region was the preserve of the Medicine Man. A wall decorated with animal skulls, bones and birds' feet announced his occupancy. Beside this lay the Dogons' burial chamber. Here the bodies of the dead were laid out on a wooden pallet before being raised by a crude rope and pulley system to their final resting place in caves recessed higher up the cliffs.

Further along we saw the Ogon — the oldest man in the village who our guide told us was 120 years old. He was performing a ritual ceremony to cure a girl of infertility. He had spread water and millet onto the earth in front of the girl and amidst many incantations sacrificed a chicken, letting its blood run into the millet paste.

Below us the tightly-knit buildings of the village formed patches in this fascinating quilt. We made our way slowly back up the escarpment in the searing midday heat. At camp, I found to my relief that CSgt Bennett was beginning to look slightly better. His eyes had lost some of their puffiness and he was more coherent if not totally logical. However, he was still very weak and in obvious pain.

The next 375 miles to Gao saw some dramatic changes in scenery. We continued east, initially through typical Sahelian scrubland and then into vast open plains. After Douentza these were studded with massive red rock outcrops towering above their surroundings. Nearer to Gao the scenery changed again — this time in favour of low dunes and coarse tussock grass. I began to feel that at last we were getting close to the real desert.

Gao had been the capital of the Songhai Empire and a dynamic trans-Saharan trading centre until it had fallen to the forces of the King of Morocco who struck south across the desert in 1591 to capture the West African gold trade. It was now a dusty provincial town with a reputation for having a difficult police force. At each of the towns that we passed through we had to complete the equivalent of full border-crossing formalities. Sometimes this was required at the police post on the entrance of a town, at the main police station in the centre and again at the police post on the way out. At the end of the day a present of some description usually eased our passage. Sometimes a Bic biro or metal badge would suffice; at others more elaborate gifts were required. Most popular of all was medicine which was rarely available to the tribespeople and always expensive. Often they would feign a headache or stomach ailment to get medicines from us for use at a later date when they would genuinely be needed. On occasion the treatment was more pressing: Matthew was once taken behind a shed by an official who dropped his trousers and displayed a most unpleasant sight — la *maladie des femmes* is a common complaint in Africa. Matthew prescribed penicillin for the sufferer and a measure of whisky for himself to get over the shock.

The night after we passed through Gao I called a team 'parley'. I aired all the grievances that I was aware of, carefully avoiding personal references, and pointed out a number of general feelings. When I had finished and invited open discussion there were few complaints. Later, round the campfire, I could feel that much of the tension had dissipated. People were laughing openly and easily for the first time for a while. I felt happier than I had since we started and hoped that we had now laid the firm foundations for a team that would work well together in the desert.

The border crossing into Niger was the usual bout of form-filling, hanging around, explaining away our army background and trying to avoid giving out any more *cadeaux* than we needed to. I had been warned by Alasdair Johnstone that the Foreign Office had said we would have to have a military escort through Niger but there was no evidence of them when we arrived. We hadn't gone far beyond the border when we came to the town of Tillaberi. The policeman at the checkpoint on the way into town was highly agitated and gesticulated wildly. He kept saying, *'Faites attention, les enfants sont engreve'.* Unfortunately neither my French nor our phrase book could decipher *'engreve'.* However his frantic miming suggested that the children were throwing rocks. Not quite sure what to expect we drove cautiously towards the centre of town. As we came over a rise the main street lay before us. In the middle of this was a group of about 200 youths aged from six to eighteen years old. They had lined rocks across the road. As we approached they repeatedly screamed out *'La route sont barree'* and waved their sticks threateningly indicating that we should turn back. I had no intention of doing so but nor did I want to charge them in case we knocked someone down or got all of our windows smashed. Instead I drove forward slowly, stopping at their barricade.

A horde of angry faces swarmed around the Land Rover, shouting and yelling at us. We all smiled as broadly as possible. I picked on one guy who appeared to be a ringleader and started to talk to him. Initially he was hostile and kept insisting that we must go back but then couldn't resist the normal African reaction to smile back. I launched into an impassioned speech saying that we were the Queen of England's personal bodyguard and had to go through. Some began beckoning us on but others became hysterical, battering the sides of the vehicle. I drove slowly forward, gradually picking up speed and praying that the other vehicles would stay closed up and get through all right. A couple of stones landed around my vehicle but the two Bedfords took a pelting. Luckily there was no damage done except for a few chips on the paintwork and Gdsm Paul Newman getting a bruised leg.

We pulled up at the Police Station. All around hundreds of stones lay where they had landed; witness to previous attacks. Inside, the police were virtually under siege conditions and appeared well and truly hassled. Our passports and vehicle documents were processed in record time save for one break whilst they all rushed outside, grabbing truncheons and riot shields to repel another attack. Needless to say our team thought the whole episode highly amusing. The soldiers, most of whom had served in Northern Ireland, were all for offering to help clear the street with a baton charge.

We stopped at the next village to buy bread. There we met the local primary school teacher who told us that the student strike was countrywide. In Niamey, the capital, the army had opened fire on the rioters killing fourteen and another 400 were reported missing. This put a rather different complexion on matters. We approached Niamey circumspectly but found it temporarily peaceful so we settled in to the main campsite and savoured proper showers and cold beers for the first time in over 3,000 miles.

We spent a day washing everything from vehicles to clothes, resupplying food, fuel and water and extricating our gleaming new petrol generator from the airport customs. Mercifully it was much smaller than the original one, which had taken four men to lift and could have powered most of the Blackpool illuminations. Despite its reduced size it had still been an impressive feat by Alasdair Johnstone to get a replacement generator out to Niamey with just over a week's warning. Aside from the physical comforts morale was considerably restored by mail from home. I got a letter from my sister Jenny telling me amongst other things that my car had been sold and my flat let — it all seemed a million miles away.

A two-and-a-half day drive north took us to the trading post of Agadez, gateway to the Sahara. Beneath the famous mosque tower the streets buzzed with activity. Hausa tribesmen rubbed shoulders with Fulani and Songhay. Set apart by their noble appearance and their own contempt for what they considered to be lesser beings Touaregs strode confidently through the crowds; tall, straight-backed men. There were many tribes within the generic group of Touaregs, each distinguished by subtleties of dress. Common to each were the voluminous floor-length robes and long head cloths wrapped many times around the head to cover all but a slit for their eyes. Both robes and head-dress were in single bold colours. Some carried ornate swords in scabbards attached to their waist. Their skin varied in colour from a light mahogany to ebony. They had fine Arabic features.

I went straight to the tourist office to find a guide for our planned journey across the Tenere. The Chef d'Office was a giant of a man with an enormous turban. He immediately asked to see our authorisation — 'What authorisation?' I queried. At that he strode off towards the police station leaving me jogging along in his wake. There the Commissioner was adamant: No authority — no journey into the Sahara. He then looked in our passports and saw that, in Niamey, they had been stamped with the next place as Nigeria. Thus he believed that we had no business to be in Agadez and should be on our way to Nigeria. I tried every tack possible: Official British Military expedition, there at the invitation of the Niger government, personal guards to Her Majesty the Queen, charitable aims — he wouldn't budge. If we wanted to visit the Tenere I had to go back to Niamey, get a letter of authorisation from the Ministry of the Interior and return. He would like to help but couldn't.

I managed to persuade him to ring his superior in Niamey but as it was Saturday and not a day of work there was no reply. I implored him to try again later and left having arranged to return at 5pm. I returned to the others to break the bad news. The thought of driving all the way back to Niamey was singularly unappealing.

At 5pm I returned to find that the police commissioner had gone home. I raced back over to the tourist office to find the Chef d'Office together with all of his family, sitting cross-legged on mats on the floor around an ancient television. They were watching the final of the national sport — a form of wrestling not dissimilar to Sumo. One of the men in the competition was from Agadez and the match was the subject of intense criticism with much roaring, sighing and jeering. In between bouts I managed to elicit a response to my questions. The good news was that we could proceed. The bad news was that we were not going to be allowed to cross the southern section from Bilma to Nguigmi. This was the hardest section and involved crossing a large sand sea. It would have been a very hazardous journey with little or no chance of outside help if anything went wrong. As it was we had permission for a 1,300-mile, sixteen-day journey which included two crossings of the Tenere. That night, as we set up camp a short distance out of town I pondered the potential problems.

Back at the tourist office next morning we set about hiring a guide. After a drive around town the Chef found a thin, young looking man to guide us. My first impression was that he wasn't particularly self-confident but he seemed to know the route. Once more at the office we were ushered into the Chef's private room. We discussed the route in detail comparing photographs with the map.

I spent the rest of the day with Hamma, the guide, going over the details of our journey. I was encouraged to see that he looked at some depth into our equipment, fuel and water carrying capacity. We were carrying a comprehensive tools and vehicle spares pack. In addition to that both Land Rovers had electric winches, one of the Bedfords had a huge mechanical winch and pulley and all four vehicles were equipped with sand ladders and shovels. We carried forty five-gallon water jerricans which could sustain us for ten days if we limited washing to one cupful of water per person per day. We hoped never to have to restrict drinking water. Fuel-wise, through a combination of extra tanks mounted on the Bedfords, we carried a total of 400 gallons which gave us a total capacity for a convoy of 1,200 miles on good roads. We didn't know how far the fuel figures would fall off in soft sand but we estimated fifty per cent. Past disasters exemplified that a failure in our calculations in any of these areas could prove fatal. Having satisfied ourselves that our safety margins were adequate we wandered through the town to have a look at the camel market.

The camel market took place on a large dusty plain on the outskirts of town. In the centre of the scene a number of camels and goats were either hobbled or tethered at random, tended by their owners. Cries of children playing rose above the hubbub. There appeared to be little in the way of transactions taking place but with the warm evening light filtering through the haze and dust there was a glimpse of the bygone way of life of these proud nomads.

Next morning, after a final flurry around the markets to lay in a supply of fresh vegetables and having topped up every available water can, we picked up Hamma. He was clutching our letter of authorisation, typed in triplicate and complete with the mandatory rubber stamps and signatures without which no African official would recognise a form's legitimacy.

Eventually we were on our way. I felt as if a great weight had lifted off my shoulders. We were driving away from intransigent officials and out into the embracing peace of the desert. We left Agadez on one of the many narrow sand tracks. After about 20 miles it emerged as a clearer route with even the occasional signpost pointing the way north to Timia and Iferouane. The ground was relatively flat, pebbled sand. We passed several palmeraies. In most, there were clusters of circular grass huts.

As we drove I questioned Hamma about his background. He had been born the youngest of a large Touareg family. His father had owned and bred camels. Typical of a Touareg family, they had lived a nomadic life moving to wherever they could find adequate grazing around the southern edge of the Air mountains. They had never stayed in one place for long before the grazing was exhausted and they had to pack up their spartan camp and move on. Hamma had never been to school and couldn't read or write. All his learning had been gathered whilst tending the flocks and listening to the older men around the campfire. He had journeyed around most of the Air and had even crossed the Tenere by camel to Bilma. He spoke longingly of his days as a camel herder before he had moved into Agadez to join his wife's family and work as a guide. Once a year, after the rains, there had been a great gathering of the Touaregs. They came together from all over the Air to celebrate the rains. There was feasting, match-making and the main highlight: camel races. The camels were specially bred for this and he spoke with as much feeling as any Newmarket trainer would about his Derby hopeful. The races were long, up to thirty miles, hard and keenly contested. He had competed for a number of years, coming second once but he had never won.

He talked of a time, centuries before, when the Touaregs had controlled most of Niger northwards from Zinder and had their capital at Iferouane. He gave the impression that there had been thousands if not tens of thousands of Touaregs camped around the oasis. The Touaregs had always been a nation of warriors. They had either attacked or demanded protection money from any outsiders entering their territory. Even paying the levy hadn't always guaranteed immunity. Then

150 years ago the French had marched in. He talked of a Great War between the Touaregs and the invaders, of many battles and great bravery. But in the end, no matter how determined the tribesmen's resistance, they were subdued by superior weaponry. Camel-borne charges were cut down in swathes by the Legionnaires' rifles and machine guns. The French had governed Niger as a colony for the next 120 years. They had reinstated the Hausas, schooled them, trained them and set them up in government. The Touaregs on the other hand had been persecuted and denied public office. Even now in modern Niger they held little political power. He could remember, aged seven, watching the French military leaving Agadez. It had taken many trucks and three days to evacuate them all. He spoke in quiet, rich tones rolling his 'r's' in a slightly guttural way. It was a version of history passed down by word of mouth from generation to generation in a sad lament to a once great nation.

At Hamma's request we had given a lift to one of his cousins and so we stopped to drop him off at his village. The menfolk were away and there were no more than fifteen women and children. Some of the women came up asking for medicines for a variety of complaints. Hamma was obviously keen that we should help so Matthew held an impromptu clinic. As throughout the Sahara we noticed a widespread problem with eye infections. They were open, friendly people — peasants among their own kind. The little children were very pretty with fine features and dark brown eyes.

The further on we went the hillier the surrounding countryside became. We crossed several dry river beds which Hamma told us would flash flood in the wet season and then dry out within hours. We stopped in one to camp the night. Setting up camp was now a familiar routine. Each person had their own task and by and large it worked efficiently.

Continuing on our route took us into far harsher terrain. The surrounding hills became steeper and higher. We crossed black volcanic rock plains which shimmered in the heat. In places there appeared to be no colour in any direction. It was hot and oppressive. At other times it was surprisingly green. We passed through a number of irrigated fields and palmeraies. We even saw a couple of patches of healthy looking wheat. Later that morning we turned off the main track and dropped down a short section to a pool in a dry river bed with a small waterfall pouring into it.

The rock had been eroded so that it swirled into smooth recesses in the centre of the watercourse and at the edge rose in small stair rods. The water was bracingly cold when we dived in. It made a pleasant setting in which to while away the hottest part of the day.

Later when it was cooler we drove on to the village of Timia. Bigger than the other villages that we had seen and flanked by large palmeraies it had a lush, comfortable feel about it. A couple of hundred feet above on a small hill sat a deserted fort — a relic from the early French occupation. This was the first place where we had to submit our papers to the police for inspection.

Next day we continued on into the Air crossing more lunar landscape. We stopped at the deserted village of Assonde. It had been built in the fifteenth century but abandoned during the Great War. All that remained now were the broken-down shells of houses. It was such a bleak, arid spot that it was impossible to imagine why anyone had ever wanted to live there.

We turned east about halfway up the range and emerged from the dark, stony wasteland into a broad valley leading out towards the Tenere. The vegetation began thinning out and dunes flanked our path. At one point we came across an enormous dune littered with rocks of white marble. The white rocks, yellow sand and blue sky stood in crisp, striking contrast to each other. We glimpsed small herds of dainty gazelles who skipped away at the first sight or sound of us. We also saw two groups of ostriches who were equally shy. Hamma told me that hunting had been banned in Niger but the twinkle in his eye suggested that this was not adhered to by the Touaregs. They liked to hunt with long sharpened poles, mounted on their camels.

Another indication of their predilection for hunting appeared next morning when a small group of Touaregs materialised out of the desert at our campsite together with their goats and dogs. The dogs looked like a form of smooth-coated lurcher and could only have been bred for hunting. The men stood off to one side with Hamma, watching aloof. The women's natural inquisitiveness overcame their shyness and they approached closer, giggling together. They seemed particularly fascinated by Tetta and Leslie and kept touching their clothes. I asked Hamma to find out if they would be prepared to sell us a goat which they did. Leaving a group to butcher the goat and look after the lorries we set off in the Land Rovers to a place in the desert where Hamma knew of some rock paintings. We let the tyre pressure down to give us better flotation over the soft sand. Even with our Michelin XS sand tyres we were finding it tough going. Three hours of driving through some stunning desert scenery brought us to a small lugga, on one side of which was a rock wall about 100 yards long and fifty feet at its highest point. There had been no track to bring us there nor had we seen signs of any other vehicle tracks. Hamma's sense of direction in apparently featureless surroundings was uncanny.

In groups on the rocks were paintings that he claimed were 10,000 years old. Some were fairly sophisticated. There were individual animals; addax, giraffe, cattle, stylised Touareg women and scenes of hunting on horseback. One rock was covered in Tamasheq writing. At the time of painting the Sahara would have looked very different. It had been fertile, green and populated by much of the wildlife now associated with East Africa. We stopped to take photographs and have lunch; an uninspiring meal of hard tack biscuits, tinned mackerel and jam. Despite the sun beating down with great intensity it was surprisingly cold due to the constant Harmattan wind that blew at that time of year keeping us in long trousers and fibre pile jackets for most of the day. We made our way back to the lorries via another open water-hole. There was no way that we would have found it without Hamma. It wasn't marked on our maps and was concealed one mile up a gulley which was impassable to vehicles. We didn't swim as he said that the water was very precious here and reserved for drinking only. As we drove on the evening light made the dunes glow pink. The sun set, a perfect fiery globe, behind the dark Air mountains. Hamma guided us faultlessly but it was with some relief that we saw the lights of camp appear in front of us.

That night there were happy faces around the campfire as Cpl Goodier handed around great, dripping steaks of spit-roasted goat. It was the first time that we had had fresh meat for several weeks. I had been concerned as to how Hamma would settle in to the group. Before leaving Agadez I had overheard muttered comments from amongst the team querying why we needed an outsider to show us where to go. His customs set him apart. As a devout Muslim he wouldn't eat pork and prayed five times per day. At the appointed times, if there was no reason to prevent him, he would walk away from the rest of us and kneel facing east. Then he would slip off his sandals and wash both feet and hands in the sand before praying. In prayer he would mouth verses of the Koran, repeatedly bowing forward to touch his head on the sand. Several of the men had reported seeing him get up at 5am to pray. At night he would set his camp slightly away from us and only then did he remove his head-dress. Not even when eating would he uncover his face in front of us. Aside from that he had a ready sense of humour and came over as a warm, kind-hearted man. He was thus accepted by most of the group despite the fact that few could speak even a few words of French and thus weren't able to converse with him. He became closest to Cpl Goodier who had broken the ice by asking Hamma to show him how to wear the head-dress and robe that he had bought. That had led to Cpl Goodier being jokingly known as 'Andy Touareg'. When 'Andy Touareg' was preparing the evening meal Hamma would set up his own ritual brewing of the Touareg tea beside him. This was an elaborate procedure. First the pot was swilled out and then

Top: Starting the trek in to the Neltner Hut; High Atlas Mountains.

Bottom: Moving up the ridge to the summit of Jebel Toubkal.

Bambara Woman, Mali.

Top: Driving through the Sahel, Mali.

Bottom: Touareg brothers at the camel market in Agadez.

Top: Touareg drawing water to irrigate his small vegetable plantation.

Bottom: The 13th century mud chateau at Djaba.

Top: Foreign Legion fort at Chirfa.

Bottom: Touareg and hunting dog on the edge of the Tenere.

Top: Another patch of soft sand in the Tenere. Cfn Heath and Gdsm Hughes dig out.

Bottom: The Tenere — 200 miles of perfect emptiness.

Stands of bamboo collapsed across the Zairean tracks.

Top: Pygmies sorting out their long nets at their camp in the Ituri forest.

Bottom: The Mountains of the Moon stretching up above the jungle.

warmed. Then the leaves were added and brewed together with mounds of sugar. The mixture was then poured from a great height and with considerable flourish into small glasses only to be poured straight back into the pot. This performance was repeated several times before the tea was deemed drinkable. The end result was about four or five glasses of very sweet but refreshing herbal tea. It became a feature of our nightly routine. Hamma would normally only brew one pot sharing it with just one or two others. Although more performance than result few people turned down the offer of one of these apparently prestigious cups of tea and most were flattered to be invited to partake.

We continued north up the east side of the Air. For the first time we began to learn some of the hard lessons of desert mobility. Initially we travelled over wide areas of soft sand but apart from the occasional bogging in we managed without any major difficulties. We were then faced by a narrow gully leading up to a fairly steep ramp of sand. The Land Rovers made it to the top with a bit of effort. Cpl Goodier took a long run at it in his Bedford and bulldozed his way over but Cpl Chesterfield, in the heavier winch wagon had no chance. He just couldn't build up enough momentum to carry the vehicle through. The vehicle was now bogged halfway down to its axles. We tried using sand ladders to get it out — but to no avail.

Cpl Goodier then took to the cab and with some fairly aggressive driving and quick gear changes managed to back it out. He took an expansive run up and charged the hill. No matter how much we all willed the lorry forward we watched as it made just a few extra yards' progress on the previous attempt before, this time, sinking right up to its axles. The mechanics then decided to try and winch it over by attaching the winch cables to the other Bedford on the far side of the obstacle. At this point everyone suddenly became an instant expert on vehicle recovery and began chipping in their ten pence worth — the result was chaos. I could see that CSgt Bennett had stepped back from the scene and was filming from the far hillside. I decided to withdraw too and watch to see how the mechanics would cope. I knew little or nothing about vehicle recovery and didn't want to get in their way. It took what felt like an age for them to sort themselves out. They found that a 1:1 pull wasn't strong enough and so began to rig a pulley for a 2:1 pull. Looking from a distance I could see just how relatively small an obstacle had stopped us. Crossing one of the great sand seas with these vehicles didn't bear thinking about.

After an hour and a half Hamma could stand it no longer and stopped them saying that he would find a way around. The mechanics looked most indignant that their high-tech solutions weren't working and they looked accusingly at me for not giving them longer to try. After another age while they packed all of the kit away, they extricated the vehicle backwards and true to his word, after several attempts Hamma led them around the problem. His eye for the ground was outstanding. He stared intently at the sand almost defying it to deny him. He would get out and scrutinise ever closer on the really soft sections.

Following this incident I put Hamma into the winch Bedford and made that the lead vehicle. This worked much better. He was able to read the ground and avoid the majority of boggings. When this didn't work the other lorry travelled a short distance behind it ready to provide an anchor from which it could winch itself back out. The Land Rovers were then free to whiz about at will. We continued on our way crossing several low but steep ridges, making progress with the occasional stop to dig ourselves out. The only near disaster came at another of these ridges. I saw each of the other vehicles accelerate to give themselves enough momentum to get over it only to grind to a halt at the top. Not wishing to suffer the same fate I wheeled round and took a long run at it, building up as much speed as I could. I hit the slope with a full head of steam, foot to the floor, in fourth gear. What I hadn't seen was that the others had all stopped, not for soft sand, but due to a near vertical drop the other side. With the speed that I had built up we shot over the crest like a cork out of a champagne bottle and then nosedived, plummeting down the far side. There was an appalling moment as everything went into slow motion and there were a couple of yells of 'Hang on!' from the front and 'Oh shit!' from the back. We hit the ground with a chassis-shattering crunch. All of the kit was hurled forward from the back and everyone was fairly shaken up but amazingly no damage was done. Another lesson learnt — recce blind hills!

For the remainder of the day we followed a broad open piste until, in the afternoon, we came to Adrar Chiriat. This large black mountain massif formed an island in the surrounding sand sea. On the horizon dunes of many different pastel shades glowed warmly as though casually dropped like so many piles of silks. Subtle pinks blended with soft oranges, rich creams and pale almost whites. In stark contrast Adrar Chiriat rose up a Tolkeinesque collection of forbidding towers and spires. We drove through a pass in the mountain. Once again I was struck by the beauty and variety of the desert scenery.

That night we reviewed some of the lessons that we had learnt and worked out a code of convoy discipline and an approach to recovery situations.

I awoke to find myself lying in a mini sand dune that had built up around me in the night. It was still very cold and blowing a gale. We shook ourselves down and huddled around the stove to eat our breakfast of coffee and porridge. We drove for fifty miles before reaching Iferouane. Although no longer the capital of the Touareg kingdom, Iferouane was a large settlement of rectangular mud buildings. There were a few stores selling dry biscuits, dates, which we later found were mostly inhabited by maggots, and more of the EEC's aid provided tinned sardines and corned beef. We were able to fill up with water for the last time before setting off into the Tenere. We drove on for another fifty miles before finding a campsite in the lee of a rock face with a small cave for a kitchen. Fetching wood for the fire we found a small, evil looking snake — probably a viper, which Hamma warned us was deadly poisonous. We had come across another snake a few mornings before: Tetta had been packing away her bed when she turned it over to find a snake curled up asleep underneath it. She leapt out from under the canopy shrieking, much to the amusement of all the soldiers. On closer inspection it looked to be a blind sand snake which had been attracted to the warmth of her body. It appeared harmless and burrowed back under the sand away from the bright sunlight.

Between us and the Tenere lay some of the largest sand dunes in the world. We drove on along a reputedly difficult piste. The only really tricky section was in a narrow gulley where sheer rock walls channelled us along deeply rutted sand. We rose all the time until we reached the Col du Temet, the highest point of our route on a saddle between two dunes. We got out of the vehicles and climbed one of these. In front of us lay one of the most spectacular views that I had ever cast eyes on. Stretching away as far as the eye could see was an endless sea of massive classical dunes. The scene brought to life every desert photograph that I had seen. Great sweeping ridges of sand snaked up to star-shaped, wind-blown summits in perfect crescents. Every shape, every shadow, every colour seemed to epitomise crisp geometrical exactitude. It was a symphony in sand.

As we drove down the far side of the col we gawped at each dune in turn as it loomed, even larger and more graceful than those previously above us. Film followed film through the cameras as we tried to capture the beauty of the place — as if we could ever hope to take it away with us. We entered one small valley carpeted with desert melons and low tussocky cram cram grass. The melons were small and circular but they are emetic and thus inedible. A lone Touareg woman stood with her herd of goats; dressed in black with her veil drawn across her face, she appeared a tragic, lonesome figure dwarfed by the vastness of her surroundings.

We made camp early in a flat-bottomed valley between two enormous dunes which rose 1,000 feet above us. Either side the ridges hummed under the force of the wind. Depending on the intensity with which it blew the sound varied from a low murmuring drone to a high insistent whine. I cleaned all of the camera equipment in a vain attempt to protect the working parts from the abrasive persistence of the sand before shooting a series of promotional shots of items of sponsored equipment with the dunes as a backdrop. Later I went for a walk alone to absorb the feeling of the place.

The next twenty-six miles continued through more grandiose, intoxicating scenery until we reached Adrar Brous, a large mountain that signalled the end of the sand sea. A long slope led up to the flat expanse of the Tenere. The winch Bedford bogged down and then in a rather ill-considered attempt to lighten its load by refuelling the Land Rovers from its entrenched position one of them bogged in as well. Only after a protracted period of digging, laying sand ladders and deflating the tyres did we gain the plateau.

Ahead lay 220 miles of absolute void. I had a mental picture of what it was going to be like but I was totally unprepared for the reality. Initially the scrubby acacia bushes gave way to tussocks of cram cram grass but after a while even that disappeared. There was no vegetation, no stones, no tracks, just emptiness. As driver of the front vehicle there was nothing to focus on. It was almost impossible to judge whether the horizon was fifty yards or fifty miles away. Patches of dark sand appeared like shadows in the dunes spooking the drivers into slamming on their brakes thinking that they were about to crash into a sand wall or plunge down a steep drop. In places the sand was undulating and yet it was difficult to determine whether you were going up or down without looking at another vehicle for comparison. Another illusion was that moving vehicles appeared stationary. Any form of perspective vanished leaving just nothingness with a line of silver mirage separating sand from sky. It was an agoraphobic's nightmare.

Hamma sat in the front passenger seat of my Land Rover staring intently forward and indicating the direction that we should take with a flick of his finger. He had no reference points and no map or compass and yet he never hesitated. I asked him what he used to guide him and he said the position of the sun and the pattern of the wind in the sand. Once he had explained how he did it I tried several times but was never able to hold a straight course for longer than a few minutes before veering off. He said that no camels crossed the Tenere by this route as there were no wells for them to take any water.

We stopped after 110 miles having made good progress. It felt very strange to set up camp whilst unable to see a single thing in any direction. However it provided perfect parascending ground. Unfortunately the conditions weren't ideal with winds gusting well above the safety limits.

Before packing up we conducted a few training practices putting individuals into the harness, letting the chute inflate and allowing them to get the feel of controlling the chute using the steering toggles whilst anchored to the ground by several of the biggest men holding them down. When they practised their flare-outs the chute collapsed and the whole lot ended up in a great sprawling heap on the ground.

We set off again across the Tenere. Once more the nothingness enveloped us. After a couple of hours I spotted an object breaking the line of silver mirage on the horizon. We turned off our course and drove over to find the body of an aeroplane that had crashed four years earlier. A simple airstrip had been marked out with forty-five gallon drums. We couldn't tell the reason for the crash but there lay the body of a small light aircraft with bent propellers and debris lying all around. In the back was a small packet with handwriting in French which said, 'To all entrants of the Paris-Dakar Rally put your mail here. Good luck'. From the wreckage we could see another much larger object in the distance.

We drove towards its distorted image, peering through our binoculars to try and make out what it was. What greeted us was a scene that could have come straight out of Mad Max. It was an abandoned oil drilling station. Five portacabins, half filled with sand, and mechanical debris in great twisted, decaying piles surrounded the main platform. We climbed up to the control room where log sheets bearing the crest of the parent American mining company were fluttering in the wind. It was an eerie place.

Later on Hamma announced that he was looking for a tree — a concept which seemed to me perverse in its difficulty. Sure enough several miles further on another distant object broke the horizon. On closer inspection it was a small isolated mound with a couple of scrubby acacia trees on top underneath which there were some marble stones. On one of the stones was inscribed 'Thierry Sabine', together with his date of birth and untimely death. Under another rock in a plastic bag were two books describing the life of this remarkable Frenchman who had founded the Paris-Dakar Rally. He had died in a helicopter crash in Mali whilst organising the 8th Paris-Dakar Rally in 1986. He had been a true adventurer and was clearly held in high esteem by both Westerners and Africans. L'Arbre Perdit du Tenere seemed a very fitting resting place and in itself a great tribute to the man. It had a special, rather humbling, peaceful atmosphere, a single island isolated in this endless nothingness.

After a brief and rather unappetising lunch of hard tack biscuits we carried on. I invested a couple of hours reading *The ABC of Paragliding* in a belated attempt to save my neck whilst Richard drove. In front, a narrow pink line grew steadily larger until we could see it as the line of cliffs or falaise that marked the far side of the Tenere. At last we had something solid to focus on. The sand gave way to a long pebbled piste leading up to the falaise. We headed towards a break in the cliff line which would lead us to the outpost of Chirfa. On the way we came across the fourth reminder that day of the dangers posed by the Sahara; the burnt-out shell of a DAF truck that had crashed and rolled, killing both occupants, whilst competing in the Paris-Dakar Rally. It was a sobering sight.

We camped in a beautiful location, nestled under the wind-sculpted pink rock of the falaise from which we could gaze out into the Tenere. Richard and I sat on stag* together from 10pm until midnight sharing a small glass from my dwindling supply of whisky and reflecting on all that we had seen.

Next day we drove the remaining eight miles across a flat plain to present ourselves to the military or Gard Nomadique at Chirfa. The outpost was built on a small hill with a stone wall perimeter and block houses on two prominent knolls with commanding views over the surrounding area. We could see uniformed guards on sentry at each of these. The whole place had an austere rather business-like feel about it. As we pulled up two men came out to meet us. The first took charge and made us move our vehicles to another place about fifty yards away. It was a rather senseless gesture but presumably designed to show us who was boss. When I explained that we were a military expedition his attitude changed completely and when I said that we were infanteers he positively beamed as he also was an infantryman. We left our passports with him having called the roll and checked off each man's face against his passport photograph.

We drove nineteen miles north, passing a couple of lush palmeraies until we came to a series of enormous volcanic plugs. The largest of these sheer-sided mountains, Ourida, towered 1,000 feet above us and must have had a circumference of well over a mile. It was a rock-climber's dream offering unlimited hard technical climbing on hot rock. We stopped in a col between Ourida and its neighbour which gave us a spectacular view along the mountain chain. Tens of thousands of years previously, when the desert was under water, this might have been the cliffs on the shoreline.

Hamma had told us that there was normally a large water source here and had said that we would be able to swim. Still on water rationing of a cupful per person per day for washing that was like pledging the earth. So it was with much dismay that we looked out over a depression of parched sand where the promised water hole should have been. In the

*Military jargon for 'sentry duty'

face of considerable disbelieving muttering he took off down the slope to the base of the depression and began digging. After going down eighteen inches he hit damp sand and another foot further down the hole began to fill with brown rather rancid water. It was deliciously cool to wash your feet in but a long step from the exotic oasis of everyone's fantasies. I felt a strong urge to get away from everyone for a while so I pottered off and scrambled up some rocks well out of harm's way to enjoy a bit of peace and solitude.

We drove along the line of volcanic plugs. In the base of two were large caves. They had impressive entranceways, vaulted like some natural Gothic cathedral. Inside they were cool. Up at the back we found tunnels where over a thousand years before four or five Toubou families would have lived. A few miles further on we came to the deserted chateaux of Djaba and Djado, built by the Toubou in the thirteenth century and deserted 200 years ago because of a proliferation of raiding Touaregs, Western slave hunters and malarial mosquitoes. The Djado chateau was much the larger of the two and had survived longer but our enjoyment of it was marred by the clouds of mosquitoes that descended on us as soon as we set foot in the surrounding palmeraie. The Djaba chateau some six miles away was very compact, much more attractive and mercifully insect free. It consisted of a labyrinth of passages connecting layers of rooms built on and around a conical hill. The walls were all mud built and the chambers appeared to have been piled on top of each other with total disregard to any plan or order. Although many of the roofs and walls had collapsed most of the framework was still in place. They must have been tiny people judging from the size of the sleeping pallets and doorways. The proliferation of rooms suggested that the chateau must have housed a sizeable community. Inside, it had a busy feel to it but from a distance, set against the mountain backdrop, with swaying palms before it, although deserted and crumbling it had a regal air.

The next day dawned 1 March — St David's Day. There was a fairly half-hearted rendition of the Welsh National Anthem at breakfast. Everyone was thinking of the celebrations that would be taking place back in Pirbright. As usual the battalion would be having a parade in tunics and bearskins. This year, as it was our 75th Anniversary, Her Majesty The Queen was to present the leeks. No doubt the whole place would be spick and span with the smell of fresh paint heavy in the air. After the parade Officers, Sergeants, Corporals and guardsmen would retire to their respective messes for lunch and more than a few drinks with their wives, girlfriends and families. I wondered if any of them would have time to spare a thought for us. I learned much later that just as the Commanding Officer was briefing The Queen after the parade, my first letter to him, outlining our progress to date, arrived and that they read it together.

Meanwhile back in Africa we left those who wanted a relaxing day to look after the Bedfords and set off in the Land Rovers to explore the Djado plateau. To get onto the plateau we found ourselves lurching up over a series of rough, stepped rock pavements and wending through narrow channels between the rock walls. Above lay a boundless wilderness of volcanic rock peaks separated by valleys and more stone pavements. We found natural arches, huge boulders teetering on slender pedestals and more caves adorned with paintings of elephants. Around the outside were strewn shards of pottery. It was a hostile, godless environment, cruel on the vehicles and with a scale that was overwhelming.

Once reunited with the others we returned to Chirfa to replenish our water from the well and collect our passports. In the centre of the village stood a fort abandoned by the French Foreign Legion. It could have been transposed straight out of the pages of *Beau Geste*: an arched entrance flanked by long crenellated walls, surrounded a small parade ground. Two palm trees grew either side of the gateway. A single layer of rooms lined the inside of the walls. At diametrically opposite corners of the square stood watch towers. All that was missing were legionnaires in blue tunics and white kepis with blancoed webbing belts and straps attaching issue grey army blankets to their backs doing drill under the Saharan sun. If only those walls could talk what stories would they have to tell? Had they faced attacks by hordes of Touareg tribesmen? What deeds of bravery had they witnessed? It was a place to stir one's imagination.

We took a further two days to drive south to Bilma. Initially we followed the line of the falaise before breaking out into the open and, at times, featureless desert. There were several villages along the route. In general they were unremarkable and rather drab; just a single street of whitewashed mud houses inside a palmeraie. The inhabitants were largely Toubou. They were a naturally attractive people. The women wore brightly coloured robes and veils. Most had a gold ring through their left nostril.

The conical hill of Pic Zoumri guided us to the village of Sequedine. Beyond we had problems with feche feche — areas of soft sand concealed by a hard crust. The Bedfords tended to plough slowly through but the Land Rovers would fall through this crust without warning and bog in straight up to the axles. If the driver didn't stop revving immediately you could see the Land Rover tensing up on itself like a boxer flexing his muscles. If the driver then dipped the clutch instead of easing off the accelerator all of the energy that had been built up would be released in a sudden explosive burst which risked shattering the half shafts.

At Dirkou we went to the only fuel dump on the east of the Tenere. It was run by a Libyan named Jerome who announced gleefully that he would accept any hard currency. He was in his sixties and proudly told us that he had served in the Arab Libyan Corps under Montgomery at El Alamein, Sidi Barani and Tobruk. His new-found friendship for us as fellow soldiers didn't extend as far as a reduction in the price of the fuel for which he charged us through the nose. Having filled up with enough fuel to recross the Tenere with a safety margin for error we continued on towards Bilma.

Bilma was the largest of the eastern Niger settlements. This was mainly due to the salines on the edge of town. The sand was dug away from large patches of ground up to six feet in depth revealing a layer of impure rock salt underneath. This was then smashed with poles into six foot by four foot pits and then flooded, forming natural evaporation ponds. By the side of the ponds lay piles of pure white salt crystals that had been harvested. These were finally ground down and sold for human consumption or remoulded into either circular nuggets or cones, that were the original biblical pillars, to be fed to the stock. Camel caravans even now cross the Tenere from Agadez to Bilma to carry back their cargo of salt. We were still eating the salt that we had bought in Bilma ten months later. Reprovisioning as always took ages whilst LSgt Jenkins and Cpl Goodier went around all of the gardens and ducas haggling for every item. Meanwhile the remainder of the team descended upon the town like a swarm of locusts in search of any luxury titbits. Some found the first cold beer since leaving Agadez whilst for others cool sweet juice from a tin of pineapple slices was nectar enough. As always we were pursued by women trying to sell us arrowheads and jewellery and children demanding *cadeaux* of money, sweets or pens.

We drove out of town to be greeted by the rather incongruous sight of a lighthouse that would have graced any channel port. It had been built by the French to guide voyagers from the Tenere to safety.

We recrossed the Tenere following the route taken by the camel caravans. Camel skeletons, lying every few hundred yards, served as grim reminders of the hardship and dangers associated with the journey. The conditions were very different to those of the northern crossing. We now found ourselves travelling along causeways between long parallel dunes. The dunes were much lower than those at the Col du Temet and seemed to flow in equally sized lines like waves on the sea. It was more interesting country but lacked the same sensation of isolation. Navigation was no easier and we had constant problems with soft sand. Our vehicle recovery techniques became swift and efficient. Often we had to dig the vehicles out with shovels or just our hands scraping away the sand and sometimes we had to lay sand tracks in relays to build a causeway out of the soft area.

On one occasion the soft sand worked in our favour as a Bedford bogged down five feet before it would have plunged down a near vertical slip face. Cpl Chesterfield, the driver, was visibly shaken. Again the monotony of the sand was playing havoc with our ability to judge distances and he had had no inkling of the danger that lay in front of him. Fachi provided the first of two havens on the route. It was a bright, cheerful place with plenty of shade in which to hide from the relentless sun. As soon as we stopped we were surrounded by an enormous crowd of children all cheering and smiling. There seemed to be an inordinate number for this small desert village. They were mainly primary school age. The girls had their hair plaited into intricate patterns or twisted to form spikes and pyramids. Hamma dealt with the formalities and the rest of us either sunbathed or took photographs.

We stopped forty miles further out into the desert to parascend. We had had several sessions and were now confident in our methods and safety procedures. Flying over the Sahara was always exhilarating but my lasting memory is of the flight the next morning. We got up at 6am, bundled all of the parascending kit into the Land Rovers and drove a short distance away from camp to a flat area between parallel dunes. I went up first just as the sun peered over the horizon. There was almost no wind. It was a stunning flight. Below me, I could see the tiny figures at the launch site, to my left the two matchbox-size Bedfords still set up with all the accoutrements of an overnight camp and spreading away into the distance the long, low lines of dunes. The glowing orb of the rising sun bathed everything in gentle orange light. Several others enjoyed similar flights before the wind conditions became too difficult.

Once we had dropped down from the dune plateau we entered a desolate, stony wasteland. A line of balises led us to Arbre du Tenere. As its name suggests Arbre du Tenere had been the site of a lone tree marking the second well of the crossing. Incredibly, despite literally thousands of square miles of space surrounding it, a lorry had driven into the tree in a sandstorm and knocked it down. There was now a rather crude metal 'tree' marking the spot. To our amazement in this terrible, bleak, windswept place there was a hut out of which emerged a Touareg and his family. He was the guardian of the well which had been sunk in 1988. The old well, nearby, had been poisoned when a camel had fallen into it and died.

We continued across plains of sharp rocks into sparse scrubland. We camped in a small depression surrounded by a few straggly trees. Some tribespeople materialised out of the scrub and sat watching us until well after dark. It felt very dirty after the crisp cleanness of the desert.

The last stage of the journey back to Agadez took us three hours in a minor sandstorm. It wasn't an attractive route and I had an overwhelming feeling of anti-climax. Back in the world of reality we needed to take on fuel, water and provisions, go to the bank and ring England to sort out the changeover arrangements and make last-minute requests for the next phase of the expedition.

When we dropped Hamma off at his house he asked us in to share Touareg tea with him for one last time. He led us through a dirt courtyard into his flat-roofed, mud-walled house. Seven people lived there: himself, his mother, brothers, wife and children. We passed through one room furnished only with two simple chairs and no decorations. In the room beyond there were mattresses or mats to sit on, a bed with no bedclothes and a metal locker — nothing else. Following his example we took our shoes off and sat down. There was a slightly wary atmosphere due to the language barrier and our lack of familiarity with the correct etiquette. A large bowl of water was passed around. One of the guardsmen washed his hands in it to the horror of Hamma's family. Apparently it was for drinking. One of the others had suggested that we should wash our feet in it but luckily no one had. I chatted to Hamma about the possibility of returning on another expedition to make a journey by camel out into the desert. One of his brothers wrote down Hamma's name and address for me so that I could write to him to make the arrangements for him to buy camels and obtain the necessary clearances. We partook of the ritual three glasses of tea and then took our leave. As we were going Hamma presented 'Andy Touareg' with one of his tea glasses as a memento. It was a touching gesture. He had been an excellent guide and had shown us what a proud, disciplined and distinguished people the Touaregs are. As we said goodbye I felt as if I was leaving one of the team behind.

Apart from reprovisioning with a mouth-watering array of fresh food Agadez proved frustrating. The bank was closed and thus we didn't have money for fuel. Water was being sold at extortionate rates and the police kept trying to move us on. We headed out of town to camp in the bush before continuing south.

We passed a number of camel caravans, their caravanniers' heads bowed against the Harmattan wind as we drove through the semi-desert towards the Tinidit falaise and on a further day's journey to Zinder. There once again our plans were thwarted. The students had declared a National Strike and everyone else had gone out in sympathy. As we completed the formalities the police informed us that the strike could well go on for several days. With the banks and Post Office shut there seemed little point in hanging around so we kept going to the Nigerian border.

Our relief at entering an English-speaking country was short-lived when the hitherto polite customs official spotted a fault on our documentation. Our carnets de passage weren't endorsed for Nigeria. No matter how hard I looked at them there was no denying that he was right. As he was refusing us entry to the country we had no option but to try and bluff our way through using the old lines of being a military expedition there at the invitation of the government. As we launched into this approach events took an even worse turn when another official announcing himself as a member of military intelligence stepped forward and pronounced that he knew nothing about us, we were clearly a threat to the national security and should on no account be admitted. At this stage all the others became very wary of us. I argued for all I was worth, dropping every name that I could think of but to no avail. I knew full well that we did indeed have formal clearance from the Nigerian Government to enter the country but with no letter to prove it and no workable telephone system available for them to contact their higher command I wasn't getting anywhere. The more I protested the more adamant the military intelligence man became and the more unhappy the customs officials looked. We were passed on up the chain from officer to officer until finally I spoke to the Commanding Officer of the frontier post. He was a most charming man who sympathised with us but wasn't prepared to go against the advice of his colleague. Eventually I managed to get him to agree to have us escorted to Kaduna, the district capital, to sort the matter out. I knew that there was a British military advisory team there headed by a Colonel. I was sure that if only I could contact them this whole horrible mess could be sorted out. We left the customs post at 7pm having completed all the formalities and thanked the customs chief for his help. Armed guards travelled in the front of each vehicle.

The roads were desperate with many complicated detours and a lot of police and military checkpoints. Our escorts proved to be a blessing acting as our passport through. We arrived at the customs depot at Kaduna at 2am and to their amazement set up camp and went to bed. In the morning events didn't go as planned. I was taken to see the Head of Customs for the District of Kaduna. As with the other officials he was polite but in view of our military status we were too hot a potato to handle. Before I knew it I found myself on the way to the Headquarters of the Military Command for the district to see the senior army officer there. There I was questioned at length by a colonel. He knew nothing about us and was instantly suspicious. After several bouts of questioning I was sent to fetch the remainder of the team. When they arrived he called for all of our passports which he then impounded pending a decision from the military High Command in Lagos. Unfortunately it was now Friday afternoon and as in all Muslim countries everyone was on their way to the mosque. We would be unlikely to receive an answer until Monday but meanwhile we were to be released into the care of the British Consulate and confined to their compound.

We were taken, once more under escort, to the Consulate. When I sat down in the cool air-conditioned waiting room it was with a mixture of relief and satisfaction that we had reached the end of the first part of our journey without any major mishap. I was sure that our present predicament would be shortly resolved. I knew we had reached safety when the receptionist offered us afternoon tea whilst we waited. The only thing that spoilt the moment was the awful realisation of just how dirty and malodorous we were in comparison to our immediate surroundings. The looks on the faces of the consulate staff as they saw the state of us and the way their noses wrinkled as they caught the first whiff of unwashed bodies was killing. It varied from mild embarrassment to the horror and consternation of a Bateman cartoon that one of Her Majesty's waiting rooms should be thus defiled.

Luckily LtCol Peter Cable and his wife Diana appeared before long. He had been expecting us and now took charge. He and I went straight around to the Nigerian colonel's house to try and resolve the passport situation but no joy there. When we returned to the Consulate the staff very kindly offered us the use of some unoccupied apartments in their compound nearby. To us it was unimaginable luxury, proper beds, rooms with carpets and most exciting of all, baths. Meanwhile the Cables were delivering mountains of fresh food to stock our fridges. They were an absolutely charming couple and bent over backwards to make us welcome. Col Peter and I worked out some of the practical arrangements whilst Diana took the two girls under her protective wing and began a serious pampering regime.

Over the next few days we began a routine of vehicle maintenance, equipment repair, report writing and balancing our accounts. There was much to be done before this team left and the new team arrived. Retrieving the passports took several attempts. On our first visit the good colonel had gone away 'somewhere' leaving them locked in his safe. In the end it took a personal visit from the Consular First Secretary to secure their release. He tried to get a letter of authorisation for us to prevent any further problems but was assured that this was quite unnecessary as the matter was now resolved. I had my doubts.

In the evenings we were lavishly entertained by the Cables and resident expatriates in their homes and clubs. The soldiers wasted no time in seeking out the bright lights. On the first night everyone had gone out to a nightclub. I had gone home early unable to resist the call of a soft bed. In the morning I got up to find all of the others ribbing one very worried-looking member of the team. Despite frequent lectures on the dangers of sexual associations with local girls he had been unable to resist the temptation of the ladies of the night and had brought one back with him. They were all joshing him that he would contract Aids. Harry backed him up by saying that she had been beautiful enough to marry. Seeing the strength of their reaction I thought no more about it.

Next night everyone went out again to the nightclubs. By any standards many of the girls were stunning and after six weeks in the desert they took on goddess qualities. It was Saturday night and the party went on well into the night. I crawled home around 5am and woke with a storming hangover. I took my time getting up and making myself breakfast but the silence from the other rooms was ominous. When I went around to wake everyone up I found that most rooms were heaving with girls. One room was like a zebra crossing! I knew that we were treading on fairly thin ice with the consular staff as it was, many of whom weren't wild about having twenty squaddies living amongst them and I dreaded them seeing this lot. Nightfighters began appearing all over the place in various states of undress shouting, laughing at each other from the balconies and teetering around in high heels. Trying hard to avoid throwing a fit I raced around telling the men to get rid of them. Luckily no harm was done.

After a final party given for us by the Cables we set off to Kano to pick up the new team. All went well: they arrived safely, laden down with enormous rucksacks that they could barely lift containing more twenty-four hour ration packs and vehicle spares. They had had to jettison most of their own personal kit in favour of vital expedition stores. Col Peter paved their way through customs, all the baggage was cleared and then we hit a problem. Immigration took one look at our military status and impounded their passports. Where was the letter of authorisation? Where indeed I thought. Once again we faced a delay. However our problems didn't stop there. Somehow our freight had got inextricably lost in the web of bureaucratic insanity at the cargo depot. Then, to cap it all, when the Phase 1 team went to catch their plane the next day there were no seats available. The previous flight had been cancelled and hundreds of Africans were literally trying to fight their way up the gangway and onto the plane.

It was another day before we sorted out the chaos, found and retrieved the freight and arranged flights. With the clock already ticking on Phase 2 and with a planned rendezvous with our Patron five days later in Cameroon we had no choice but to leave the Phase 1 team, installed in the Kano campsite, to their own devices. They had a two-day wait before the earliest possible flight but in the event, to add insult to injury, the Harmattan struck, closing the airport due to sandstorms and it was a week before they left. We bade a sad farewell to Peter Cable. He had been so enthusiastic and over the previous week had baled us out of many problems. Turning south we drove on towards the next leg of our adventure.

Chapter Two
Pygmies and Primates

Phase 2

Captain John Warburton-Lee, Welsh Guards, Expedition leader
Captain Richard Gaffney, Welsh Guards, Second in Command
Captain Matthew Roberts, Royal Army Medical Corps, Expedition
  doctor
Colour Sergeant Alan Bennett, Welsh Guards, Senior Non
  Commissioned Officer
Miss Tetta Nicholls, Expedition secretary
Lieutenant Mark Jenkins, Welsh Guards
Petty Officer 'Bogey' Knight, Royal Navy, Mountaineering instructor
Sergeant Martin Damms, Royal Electrical and Mechanical Engineers,
  First mechanic
Sergeant 'Taff' Jennings, Royal Engineers
Lance Corporal Chris Buck, Royal Electrical and Mechanical Engineers,
  Second mechanic
Lance Corporal 'Flapper' Farmer, Royal Engineers
Corporal John Violett, Royal Corps of Transport
Lance Corporal Kev Keepin, Welsh Guards
Lance Corporal Mike Williams, Welsh Guards
Guardsman Andy Simmons, Welsh Guards
Guardsman Ray Williams, Welsh Guards
Guardsman Jason Hills, Welsh Guards
Guardsman Chris Davies, Welsh Guards
Craftsman Andy Howard, Royal Electrical and Mechanical Engineers,
  Third mechanic
Miss Sue Patchett, Weston Spirit

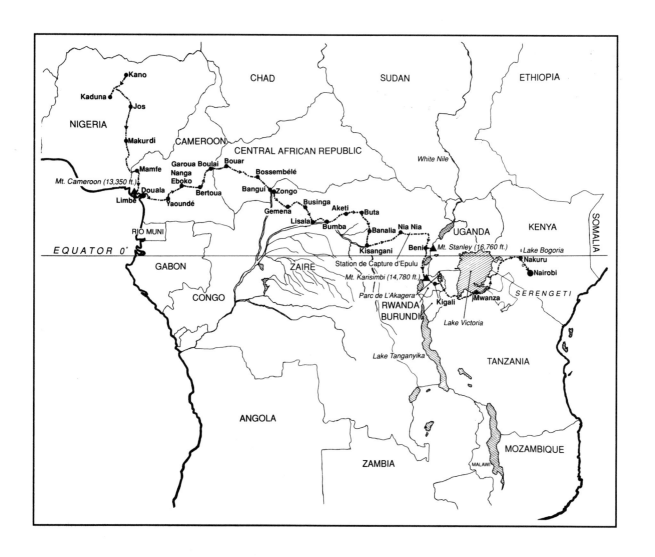

The first few days of the phase were a race to get down to Cameroon in time to meet our Patron who was on a Royal visit. We drove hard for two days through southern Nigeria to reach the border at Ikom. The new team were a bit shell-shocked by the speed of events and the lack of any chance to settle into their unfamiliar surroundings but made the best of it. Following a relatively straightforward path through the border formalities we sped on. After a few miles there was a small town. I stopped, in my Land Rover, to let the lorries catch up. As we were about to pull off again I noticed a tiny white Suzuki jeep racing towards us flashing its lights and hooting its horn. Just resisting the temptation to scoot off, lest it was immigration officials having noticed some problem with our paperwork, I waited to see what the problem was. The Suzuki screeched to a halt and to my amazement out clambered one of the fattest Africans that I have ever seen. His great bulk seemed to strain every seam of his clothing. Dabbing furiously at the rivulets of sweat which poured down his flabby jowls, with an already drenched handkerchief, he asked if we were the Roof of Africa expedition to which I replied that indeed we were. He then announced himself as the Chief of Police for the local district and asked me to accompany him back to the police station which we had just passed. Full of dread I did so. However, once inside, my misgivings were quickly allayed as he made a very long-winded speech of welcome saying how honoured he was to receive us.

Two days later we drove into Yaounde, the capital of Cameroon, on the sole serviceable tarmac road in the country. There was an almost carnival atmosphere in the city with the Royal party due to arrive in a couple more days. At the Embassy arrangements were frenetic. To our great fortune the Defence Attaché was a Welsh Guardsman, Colonel Simon Fordham. Simon and his wife Suzy, together with the expatriate employees of British American Tobacco were amazing and threw their houses open to us.

With the race to get to Cameroon on time I was still getting to know some members of the team. Certain characters emerged quicker than others. Amongst them the most colourful was Cpl 'Flapper' Farmer. 'Flapper' was a forty-two-year-old blacksmith in the Royal Engineers who worked as a part-time gamekeeper when he wasn't at his forge. He spoke with a soft West Country burr but a rather bulbous nose and a mischievous twinkle in his eye betrayed a penchant for strong liquor and an almost unfailing ability to get into trouble. Towards the end of dinner, by that time considerably refreshed, he leant across Suzy Fordham, leered at her bosom and fixing her with a bleary, rather schoolboyish expression, announced, 'I would just like to say that you have got a marvellous pair of tits'. As he slumped back in his seat I once more blessed the angelic nature of soldiers and prayed for the floor to open up and swallow me.

We were due to meet the Prince of Wales during his tour of the botanical garden at Limbe, an attractive if rather decaying coastal port in the shadow of Mt Cameroon. On arrival we went to see the curator. I had anticipated a heavily bearded, eccentric figure. In fact Mark Bovey was in his early thirties, clear of bristle, utterly down to earth and on attachment from Kew Gardens. He led us through the wonderful collection of exotic flora to our appointed spot. We found ourselves between a natural amphitheatre reverberating to the sound of tribal dancing and a collection of bemedalled old comrades from the African Pioneer Corps led by a hysterical figure, enormously fat and clad in long white robes topped with a fez hat. He was full of bonhomie and insisted on us having a joint group photo.

When Prince Charles arrived, surrounded by a throng of security men, soldiers, press and extravagantly dressed officials, including a heavily perspiring Simon Fordham, the visit seemed to pass in a flash. In fact he spent a quarter of an hour with us. His opening line was, 'I am amazed that you have made it so far' — that makes two of us I thought to myself as I briefed him on our progress to date. He then went around and had a few words with each of the team members before being swept off towards the old comrades. When the last of the entourage had disappeared there was much excited comparing of notes and experiences before everyone split up to savour the delights of Limbe at night in their own way: I headed off with a few others to the Atlantic Bay Hotel to gorge ourselves on prawns and barracuda washed down with ample quantities of wine and to ponder our next challenge.

Mt Cameroon rises like a great pimple out of an otherwise flat coastal plain. The ascent of the 13,350 foot summit, Fako Peak took us two days. It began with a narrow trail which wound its way up through heavily vegetated rain forest. It was very humid as we walked through tall grasses and ferns beneath wide-trunked trees draped in lianas, themselves clad with dangling mosses. Splashes of colour were provided by orchids nestling in the forks of trees. After a couple of hours we crossed the only stream on the mountain by a wooden hut and then shortly afterwards we broke out onto a seemingly endless, steep, open slope covered in loose volcanic shale. The grass had been burnt off leaving short blackened tussocks which added to the oppressive feel of the place. The trail continued relentlessly upwards for several thousand feet before we arrived at the second hut. There we rested and had a hot meal before continuing on about 3,000 feet up to the third and final hut at just over 12,500 feet. We spent the night, competing for floor space to lie on, before completing the final 700 feet of ascent over gently undulating moorland. There was a strong, cold wind and we huddled down into our

Goretex jackets. The sun had risen behind us as we climbed and now bathed the mountainside in an orange glow, highlighting the cumulus clouds beyond. To the west the Atlantic Ocean was covered by low cloud but we could see a dramatic drop down to an uneven plain below. A steam trail rose indicating some minor level of volcanic activity. The last eruption had been in 1982. The descent was one long knee-jarring nightmare. The steepness allowed no opportunity for a break to ease taut muscles and our feet grew hot and sore walking on the unyielding larval rock.

We headed back to Yaounde where once more we installed ourselves with the Fordhams and BAT. I rang the expedition office in Pirbright. Alasdair seemed to be very pessimistic about life. Our finances were beginning to appear very shaky. We tied up as many loose ends as we could as I wasn't sure when I would next be able to contact him. Having packed the vehicles with all of the supplies we could fit in we took our leave of the Fordhams and set off towards Central African Republic and Zaire, very aware that this was the last point of real civilisation until we reached Kenya in two months' time.

The tarmac soon ran out and we were quickly bumping our way along narrow dirt roads en route for Nanga Eboko and Garoua Boulai. Either side of us thick bush merged into semi-tropical rain forest. Just beyond Bertoua, on the second day, I stopped as usual to let the convoy catch up. When after three-quarters of an hour no one appeared I turned back dreading what I might find, only to meet the convoy limping towards me a few miles further back. I could see straight away that the leading Bedford was misshapen. The windscreen had been smashed and a great gash ran through the metal front of the cab splitting the 'ICI Pharmaceuticals for World Health' sign in two. Cfn Howard had pulled out to overtake a broken-down local truck. As he did so the driver rolled the spare wheel out into the road directly in front of him. He swerved to avoid it but in doing so lost control and had hit the parked vehicle. The Bedford was driveable but in a bad mess and with rapidly building cloud threatening rain we had to stop to make some basic repairs to safeguard the now exposed electrics. Luckily Sgt Jennings was, amongst other things, a panel beater and welder so he, Sgt Damms, our chief mechanic on the phase and Flapper set to. They managed to pull out the worst of the creases with one of the Land Rover's electric winches and sledge-hammered the rest into some semblance of shape.

We set off again with the damaged truck leading the convoy. Cpl Violett drove and I sat beside him reading the map. We hadn't been going long when the heavens opened in a true tropical downpour. Despite our Goretex suits we were soaked. The concept of crossing the jungle in the wet season with no windscreen didn't bear thinking about.

That night we pulled off the road into a small quarry to make camp and set about making more permanent repairs. LCpl Buck sat in my Land Rover chasing an elusive electrical fault. At midnight when I turned in he still had the dashboard in pieces, the steering wheel removed and with furrowed brow was consulting the Land Rover maintenance manual. Cfn Howard had been given all of the dirtiest maintenance jobs and was suffering a torrent of abuse about green drivers not being able to handle a man's vehicle, much to the amusement of the others and his own chagrin. Meanwhile Sgt Jennings and Sgt Damms attacked the damaged Bedford. They worked through most of the night panel beating and covering the tear with epoxy dough and fibre glass. By morning they had strengthened the cab front, window frame and dashboard, waterproofed the sensitive areas and, although it still looked far from right, they had got the vehicle into a safe driveable condition.

We hadn't gone far when we were stopped by the first in a succession of policemen who informed us that in their country it was illegal to drive with no windscreen. He then set about trying to extort the largest possible fine. Each time we were stopped it required a long series of negotiations until a mutually acceptable arrangement was reached. The border crossing at Garoua Boulai was the normal chain of aggravations, form filling, transcribing information into ledgers and referral from one official to the next to explain for the umpteenth time who we were and what we were up to. Patience has never been my foremost virtue so when we were issued with a second set of forms demanding physical descriptions including size of nose and breadth of forehead it was all that I could do not to explode. The Central African Republic side was even worse and it was only after a considerable number of *cadeaux* had been passed that we were able to proceed.

CAR has an unhappy history characterised by slavery and oppression. It has been successively raped by the ancient Egyptians, Islamic conquerors and French colonialists. Even after independence it has suffered the harshest repression during the thirteen-year reign of terror under the most infamous of Africa's dictators, Jean-Bedel Bokassa. It is a small but potentially wealthy country with valuable mineral resources but even now it is in a state of total decay under a corrupt and ineffectual government propped up by the visible presence of French Foreign Legionnaires. Bangui, the capital, has a reputation built mainly on stories of theft and murder. There is a pervasive air of corruption, oppression and fear.

Next day we set about finding some material with which we could cut a replacement windscreen. The cab front had been so badly damaged that despite all of our repairs it would never be able to hold a glass window in place again. I took a Land Rover into town to shop and scour the markets for a sheet of perspex. We found an ironmongers' shop in the centre of the city. I went in with Sgt Jennings and Sgt Damms leaving Tetta to watch the vehicle. The negotiations were protracted. Materials were scarce and a sheet the size we needed was going to cost £200. To make matters worse they weren't prepared to cut it to shape for us and without the right tools our mechanics risked cracking the perspex if we cut it.

We went outside to deliberate and found Tetta in floods of tears. As soon as we had gone into the shops and out of sight she had been surrounded by a group of youths. One had started letting down the Land Rover tyres. When she went to stop him another got in by the back door whilst others jumped up onto the roof to see what was in the roof rack. Alone she hadn't stood a chance. A policeman had seen what was going on but hadn't helped and then a French woman pitched in and by delivering a high velocity burst of local dialect, got rid of the youths but then rounded on Tetta for being stupid enough to stay in a vehicle alone. I had never considered such a problem but it was a salutary lesson learned the hard way.

We were held up from leaving CAR as a result of a diplomatic deadlock between ourselves, backed up by the British Honorary Consul, and the Zairean Embassy which refused to issue us with a *laissez passer*. What had started as a perfectly innocent attempt to get a written authority to help us avoid another situation like the Nigerian débâcle now took on epic proportions. By Wednesday with the end nowhere in sight and the Zaireans alternately prevaricating or simply leaving their office to avoid a confrontation I decided to press on regardless.

We processed our passports through customs and loaded the vehicles onto a shallow draught ferry. As we crossed the Oubangui River I prayed that we would be able to get past the Zairean officials on the far side. I could see a soldier ominously waiting for us on the south bank. Once on the shore the Zairean officials were instantly suspicious of our military status. They searched all of the vehicles very thoroughly, ostensibly for guns and grenades or so they claimed, but it soon became apparent that they were looking for suitable 'presents' which would either be forthcoming or we wouldn't be allowed to proceed. Then they produced an old battered school exercise book in which was written a list of tariffs in scruffy freehand. It was a great relief when we eventually got under way. We had been warned that a regular trick was to hold travellers at the border until nightfall and then follow them to their campsite and rob them so we broke our golden rule and drove for several hours after dark to get well away.

The first obstacle was a tributary of the Oubangui River at Bogilima. The stanchions of an unfinished bridge rose up out of the river. To one side was a small flat-bottomed ferry and beside that a comically small, Capt Pugwash style, tug that must have been a contemporary of *The African Queen*. It took forty minutes to find anyone who knew the whereabouts of the tug driver and his assistant. Eventually they arrived at a slow amble and then it took another half an hour using our vehicle batteries and fuel to coax the tug into service. It required two crossings to carry our four vehicles across the river.

The next sixty-five miles of road, to Gemena, was in fairly good condition and we covered it in a couple of hours. It was a sprawling, open town and home to the first of the BAT depots on our route.

Beyond Gemena the road conditions deteriorated. The track became narrower, rougher and in places deeply rutted. Our speed halved to about ten miles an hour. We passed through Karawa and Businga. In one village the children held up a tiny antelope that they had caught. It was a blue duiker, with a glossy coat and little hooves that were no bigger than the knuckle of my first finger. The jungle became much denser, at times encroaching upon the tracks. In places the road tunnelled its way beneath great interlocking stands of bamboo. Butterflies billowed up in brightly coloured clouds from the puddles and streams, a myriad of cream whites, bright blues, primrose yellows, vibrant reds and mottled browns.

At Lisala we saw the great Zaire river for the first time. The far bank was at least half a mile distant. Beyond, the jungle stretched away to the horizon. Pirogues poled their way between the islands. We could see for miles up and downstream which emphasised the enormity of the river. The route on to Bumba continued much as before. At one point we had to bypass several trucks either side of a bogged tractor and trailer. On this occasion we managed to force our way through the bamboo at the side of the track but high mud walls would normally have prevented us leaving the track.

Bumba was another large open town on the north bank of the Zaire River. We made straight for the BAT depot. I sent Richard off to speak to the manager whilst I retired to a quiet spot with our short-wave radio clamped to my head. It was Saturday 7 April — the day of the Grand National. My cousin, Marcus Armytage, was riding but I wasn't sure on which horse and the BBC World Service commentary cut out the preliminaries and started as the race began. It was an exciting race. I heard the horse Gee A's name called up at the front a couple of times and wondered if, as in the last two years previously, Marcus's sister Gee Armytage was on board. The leader for the first two circuits fell and a horse called Mr Frisk came to take the lead. Coming on up the final straight he was challenged strongly by Durham Edition but held on, winning by a length. I still didn't know what had happened to Marcus. The reception was poor and the commentator's voice kept disappearing beneath the static. Finally he read through the order, 4th, 3rd, 2nd and Grand National Winner 1990 Mr Frisk ridden by the amateur rider Marcus Armytage. Even writing now my eyes fill with tears as I think about it. To win the Grand National is the greatest dream of any jump jockey, amateur or professional, and he had done it. For the first time on the expedition I longed to be back in England. I would have given anything to have been there and been able to watch the race. It made me very homesick for my friends and the way of life I had left behind.

Poor Richard, meanwhile, had been desperately trying to explain away my rudeness to the BAT manager by regaling him with stories of our exploits in his best French. I tried to join in the conversation but I couldn't concentrate. In my mind I was miles away on a windy race track outside Liverpool. He had actually done it!

We sorted out our administration, took on more fuel and water and carried on the next day towards Aketi. It was Palm Sunday. The road was full of small children waving palm fronds as we passed them on their way to church. The small mud and thatch churches were lavishly decorated with greenery and flowers. In every village they were packed with people. Fabulous strains of gospel singing filled the air. It all sounded such fun. We got a wonderfully warm welcome wherever we went. We stopped at a place where the road crossed a stream. A clear pool of water had formed. The cool water was marvellously refreshing. There were lots of children in the water so we had an impromptu game of water volleyball amidst much splashing and diving.

For the next couple of days we made slow progress. There were frequent deep potholes with walls often higher than the Land Rovers and semi-filled with rancid, stagnant water. The jungle closed in on us. Where the bamboo stands had collapsed blocking the road we had to cut a way through with axes. It was hard to find any space to pull off the road and make camp. We stopped late one evening. Clouds of fireflies danced around us. A distant storm sent flashes of lightning across the sky every few seconds.

Buta appeared: another run-down town. It had a depressed rather dissolute air. My impressions were confirmed when we were offered both drugs and illegally hunted leopard and okapi skins. It was sad to see the badly cured and creased skins of these fine and rare animals pegged out to dry in a fly-blown backyard ready to be carried illicitly, by passing lorry drivers, to Kinshasa where they would be sold for £400-500 per skin.

We crossed the Banalia Ferry with ninety miles to go to reach Kisangani. In most of the villages lorries were collecting piles of freshly cut wood. Men were walking down the lines of houses paying off each of the villagers in turn. The further on we went the more congested the road became with bicyclists and people pushing handcarts laden with vegetables for sale. The outskirts of Kisangani were marked by a large metal girder bridge crossing over a hydro-electric installation. We couldn't fit inside the tiny courtyard at the BAT depot so we went to the overlander's campsite at the Hotel Olympia. We settled in, rather swamping the small camp ground. The showers and loos were a serious health hazard but there was a bright bar selling cold beers and a restaurant service providing steak and chips.

We had a late start in the morning, not least because we hadn't moved our watches forward at Banalia, which marked the boundary of a time zone. As soon as we surfaced the usual plague of artefact sellers, black market money dealers and local tailors descended upon us all clamouring for business. Out of the midst of this mêlée appeared a self-appointed Mr Fixit character called Eugene. He had been recommended in *Africa on a Shoestring*. Unfortunately as a result of this he had become an ingratiating little man who had adopted rather flash Western dress and a quasi-American accent. He offered his services with much largesse claiming to be able to arrange fuel, spares and money-changing for us at 'very special, low prices' and then attempted to curry favour by disassociating himself from the other Africans and bad mouthing them in a stream of obscenities all put on for effect. The covetous glint in his eye belied his stated intent so that by the time that Richard, who was now well used to the street rates, had got his calculator and gone to town on him he had some of the wind taken out of his sails.

I was about to set off in search of the British Consulate to register our presence when the Consul himself hove into sight. He was a charming Belgian expatriate, called François Senneque. He was a sixty-plus retired businessman who spoke English in a rather quaint old-fashioned way. He had been expecting us and offered us the services of his African assistant James, to show us around. With Eugene and James as guides we set off to the bank, post office and markets. I went on with James to the BAT office where to my dismay they told me that it was quite impossible to ring Europe in the daytime and only rarely possible between 2 and 3am. We had been out of touch with England for three weeks and I was desperately keen to speak to Alistair. François arranged for me to send a telex from the Belgian Consulate but I wasn't overly hopeful of it reaching its destination as it had to be relayed four times before it would reach Pirbright.

Richard wasn't having much more luck at the bank which took four hours to cash travellers' cheques. In the campsite the mechanics were still working on one of the Bedfords which had developed a serious fuel feed problem. They had been at it for most of the night and had stripped the fuel system down and changed the pump but still hadn't got the gremlin out of the system.

In the afternoon we went down to see the Stanley Falls. The falls spanned the half-mile-wide frontage of the river with a drop of around fifteen feet. The locals had constructed an ungainly framework across the river from which they dangled conical fish traps. In amongst this, native fishermen threw themselves into the fast white water, casting their weighted nets. Standing by the falls I had a feeling of being at the very core of Africa. My mind flooded with the evocative images of H. M. Stanley's travels through this region. The early explorers had literally had to fight their way through in the face of frequent attacks by hostile tribes and rife disease. They had faced real privations and as their numbers dwindled it must have taken great courage to carry on towards their goal. Kisangani had formerly been named Stanleyville in his honour.

François arrived to take Richard and I out to dinner in an open-top, classic Jaguar. We were joined at his house by the Belgian Consul, an enormous caricature of a man, ex-military with a huge walrus moustache and a strong Inspector Clouseau accent, and the Belgian head of Skol. To the accompaniment of many whiskies and some fairly bawdy humour they reminisced fondly about the days of Belgian colonialism in what was then the Congo. François talked of times when all the towns were smart, bright and clean, Stanleyville had restaurants and hotels to match those of the main European cities and all the services had worked efficiently. He remembered being able to drive his Jaguar all the way to Goma. Now the same journey was a serious challenge for a four-wheel drive vehicle due to the state of the roads. It was an evening charged with good humour, rich stories and much nostalgia but in a sad way was something of a lament for what once had been — albeit just from one viewpoint.

After two days of driving through yet more bamboo tunnels and dense jungle we arrived at the Station de Capture d'Epulu. It was a beautiful spot to camp, mown green grass with rondavels, under which to cook, beside a series of rapids in a jungle river. The Station de Capture had been funded by a rich American to capture okapis, breed them in captivity and then send their progeny to zoos around the world. Okapis are only found in Zaire. They are curious looking creatures whose closest relative is the giraffe. Members of the antelope family, they have long extended necks, big ears and stunted horns with something of a moose-like nose although not so pronounced. Their bodies are brown and their legs striped. There are many in the Ituri forest although due to their solitary nature they are rarely seen. They are trapped in large, camouflaged pits dug under their known routes. The Station had just bred its first baby okapi in captivity. Apart from the okapis there were blue duikers in cages, mangabeys high in the jungle canopy above and chimpanzees which rushed around doing somersaults, hugging us, undoing shoelaces and stealing cameras.

In addition to the okapis, forest leopard, various primates and other wildlife, the Ituri forest is inhabited by Pygmy tribes. The Pygmies have a fearsome reputation and a history characterised by stories of cannibalism. They are essentially hunter gatherers who have populated the forests of Equatorial Africa for thousands of years. With the march of progress and the development of other tribes the Pygmies have retreated deeper and deeper into the forest.

We had arranged with the rangers at Epulu to go and visit a group of Pygmies living near the edge of the forest. We each packed small rucksacks with bivvi bag, meraklon liner, waterproofs, mosquito net, torch, cooker and food and clutching our cameras set off with two rangers as escorts. A small group of Pygmies consisting of one adult and four children were waiting to guide us. Two of the children led the way into the forest. The path was narrow and twisting, barely distinguishable from the many game tracks that crossed our way. The Pygmies, agile and sure footed, seemed to melt into the forest. We blundered along behind bending low to crawl under fallen logs and tripping over roots.

One of the two boys leading us was carrying a cask of beans on his head. The other held a jar of jam. The one with the jam plucked a leaf from a large bush and without checking his pace fashioned a small carrying handle to fit the jar. They both stopped at each pool of water that they came to and drank using a folded leaf as a scoop. Although neither appeared more than seven years old they never hesitated at a track junction. They called out often in a hollow whooping sound. This would often be taken up by the other Pygmies in the group and was occasionally answered by unseen voices. Many of the trees were well over a hundred feet high and had extensive parts of their root system above ground. Whenever they came to a suitable root they would whack it with a stick. I presumed this banging and whooping was to frighten off any leopard that was in the area.

After an hour and a half we crossed a large log over a stream and came suddenly upon the Pygmies' camp. It was in a small clearing in the forest about thirty yards in diameter. Around the edge was a circle of ten huts. They were constructed of a dome-shaped lattice of light sticks into which was woven a covering of leaves. Each hut had a small fire burning outside it. Inside some had cane litters, otherwise there was nothing bar a collection of blackened pots and pans. In the centre of the clearing was a larger fire around which was grouped some crude wooden seats. The majority of the Pygmies present were women and children. I assumed that the men were out in the forest. We were introduced to the chief who was the smallest of the adult males. He stood about four feet six inches with grey hair, fuzzy beard and short hairy legs. He grinned, shook hands with all of us and called for chairs to be brought for us. They were cleverly made from local materials but excruciatingly uncomfortable. As we sat around the fire, chickens, puppies and children ran all around us. The Pygmies talked fast in high piping voices and laughed a lot. Whilst we had a snack some of the men prepared their long nets for the afternoon's hunting. I noticed that they had strangely developed breasts with nipples like women. Many were toothless.

When they were ready we cached our packs and set off into the forest behind them. Once we were well away from the camp they stopped and pegged out the nets in a line covering a frontage of a couple of hundred yards. The nets had a two-inch string mesh and were set three feet high. We were then settled down and motioned to be quiet whilst they disappeared into the forest. There was absolute silence for a quarter of an hour but for the cry of birds high above in the canopy and the whine of mosquitoes. Then we could hear them whooping in the distance. They had fanned out and were now beating their way back towards us. As they approached there were some excited shouts and our guard took us over to see one of the Pygmies disentangling a small blue duiker which was rapidly dispatched with a sharp knife. Although they reset their nets they only caught the one duiker.

Back at their camp the Pygmies began preparing their evening meal. Pans of strangely coloured beans, rice, mangoes, dried fish and duiker's head all bubbled away on different fires. As it got dark the remaining menfolk returned until there was a total of about forty Pygmies. Some lay back in their seats smoking marijuana in water-filled cane pipes. With no warning a storm broke. Thunder, lightning and lashing rain sent everyone diving for cover in the nearest hut. Tetta, Cfn Howard and I ended up in the same one which, bar a few drips, remained fairly dry. After a while the family whose hut it was appeared. We got up to leave but they indicated that we should stay.

The father of the family moved the fire inside which instantly filled the hut with smoke but when he moved aside some of the leaves in the roof he reduced it to an eye watering but bearable level. The hut was no more than five feet in diameter and four feet high. I lay along one side with my feet sticking out of the door. Tetta lay beside me and Cfn Howard lay at right angles above our heads. The two adult Pygmies sat smoking their hubble bubble pipe whilst the children snuggled up as close to Tetta as they could, trying to edge her off her Karrimat. It was nothing if not cosy.

I woke after a brief, rather uncomfortable sleep at about 10pm to hear all the Pygmies outside singing and dancing. The rain had stopped and they were in a circle around the main camp fire. Some played animal skin drums whilst others danced in a shuffling, stamping motion with bells and rattles attached to their legs. The singing was rhythmic and melodic, interspersed with much whooping. As the night wore on and more dope was smoked the tempo died down and the songs became somehow haunting. As I drifted off to sleep my last thought was to wonder whether if I pinched myself I would wake up and find myself in bed in Fulham and that the whole expedition was just a dream.

We were woken at 4.30am to find that all the Pygmies were outside and the singing and dancing had recommenced. It was certainly a most unconventional start to Easter Day. I lay dozing and listening to their rich, harmonious singing. It was all just as enthusiastic and with as much gusto as the night before. Once it was light we had a brew, took some last photos and leaving whatever was left of our ration packs with the Pygmies bade them farewell and set off back on the trail with a couple of guides. On the way back I chatted to Jean Marie, one of the rangers, who talked about the Pygmies' way of life.

They move camp every few weeks once they have exhausted the natural food supply in the area. When they move they take only their cooking utensils, building new huts and furniture in each place. A Pygmy can take up to three wives although this is rare. If he wants a wife he would swap a sister or niece with that of another Pygmy. He said that they can live up to seventy or eighty but I doubted that. Back at Epulu we packed up our own camp and set off along the road to Mambasa. We passed two groups of Pygmies dancing down the road. They were in columns behind their drums and covered in black and white markings.

For the next two days we continued eastward on deeply pot-holed jungle roads until we emerged into more open country. The forest gave way to fields of maize and coffee plantations. It was very noticeable that the village markets were fully stocked with fresh vegetables: leeks, potatoes, onions, aubergines, cabbages, rice, bananas and beans of all descriptions competed for space on the stalls. The people wore brighter coloured fabrics and spoke Swahili. The whole area had an East African flavour to it.

We stopped at Beni to refuel and check in with the BAT office before heading on towards the Ruwenzoris and our third mountain objective. The Ruwenzoris are more evocatively named The Mountains of the

Moon. Their shrouded summits have long held a certain mystique amongst mountaineers. When the early explorers reported seeing snow-capped peaks in the middle of Africa just north of the Equator they were pilloried by the Royal Geographical Society. Many romantic legends have been attributed to them not least that they hid the source of the River Nile. Anyone who ventured there found a strange domain of harsh climate and bizarre flora.

As we crested the hill to the east of Beni we got our first view of the mountain range, or more accurately the bottom of it. The remainder was lost in black storm clouds. Claps of thunder roared overhead and lightning struck the plain in front of us with bolts of energy that exploded on impact throwing up dirt and smoke. It was an ominous sight.

We stopped and watched awhile before making our way gingerly across the plain towards Mutwanga in the foothills of the Ruwenzoris. We slipped and slid our way along the black cotton track to the home of Patrick Ingels, a rather colourful Belgian expatriate, to whom François Senneque had given us a letter of introduction. Patrick's grandfather had built up a large coffee plantation and established a fine hotel but the latter had been expropriated by the military and now lay in ruins. Patrick continued to farm coffee. He was reputed to have five African wives and many children. He very kindly let us set up base camp in some outbuildings.

Next day after a quick breakfast and last proper wash and shave, we taped our feet up and then loaded all of the rucksacks onto the Land Rovers. At the Park Headquarters there was no sign of our guide and porters so I sent PO 'Bogey' Knight into the nearby village of Matsora to look for them whilst I tried to get some sense out of the Park Warden. Eventually he appointed a new guide who chose his twenty-seven porters from the motley looking crowd who were hanging around. When he told them to go and get their kit they all took off towards the village at a run. Things seemed to be moving. I drove down to the village to oversee the next phase of the operation — the purchasing of the porters' food allowance — only to find, to my horror, Bogey together with the original guide and his twenty-seven porters. We now had all the ingredients of a fiasco. A massive row broke out with everyone shouting at once. In the end it was only by making the entire group fall into ranks like a drill parade that we were able to regain some semblance of order and select the fittest looking men to be our porters.

Purchasing the porters' food took another age and involved more protracted negotiations. There was a fixed daily allocation of rice, mealie meal and meat. Thus when the guide asked me to drive up to a hut just out of the village to pick up some other rations I envisaged us loading up sacks of flour and dried fish. What I certainly hadn't expected was to be confronted by a large, very live pig which let out ear-splitting squeals as it was bundled into the back of the Land Rover. At this point I gave up totally and collapsed in hysterics. The whole scene had degenerated into a farce.

Eventually we got the whole ensemble to the start point. We issued loads to the porters. Each rucksack was weighed by hand amidst much hullabaloo. The guide then announced that he wanted four extra porters to carry the porters' food. This was a total scam as each man was supposed to carry his own rations in addition to his load. Another great indaba ensued with everyone shouting their support. Faced by mass opposition to my protests of fair play, as it was 12.15pm and we had still not taken a single step upwards I capitulated. There was practically a fight as people clamoured for the jobs.

Finally the entire circus set off: fourteen of us, thirty porters, guide and pig. It looked like an army on the move. I had never climbed with porters before. As a soldier I felt slightly uneasy with the idea of other people carrying our kit. I could see that several of the other soldiers felt the same. The weight of the food and technical climbing equipment fully justified this apparent luxury and it didn't take us long to get accustomed to the idea. Any remaining feelings of guilt were dispelled at the thought of the Duke of the Abruzzi on his pioneering expedition to the central peaks in 1906 who had used 150 porters for his party of twelve Europeans of which four were themselves professional Alpine guides.

The first day's climb took us up to the Kalongi Hut at 6,700 feet. The route rose steeply for the first two hours, climbing up through small cultivated patches of cassava, sweet potatoes and bananas. Women came out of the rondavels to chatter and give their menfolk a drink or a banana. It was very humid and we poured with sweat. We took a break at the Guides Hut and then followed the route as it disappeared into the jungle. At this point the heavens opened in a torrential downpour which lasted for over an hour instantly soaking us and turning the path into a mud slide. The gradient eased up as we wound our way through ever more extreme vegetation beneath the canopy. A profusion of wild flowers gave way to head-high grass and giant ferns with fronds twice the height of a man. For several miles we ducked under colossal leaves and scrambled over fallen branches. Although thoroughly chilled and plastered with mud it was a fascinating walk through this surreal plant world. My musings were frequently interrupted by indignant squeals of protest from the reluctant pig as it was manhandled over yet another obstacle.

To my amazement the hut, when we reached it, turned out to be newly built in Scandinavian style with wood framework, bunks, tables and benches. Most importantly it was dry inside. We quickly got a fire going to dry all of our kit. As one wag rather sarcastically put it, 'it was the best house that we had seen in all of Zaire'. Although the rain eased off thunder and lightning continued throughout the night.

The second day's climb took us up out of the grasses and ferns and into a wild profusion of bamboo stands, nettles and tangled mimulopsis. We had begun to ascend a steep ridge which kept the path above the worst of the surrounding bogs. After an hour and a half we came to a small platform where all the porters had stopped. They were playing a basic wooden xylophone with sticks. Behind there was a tiny twig shelter, about two feet high, where each placed a small offering of flour to the mountain gods. Our guide asked us to leave gifts of money or cigarettes. Several of the team scoffed at this but although not particularly superstitious I felt that we had enough on our plate without offending the gods — more to the point one mountaineering fall is quite enough!

The bamboo gave way to low trees and large beds of mosses and then, higher again we came to the tree heathers. We found ourselves, like Lilliputian figures, clambering amongst outsized Scottish heather. The main stalks rose full twenty feet, branches were draped with beards of lichen and gnarled roots protruded from the ground in a tortuously twisted mesh seemingly floating on a sea of glutinous black mud. Any forward progress was by a combination of hopping from root to root whilst hauling up on those above. Cloud hung in dense pockets suffusing the atmosphere with a damp greyness. Occasionally we caught glimpses of other jungle clad ridges stretching up into the cloud. The Mahungu Hut was on a prominent knoll at 10,936 feet with a commanding view back down into Zaire. By the time we arrived the porters had a fire burning. A couple of the team had mild headaches. Having settled in we spent the rest of the afternoon usefully with Bogey giving a refresher course on knots and belays to ensure that we all conformed to a common system on the mountain. The guide appeared with several porters in tow asking for the doctor. On the whole the Bakonjo tribesmen were a very hardy but good-natured race. Many climbed barefoot with only the most meagre clothing to protect them against the cold and wet. Almost all showed total disdain for the advanced Karrimor rucksacks with which we had provided them by ignoring the highly adaptable and developed carrying system, preferring to walk with them either balanced on their heads or supported by a rope of banana leaves around their foreheads. Of the ones that Matthew saw two had malaria, one a headache and one, not surprisingly, had a rucksack burn on his back.

Day three saw us splashing our way on up the ridge amidst more deep

Left: Matthew Roberts sheltering from a tropical downpour in a village church at the foot of the Ruwenzoris.

Below: CSM Bennett sorting out mountaineering equipment prior to our ascent of Mt Stanley.

Lt Mark Jenkins on the walk in to Mt Stanley.

Gdsm Williams negotiating a roped section on the walk in to the Moraine Hut.

Top: Matthew Roberts and PO Bogey Knight attend to an unconscious Gdsm Hills.

Bottom: Gdsm Hills is lowered down the rock face by PO Knight with Matthew Roberts and the author attached to him.

Top: Cpl Keepin resting on the way down from Mt Stanley.

Bottom: Mountain gorillas in the Virunga, Rwanda.

Top: DSgt Coull bouldering on Mt Kenya with the peaks of Batiaan and Nelion in the background.

Bottom: Bdr Lawes ice climbing at around 15,500 ft on the Lewis Glacier.

Bongo Woodley on our first attempt of the SE face on Nelion with Pt Lenana in the background.

We climbed rope length after rope length; Sgt Nundy.

mud and tangled roots. The path became tighter and more treacherous and the vegetation more varied and extreme. The heather became thicker, roots more protuberant, and deep moss beds carpeted any available space. Pink orchids, orange and yellow flowering hypericum and purple berried rhododendrons provided splashes of colour.

At around 13,000 feet the tree heather gave way to lobelia, giant groundsel and then a blanket of helichrysum bushes with their everlasting white flowers. A gradual slope brought us up to a plateau from where we got our first clear view of the glacier-capped peaks above. The Kyondo Hut at 14,119 feet, a solid stone-built structure, signalled the end of the route for all but four of our porters. We paid them the agreed rate of Z3,000 (£3.50) for their four-day contract. I was glad that my porter, Constant Mambati was to remain with us. Older and tougher than the rest, he had climbed fast and each day I had reached the hut to find my rucksack on what he considered to be the best bed. The four porters that remained wouldn't go any further but were kept to help carry down the technical equipment and more importantly as a back-up in case of any problems. We were now a long way from any assistance should there be an accident higher up on the mountain.

The plan for the next day was to carry sufficient ropes, food and technical climbing equipment to the Moraine Hut, 14,149 feet, cache it there and spend the rest of the day looking at routes and practising our climbing techniques on ice. Sgt Jennings and Sgt Damms were suffering with severe headaches so we left them behind to have an easy day and acclimatise gently. The track to the Moraine Hut contained a number of near-vertical sections protected by fixed ropes and wire handrails. The setting was sensational as we pulled our way across a cliff face with the mountain massif opposite and hundreds of feet below us the dark waters of Lac Vert. With heavy rucksacks full of all shapes of climbing impedimenta a couple of people got slightly gripped as they teetered across some of the airier spots. Once over these the route carries on over undulating ground tightly flanked by lobelia and groundsel until it emerges at an enormous boulder field. High up on the northern side of this glacial moraine is perched the Moraine Hut. A small simple wooden structure of one room and furnished by a single table it appeared very vulnerable in its harsh surroundings. From the rock platform on which the hut sits we could scrutinise the various routes open to us.

Mt Stanley has nine peaks over 16,000 feet. We were sitting opposite the northern group of Albert, Margherita and Alexandra of which Margherita is the highest in the chain. Straightaway we could see that the glaciers had receded a long way in the forty years since the pictures in our guidebook had been taken. Gaining the foot of the various glaciers would now involve some tricky scrambling up faces of shattered, friable rock. The supposedly straightforward Stanley Glacier Route in particular looked to have a difficult start that would be hard to protect. Immediately in front of us the West Face of Margherita offered a fine line ascending directly up steep snow fields but I was concerned by stories that we had heard of avalanches and stonefall sweeping the face.

After a brew we made our way over to the base of the Margherita Glacier where everyone fitted on their crampons and Bogey took them through the techniques of walking in crampons, using ice axes and placing ice screws. Having finished we cached the equipment at the Moraine Hut and made our way back to Kyondo. On the way back Gdsm Williams had very bad headaches and found problems concentrating on placing his feet.

Bogey and I chatted through the plan. We decided to split the team in two, make an early start in the morning with those who hadn't shown any problems with altitude acclimatisation and attempt to reach the summit by the Margherita West Face. Having woken up regularly every half-hour throughout the night I missed the 4am reveille and was woken from a most bizarre dream by Gdsm Andy Simmons. We had a brew, forced down a packet of porridge each and filled our flasks before setting out just as it became light outside. Everyone was feeling good and we covered the rope sections easily reaching the Moraine Hut after two hours.

We sorted out the technical gear from our equipment cache, donned our harnesses and started making our way along the ridge line that led up to the base of the Margherita Glacier. From the hut it had appeared to be a straightforward walk but after a while we found ourselves on a tricky scramble. Matthew and I went in front, scouting for the safest line whilst Bogey brought the others up on a rope. It took an hour to scramble the 450 feet up to the glacier. Once there we all put on our crampons and then roped up in two ropes of four. As we began the sun was just peeking over the summit but it was frequently blacked out by bands of fast moving cloud overhead. The start of the glacier was steep, hard ice. It wasn't difficult but at the beginning of the day the guys were unrelaxed and awkward. Matthew fell almost immediately and with no cry of warning almost pulled me off. After a while we began moving better in our rope teams but progress was painfully slow. The summit ridge looked a very long way above us.

After the first three hundred feet the angle eased off and I hoped that we were going to be able to pick up our pace. Unfortunately the snow on the top of the glacier was deep and soft. With every step we sank in up to our knees. As the temperature rose and we flailed our way through the slushy snow we poured with sweat. Suddenly Gdsm Hills called out that he was feeling nauseous and had a headache. Matthew went to have a look at him.

When he came over to talk to Bogey and me he said that Gdsm Hills was suffering from altitude sickness and that he wasn't going to be able to climb any further. We sat down in the snow to take a rest and to consider the implications of this. There seemed to be no option but to take the whole group down. We certainly couldn't let him make his own way down and we couldn't leave him where he was. Of all the group I was surprised that it was Gdsm Hills who had problems. On the previous four days he, Cfn Howard and Gdsm Simmons had climbed much faster than the rest of the group and none of them had suffered any problems with headaches. Our first summit attempt hadn't got very far. Having said that I consoled myself with the thought that if one of the group was showing outward signs of altitude sickness several of the others were probably suffering milder symptoms so if we all went down it would avoid any further problems and give us another day's acclimatisation.

As we were discussing our best line of retreat Matthew suddenly yelled and pointed to Gdsm Hills. He had passed out and was now lying face down in the snow. Matthew and Bogey raced to him. He wasn't breathing so they pushed a hollow breathing tube down his throat to clear an air passage. He began to breathe but remained unconscious. His condition had changed dramatically for the worse and he was now suffering advanced pulmonary oedema. We had to get him to lose altitude as quickly as possible or face a deterioration in his condition which would lead to coma and ultimately death.

We strapped him into a makeshift stretcher of rope and slings secured by karabiners and began to carry him back down the glacier. It was a fairly hazardous operation as the novices were still awkward and unsure with their crampons and ice axes. At one point Cpl Violett tripped over the points of his crampons and began somersaulting down the slope nearly pulling all of us with him. We reconfigured our system so that Matthew and Bogey manhandled the stretcher with Cfn Howard and I acting as brakes in case of any further slips.

By the time we got back down to the rocks Gdsm Hills had regained consciousness but not lucidity. He was very cold and shivering uncontrollably so we got him out of the harness and into a duvet jacket and bivvi bag. We packed two people either side of him to give him some bodily warmth. Matthew began to force feed him warm brews from the flask; meanwhile Bogey and I began to rig a rope system to negotiate the next stage. To get everyone including the stretcher down the 450 foot scramble we needed to lower people down a rope-length at a time. Cpl Violett went down first; one rope-length so that he could relay messages.

Then Mark Jenkins went down two-rope lengths to find a ledge that we could rest the stretcher on.

Cpl Howard went next carrying both his own and Gdsm Hills's rucksacks, squawking protests all of the way. Then with those three positioned at strategic points on the rock face it was time to get Gdsm Hills down. We put him back into a full body harness and then trussed him inside a bivvi bag with more slings. It may not have been overly comfortable but it provided a secure anchor point to lower him on and he was in no danger of falling out. Speed and safety were our prime considerations. Initially we tried lowering him with me strapped on to guide his body down but it quickly proved to be unmanageable. Matthew clipped on as well and between us we were able to protect both his torso and legs from the rocks. It was testing on our legs and nerves as we lurched our way down desperately trying to maintain our balance and drag his body over endless rock projections. Each move was made slowly and deliberately. At the end of the first rope-length the knot joining the two ropes jammed in the belay and we were left suspended in space for about ten minutes as Bogey sorted out the problem.

Once we were safely lodged on the platform at the end of the second rope-length Bogey lowered Gdsm Simmons and Cpl Violett down to us and then abseiled down himself. Inevitably without a figure of eight descender the ropes twisted and it took some time to untangle them. I rigged another belay for the next stage of the lower. In an attempt to speed things up we tried lowering Matthew on his own with the stretcher but it didn't work so I went down on a prussik to help out. Fortunately by the time that we reached the ground the second team, who were on their way up to spend the night at the Moraine Hut prior to their summit bid, had seen us and came across to help. As soon as Gdsm Hills was down they carried him over to the hut. I waited to see everyone else safely off the rock face.

Back at the hut, although initially very cold, after a couple of hours in a sleeping bag and plentiful hot drinks Gdsm Hills was much better. He couldn't remember anything of the rescue which, all things considered, was probably just as well. Matthew decided to keep him at the hut for the night and send him down to the Kyondo Hut the next day. Meanwhile all was not well with the second team. They had left Cpl Keepin at the Kyondo Hut still suffering with the altitude. It had taken the rest of them four hours to make it to the Moraine Hut. Sgt Damms, Sgt Jennings and LCpl Buck were all now feeling rough and although he wouldn't admit it Gdsm Williams didn't look so good. The only one in any shape to climb was Richard Gaffney. From the first team several people looked fairly shaken by the day's events. In fact having taken a casualty amongst a novice group in a difficult position the rescue had gone very smoothly.

Bogey and I walked down to the base of the Stanley Glacier route. From close up the rock approach didn't look quite as steep and imposing as it had from the hut. Back inside we outlined our plans to the others. We would make another early start and attempt to reach the summit with a small team consisting of Bogey, Richard Gaffney, Mark Jenkins, Cfn Howard and myself by the Stanley Glacier route. As we turned in the wind was howling outside and flurries of snowflakes obscured the mountains.

Bogey got up first at 4.30am and went outside to see what the weather conditions were like. The wind had been buffeting the frail wooden hut for most of the night so I rather expected him to return saying that it wasn't fit for climbing and that we would postpone our planned summit bid. I was just snuggling back down into my sleeping bag when he came bounding back in saying, quite to the contrary, that it was fine and we needed to get moving. We were all slow and by the time that everyone had had breakfast and filled their flasks it was 6am.

We made our way across the difficult boulder-strewn amphitheatre to the foot of the rock face below the Stanley Glacier. The first section was an easy scramble up a series of gullies but we then came to a large bare block devoid of any decent holds. With cold fingers and stiff bodies we gingerly edged our way around the block following any available line of weakness until we reached the top of the glacier. We put on harnesses, ropes and crampons and then began front pointing our way up the bottom section of the steep, hard ice. I had Richard and Mark following on my rope. Unused to trusting two short metal spikes on the front of their crampons to support their full body weight neither was enjoying the steepness.

After 150 fairly tense feet of ascent the angle eased and we found ourselves floundering in the same deep, wet, sugary snow that we had encountered the day before. We were now around 14,500 feet. For the next couple of hours we waded slowly up another 1,000 feet. We stopped frequently to change the lead and thus share the energy-sapping trail breaking. As we climbed cloud closed in around us, until at times we couldn't see more than twenty feet to our front. We came out onto the plateau at the top of the glacier at 9.30am. We could just manage to make out the ghostly shadow of Moebius, one of the southern peaks, over to our right. We were standing on the border of Zaire and Uganda at 15,500 feet. To get to Margherita Peak we had to drop down into Uganda circumventing the East Ridge of Alexandra Peak, cross the heavily crevassed Margherita Glacier and then climb the East Ridge of Margherita to the summit: all of which was a great deal easier said than done in view of the prevailing conditions and the antiquated and questionably accurate map that we had managed to find. A brief window in the cloud allowed us a glimpse of our route and the chance to take a quick couple of bearings. From then on the visibility closed in and it was a question of navigating by sense and memory.

We descended sharply alongside the rock wall that formed the East Ridge of Margherita. Great towering sculptures of rime ice appeared eerily out of the gloom. We were now out of sight, even in clear conditions of those watching from the hut and with the two mountaineering instructors on the climb we could not expect any outside assistance if we got into problems. The Margherita Glacier was lacerated by frequent open crevasses. We zig-zagged our way across, detouring around the wider crevasses and jumping the smaller ones. Our senses were alert to the tell-tale signs of hidden fissures or weak snow bridges. On the far side of the glacier we had to contour around one enormous last crevasse which guarded the approach to Margherita's East Ridge. After a delicate traverse along the steep ground ridge-side of this gaping chasm we gained the East Ridge by a short snow-filled gully. The final 1,000 feet to the summit was up the broad, relatively easy angled ridge bypassing heavy cornices and ever more elaborate sculptures in windblown ice. At 1.30pm we pulled our way over the last rock section and onto the summit. Windows in the cloud gave us impressive views of the neighbouring Albert and Alexandra Peaks. I felt a great sense of achievement mingled with relief that despite my earlier doubts we had made it. Our third mountain objective was in the bag. However we now had to concentrate on getting back off the mountain safely. If we didn't hurry we would be faced with the unappealing prospect of a long cold night in a snow hole with only our duvet jackets and bivvi bags for warmth. Set against that I was all too aware that the majority of mountaineering accidents occur during descent when tired minds and bodies lose their concentration and a fatal slip occurs.

After a quick brew and a bar of chocolate we took some photos and turned to start back down the ridge. The weather cleared slightly and we had some fine views away into Uganda. The jungle looked somewhat incongruous from our icy vantage point. We made good time down the ridge. I belayed Mark and Richard down the snow gully and then followed them down on a line from Bogey. I untied from Bogey's rope and then the three of us began to traverse above the large crevasse. As we were heading downhill, Mark as least experienced went at the front with Richard in the middle and myself at the back as anchor. Mark stopped to jump a fault in the snow and as he did so the entire snow face sloughed off beneath him. One moment he was upright and the next he was plunging uncontrollably down towards the yawning void. As if in slow motion I saw Richard get ripped off his feet and tumble after him. I dived into the snow pressing down on my axe with every ounce of my strength. I waited as the rope went tight fully expecting to be pulled after them. My face was pressed into the snow and I was panting with the effort. The rope was singing taut between us. Richard had managed to get his axe into the ice but Mark was dangling free over the drop. I scarcely dared breathe lest our fragile grip was lost. I shouted down to the others not to move as much as an eyelid but to hang on. Meanwhile I managed to get a prussik loop on to Bogey's rope and thus make us safe. I backed myself up again on Bogey's rope to make doubly sure and then began to try and get Richard and Mark back up the slope. Richard managed quite well but Mark, who was clearly shocked and on the steepest ice, was flailing his ice axe ineffectually. With Cfn Howard's added weight we managed to heave them back up. It had been a close shave.

Bogey climbed down to join us and then led precariously across the now bare ice above the crevasse. Each of us issued a heartfelt sigh of relief once we had passed the danger spot. Regaining the Stanley Plateau was a long hard slog through the soft snow. Throughout the day the temperature had risen and snow bridges weakened so we had to be very wary of crevasses. Mark seemed to be walking in a permanent daze. I had to keep shouting at him to try and get him to snap out of it, concentrate on placing his feet and watch for signs of danger. We made our way slowly down the Stanley Glacier. The last section of steep ice was fairly hair-raising. Reversing this, with one man less than *compos mentis*, fairly concentrated the mind. Richard looked very unhappy — he said later that he had been sure that Mark was going to fall and that we would never have held him. As we reached the rocks the light was fading. Cloud had closed in around us once more and it was half raining half sleeting. We could see a bonfire, but we were still a long way from safety.

We took off our ropes and crampons and began slowly climbing down the rock face. Climbing downwards is hazardous at the best of times but in the dark on wet rock it was no fun at all. I took a rope off Bogey on one section that I would normally have climbed with no problem. We managed to cross into a snow gully and slid down on our backsides, using arms and legs as brakes. Occasionally we would lose control and career down, although only for a short distance at a time, it was pretty hairy. Cfn Howard and I went ahead with Richard following some way behind. Mark was making hard going at the back and Bogey, reliable to the last, was coaxing him down. Below the snow gully we had to scramble down some awkward rock gullies. It was now pitch dark. We were cold and wet through. Our head torches cast feeble pools of light on the rocks below. Eventually we reached the bottom. The walk back over the greasy lichen-covered boulders to the hut seemed to go on forever. Some of the others came down from the hut to help but we just lumbered past. In the hut we collapsed totally exhausted. It was 7.30pm, some thirteen and a half hours after we had set off. I just sat and ached until Cpl Violett pressed a brew into my hands. As each member of our tired band came in, a stream of expletives summed up their feelings. Mark came in last. Matthew had carried his rucksack on the final section. He just sat and stared, lost in a world of his own. The others gave us brew after brew and then cooked us a meal. Bogey said it was the hardest day's mountaineering he had ever had.

Outside the weather was getting worse with howling wind and rain. We stripped off our wet clothes, threw the hardware outside and packed everyone into the small hut. I couldn't think of anything but sleeping. There was no way we were going anywhere the next day.

I woke at about 7am and then lay dozing. No one showed any inclination to get up so we were all still in our sleeping bags when Sgt Jennings arrived carrying extra food up from Hut 3. He was his usual chirpy, efficient self beavering to help others. At Hut 3 Gdsm Simmons was feeling rough and Sgt Damms and Gdsm Hills were still weak so he intended to load them up with spare kit and send them down the mountain.

We discussed plans for the following day. Matthew, Gdsm Williams, Cpl Violett and Cpl Keepin were all keen to have a go at the summit. Neither Bogey nor I fancied slogging our way back up the snow faces of our two previous routes so that left the north ridge of Albert. It was a long rock ridge of about severe standard. From the summit of Albert a short traverse led to the Margherita summit.

I felt very lethargic all morning and drifted around drinking brews and fantasising about fresh food. I had developed a craving for egg 'banjos'. Richard, Cfn Howard and Sgt Jennings left together, Richard with a rather pitying backward glance at me. Mark stayed on for a couple more hours before following them. He still seemed shocked from the previous day's dramas and couldn't get his act together. In the afternoon, Bogey instructed everyone on placing pitons, belay techniques and multi-pitch abseiling. Later it rained heavily.

Bogey got up at 4.30am to check the weather and came back in saying that it was freezing cold, with high winds and driving wet snow. A lot of snow had fallen in the night. On the ridge the rock would be cold and slippery low down and verglassed* higher up. It was certainly no weather to be starting a route with novices. Instead of going back to sleep we had

*'Verglas' is a film of ice on rock

a brew and chatted. We had reached the end of our permitted time on the mountain, a major cold front appeared to be settling in and so with the summit climbed I decided to evacuate the mountain. Once it was light we loaded up all of the technical kit and set off down towards Hut 3. The weather cleared for a while giving fantastic views of the mountain. I had a great sense of fulfilment looking up at its massive form. It looked very fine with fresh snow clinging to its flanks and the glaciers glistening in the sun. We made our way down to Hut 3 and then on to Hut 2 through frequent heavy downpours. The path had turned into a quagmire and as we lurched down from root to root we became caked in mud. We spent a very mellow evening in the Mahungu Hut.

We continued on the next day in similar conditions. As we descended everything became more vivid and prolific — noise, colour, vegetation. We caught flashes of parrots and monkeys high in the canopy overhead. We walked in a full-blown tropical downpour for most of the day. I stopped at the Guides' Hut for a brief respite from the deluge to be met by Constant, beaming from ear to ear, proffering a calabash of chibuku — the strong locally brewed millet beer from which he had clearly been freely imbibing. The last section down to the Church was one long wet mud slide. Cfn Simmons was waiting with the Land Rover to run us back to camp. There, morale was high. CSgt Bennett was piling cloves of garlic into a freshly butchered goat which he assured us, along with potatoes and cabbage, was made to his mother's special recipe and would make the finest stew we had ever tasted. I offered a silent prayer of thanks to Mrs Bennett for bringing up her son so practically, and meanwhile set about demolishing anything else consumable that I could lay my hands on.

For the next three days we drove south into ever more fertile country until we reached Goma on the Zaire/Rwanda border. Rwanda brought instant order out of chaos. Zaire's abominable mud tracks gave way to even tarmac roads, the border town of Gisenyi was clean, tidy and well provisioned and for the first time in six weeks I was able to ring the UK. I got hold of Hugh Boddington, the Adjutant, first, then Alasdair Johnstone and finally the Commanding Officer. There was much news to pass in each direction. On the expedition front the finances were still dodgy but not critical. However they did have some serious news. Following our failure to link up with the non-existent military escort in Niger and our problems in Nigeria we weren't going to be allowed back into either country. We would have to re-plan the last phase of the expedition. That night we camped at a small site on the shore of Lake Kivu.

Our next objective, Mt Karisimbi, lay in the Virunga, a range of eight volcanoes which form the southern extreme of the Ruwenzoris. We drove northwards between tightly terraced hillsides. Every available inch of ground was cultivated. The plots were ordered and the crops of tea, maize, bananas and vegetables well tended. The general ambience was of highly organised productivity. The cloud-capped summits beckoned us forwards. We camped in the grounds of a small mission in Ruhengeri whilst we made arrangements for the climb. I hoped to climb the neighbouring summit of Bisoke and trek to see the mountain gorillas that inhabited the lower slopes.

The ascent of the 14,800 foot Karisimbi took us two days. We drove up through banana plantations and fields of pyrethrum flowers to the road head. From there we trekked up a steep mud track flanked by powerful stinging nettles to the 10,000 foot saddle between Karisimbi and Bisoke. Nestling amongst a copse of hagenia trees were a few painted corrugated-iron huts. This was Karisoke, the research station built by Diane Fossey, as a base for her studies into the mountain gorillas. She had spent eighteen years living in this cool, ever damp environment identifying, studying and protecting her beloved gorillas. It had been a brave venture in the face of considerable physical and political adversity and had ended tragically with her savage murder by poachers in 1975.

We turned away from Karisoke and up into the tangled forest of hagenia, groundsel and wild tobacco that were rooted in the bog covering the lower flanks of the mountain. Black-headed duiker and bushbuck skittered away on our approach and we saw plenty of hyena and buffalo faeces. A further hour and a half brought us to a small metal 'hut'. We pitched our tents to enjoy a wonderful sunset. To our west Mikeno was wreathed by wisps of cirrus and crowned with a rainbow. To our north lay the summits of Bisoke, Sabinyo, Cahinga and Muhabura, sentinels watching over the Rwandan countryside.

Next morning, after a three and a half hour slog up tussocky grass slopes into thick cloud we reached the summit rocks. A large radio antenna was surrounded by a few ramshackle huts. I waited for a while, huddled into my Sprayway jacket against the biting wind, hoping for the cloud to clear but to no avail. Back at the camp we split; one group went down whilst I carried on with another to climb Bisoke. I wanted to photograph the small lake lodged in the summit crater but once again we were frustrated by cloud. Down at the Mission all was not well. Several of the group had been suffering to a greater or lesser extent from diarrhoea and vomiting. LCpl Keepin had been laid so weak that to his great disappointment he had been unable to come up the mountain. Once we had left he had got worse and become delirious at one point. Gdsm Hills had also stayed down. He had contracted a chest infection which had induced an asthma attack. Matthew had put him on a drip and for once even his relaxed demeanour slipped into concern. I looked forward to leaving the jungle behind and taking the team into the healthier atmosphere of East Africa.

Before we left we arranged to track one of the families of mountain gorillas, living in their bamboo retreat on the flanks of the volcanoes. We were split into groups of six and briefed carefully by the Park Wardens. At no time were we to talk, smoke or use flash guns and if we found the gorillas we were not to make any sudden movements. Should any of the gorillas charge us we were to get down, avert our eyes and stay put. With that last rather sobering thought in mind we went off into a forest of bamboo behind our guide. It was dark inside but between the bamboo stands the forest floor was reasonably clear. We emerged into an area of dense, tangled undergrowth which frequently reached over our heads. We wore jackets and thick trousers as protection against the powerful nettles. Trees had been brought down in storms and were now enmeshed in the undergrowth. It was like one long assault course as we battled our way over, under and through the vegetative morass.

After a rather sweaty hour we came upon an area where much of the undergrowth had been flattened. Our guides pointed out nests in the damp vegetation where the gorillas had spent the previous night. Mist hung in dense pockets all around rendering the forest damp and oppressive. We moved on carefully, senses very much alert, following the trail of destruction and faeces left by the gorillas. The assault course resumed as we followed them into even more impenetrable country. Piles of steaming faeces signalled that we were getting closer.

As we approached our guides began emitting low, hollow grunts emulating the gorillas. We strained to see and then there in front of us, framed in the mist, was a young male. He stood a full four feet tall and appeared almost as broad. We edged forward until we could see the majority of the group. Gorillas were all around us. At the back of the group an enormous male sat surveying the scene. The silver hair on his back and sides and his massive brooding form set him apart as the patriarch. Mothers watched over their young who gambolled and cavorted with each other. They seemed quite unperturbed by our presence and came right up to us showing off for the camera. Less welcome was the attention of the first young male that we had seen who now launched several charges. Crouching down in the face of these, with images of being pummelled to death by a 400-pound gorilla racing around in your mind, your heart was in your mouth and your resolve taxed. When the silverback decided that it was time to move on he went around the group delivering powerful kicks with his hind feet to motivate individuals into action. We followed them for an hour, observing and photographing. They rarely stayed still for more than a few moments but lumbered slowly on. Small groups would stop to feed, groom each other or play and would then chase after the rest. The air reverberated to the sound of crashing undergrowth, snapping branches, chomping, chest beating and the shrieks of infants. The young were enchanting as they rode on their mothers' backs or climbed stands of bamboo until the slender stems could support them no longer and they crashed, squealing to the floor. The sheer size of the adults was intimidating yet they moved with determined grace. There was an air of great intimacy about the group. One hour flashed by. Reluctantly we were led away by the guides. I felt tremendously privileged to have observed at such close-hand these rare animals in their natural habitat. As we scrambled back out of the forest it was good to ponder that although recently the mountain gorillas had been on the verge of extinction their future was now assured through well-managed, successful conservation.

Before leaving Rwanda we drove north-east to Parc de L'Akagera, a little- known game reserve tucked up against the border with Tanzania. Open, rolling hills leading to a long scarp which in turn overlooked a series of lakes, contained a magnificent array of wildlife. It was wonderful wild country, and when we weren't plagued by tsetse flies it was a real pleasure to enjoy the wildlife in such a remote setting.

We crossed into Tanzania at the Chutes de Rusumo. The river was in full spate and the waterfall resultingly powerful as we crossed the bridge over the river which took us through an area of no man's land. As we skirted the southern edge of Lake Victoria we came across some of the worst driving conditions anywhere in the continent. Once perfect tarmac roads had decayed until they were now far worse than even some of Zaire's mud tracks. At Mwanza conditions reached an all-time low with sheer-sided potholes up to three feet deep which threatened to smash fuel lines, drive shafts or axles if drivers lost their concentration. We carried on past the western extremity of the Serengeti, past Musumo and back onto desperate mud tracks. The journey to the Kenyan border was a catalogue of frustrations, awkward tolls, blocked routes, vehicle recoveries and wet conditions.

Once in Kenya I felt as if a large weight had been lifted off my shoulders. For the time being we were in a country of relative civilisation. We drove on good roads, through beautifully manicured tea plantations to towns that were well kept and well stocked. Before heading to the army base at Kahawa we spent ten days exploring some of the lakes of the Rift Valley. At Lake Bogoria we saw vast flocks of flamingos lining the shore in a great pink ribbon, congregated so densely as to carpet areas of the lake. At Lake Nakuru pelicans chased shoals of fish, in a frenzy of feeding whilst waterbuck and impala lined the shores and further into the bush we caught glimpses of rare leopard and rhinoceros. At Lake Naivasha some of the team fished whilst others climbed to the top of Mt Longonot. It was a very relaxing way to end what had been a fairly hectic three months.

Chapter Three
High Snows

Phase 3

Captain John Warburton-Lee, Welsh Guards, Expedition leader
Captain Richard Gaffney, Welsh Guards, Expedition Second in
 Command
Captain Matthew Roberts, Royal Army Medical Corps, Expedition
 doctor
Company Sergeant Major Alan Bennett, Welsh Guards
Miss Tetta Nicholls, Expedition secretary
Drill Sergeant Colin Coull, Scots Guards
Sergeant Mark Ward, 29 Commando Regiment, Royal Artillery
Sergeant Allen Thubron, Royal Electrical and Mechanical Engineers,
 Chief Mechanic
Lance Sergeant Andrew Brown 16, Welsh Guards
Bombardier Peter Lawes, 29 Commando Regiment, Royal Artillery
Sergeant Andy Nundy, Royal Air Force Mountain Rescue Team
Corporal Ken Winch, Royal Electrical and Mechanical Engineers
Corporal Alan Williams 15, Welsh Guards
Captain Carolyn Ellis, Queen Alexandra's Royal Army Nursing Corps
Lieutenant Richard Stanford, Welsh Guards
Sub Lieutenant Mike Baker, Royal Navy
Guardsman Sid James, Grenadier Guards
Guardsman 'Dinger' Bell, Coldstream Guards
Guardsman Peter Rothera, Welsh Guards
Steve Edwards, Weston Spirit

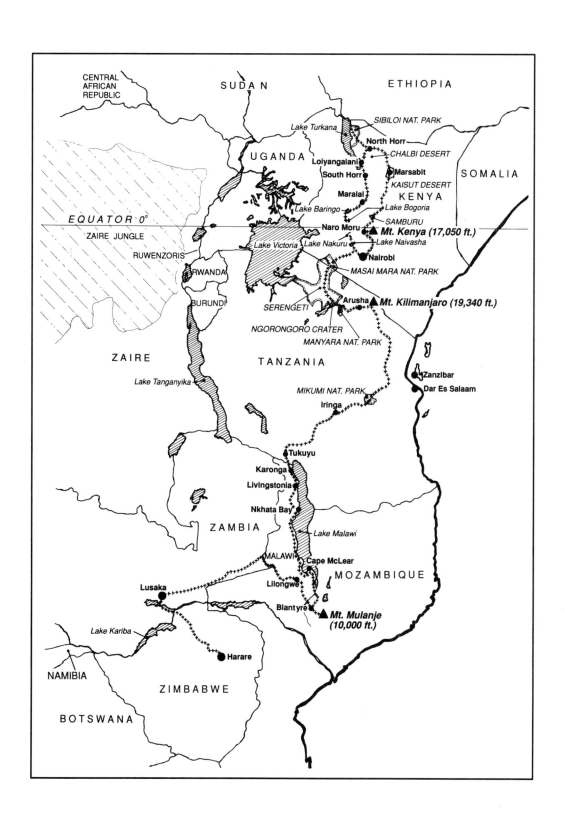

The Phase 3 team flew out to Nairobi on the last day in May. This was to be the main mountaineering phase of the expedition, tackling the last three peaks including Mt Kenya, the most technically demanding of all our mountain objectives. Amongst the new team were several familiar faces from one of our two training expeditions to climb Mexico's volcanoes in 1989. There was a breadth of experience. The most capable was undoubtedly Bdr Pete Lawes, a sound technical climber on rock and ice. He had climbed extensively in Britain, the Alps and Norway and had co-led the first Mexican trip with me until he had been injured by a rock fall at around 16,000 feet on Popocatepetl from where we had had to rescue him throughout a very long night. Sgt Mark Ward, another Mexican veteran, was Lawes's closest friend and permanent climbing partner. Sgt Andy Nundy, whom I didn't know, came from the RAF Mountain Rescue Team. Although well experienced in the art of mountain rescue in Britain he had less experience of climbing on bigger ranges abroad. Lt Richard Stanford had very much the same approach to life as me, with a similar mountaineering background, and had led several expeditions of his own. Richard had put a lot of work into the planning of this part of the expedition and had flown out to Kenya early to make preparations in advance of the team's arrival. The remainder, whether old friends or new acquaintances, were all novice mountaineers. I was under no illusion about the task ahead if we were successfully to achieve all of our aims.

We spent two days at Kahawa, briefing, planning and preparing our equipment for the first mountain. After five months on the road, living, eating and sleeping constantly cheek by jowl I had decided to send each of the other permanent team members off for a break. Matthew had gone first in order to be back for Mt Kenya. He had last been seen sporting an enormous schoolboyish grin as he disappeared into an exceedingly seedy Nairobi bar described in our guidebook as 'a hang-out for pimps, prostitutes and low-life whites'. I often felt that he was frustrated by the lack of freedom of action on the expedition but he returned with recharged batteries ready to tackle the mountain. Richard's sister Miranda and CSgt (recently promoted to CSM) Bennett's girlfriend Debbie had both come out on a short visit so they, together with Tetta, all took off towards the coast having dropped the remainder of us at the base of Mt Kenya.

Only just south of the equator, Mt Kenya rises to 17,050 feet. The central massif is a veritable climber's paradise of granite towers, knife-edge ridges and steep rock walls intersecting hanging glaciers. The two main peaks, Batiaan and Nelion, offer a tremendous variety of challenging rock and ice routes. To reach the summit of either requires sustained technical climbing of at least severe standard. The third highest and most frequently ascended peak, Point Lenana, at 16,355 feet, is little more than an arduous trek. We intended to climb that first, by way of acclimatisation, and then set about tackling the main summits.

We drove up from Naro Moru to the Park Headquarters where we met the new warden Bongo Woodley. Bongo was following in the footsteps of his father, Bill Woodley, an expatriate who had himself been warden of Mt Kenya and the Aberdares thirty years previously and now led the anti-poaching campaign in Tsavo. Since Bill Woodley had left there had been a variety of wardens. In the early seventies an American, Phil Snyder, had taken on the job. Snyder was an accomplished mountaineer and had pioneered a number of hard new routes on the mountain. He had also built up a proficient mountain rescue team. Since then, through increased pressure of tourism, lack of funding and poor management the Park and its infrastructure had degenerated. All of the old mountain rescue team had been posted to other areas, the rangers' standards of mountaineering had dropped and the huts were in an appalling state. Bongo had been appointed by Richard Leakey, the new Minister for Wildlife, to sort the park out. Richard Stanford had got in touch with Bongo and suggested that in return for him waiving our entry fees we would help train the nucleus of his new mountain rescue team. It was an arrangement that suited both sides well.

Of the four African rangers that Bongo attached to us, two, Sgt Duncan Karinga and Cpl Thumbi Mathenge, had been in Snyder's original mountain rescue team. Although both were now fairly long in the tooth Bongo had asked for them to be posted back to Mt Kenya to be the mainstays of his new team. They knew the mountain intimately and had put up several new routes with Snyder. The other two were younger men and total novices.

Our team set off on the five-mile walk from the Park gate to the Meteorological Station at 10,000 feet. I drove up with all of the equipment but, even with my acclimatisation, I felt fairly light-headed as I unloaded it. I then went back down to sort out porters and arrange some of the administrative details with Bongo. Over the next couple of days we carried all of the food and technical equipment in two loads up through the 2,000 foot vertical bog, along the Teleki Valley, past Mackinders Camp to our mountain base at the Ranger's Post at 13,500 feet.

We were nestled into a steep-sided grassy valley the head of which was dominated by the two towering peaks of Batiaan and Nelion which were in turn split by the long ribbon of ice that leads up the Diamond Couloir. It was an inspiring view. The two great sentinels had a special magnetism and whatever we were doing our eyes kept being drawn back to them. It seemed as if they were issuing a constant challenge to us.

We spent a day practising our rock climbing techniques on the low-lying crags in the valley. The rock was extremely scrappy and we had to be careful not to send mounds of loose shale cascading down on those below. Having spent some time bouldering and sorting out basic style and methods we set up some top ropes. The rangers were the first to volunteer. Both Sgt Duncan and Cpl Thumbi were confident and determined to prove themselves. Cpl Thumbi cut a hysterical figure. To look at he appeared a most unlikely climber. His short, almost circular figure was exaggerated by an enormous baggy set of breeches made from World War II battledress trousers. On top he swathed himself in as many clothes as he could lay his hands on with a balaclava permanently crammed over his head to complete the ensemble. As this ball of garments was propelled upwards by stubby arms and legs it appeared to defy all logic or physical laws and attracted a fair amount of ribaldry. Thumbi, who was quickly proving to be quite a character, wallowed in the attention and played to the gallery. Carolyn Ellis, in total contrast, had elected to wear a pair of body hugging Lycra tights and held the men's rapt attention as she scaled the rock face. Richard Stanford brought operations to a total standstill by quite unconsciously advising her to overcome a difficult move with the words 'There is a great crack between your legs, reach up with one leg and stand in it'.

Carolyn was already showing herself to be a very determined lady who whilst maintaining her femininity refused to accept any concession for being a woman. As a trained nurse she was well used to looking after herself and it was a joy to watch the ease with which she put down any cheek from the men. After a useful training session we retired in the face of heavy hail.

The next stage was to move higher up the mountain onto the glaciers to work on our ice climbing techniques and build up our acclimatisation. I intended to take one group with Bdr Lawes up to the Lewis Glacier from where we would also climb Pt Lenana. Meanwhile Richard Stanford and Sgt Nundy would take their group to work on the Tyndall Glacier and then follow us a day later for their ascent of Pt Lenana. I then intended for all of us, having spent two nights at 16,000 feet to go back down to the Rangers' Post to select teams and sort out kit for the main summit bids.

Next day we were away from the Rangers' Post by 8am. We followed the left-hand side of the valley avoiding a steep scree slope between some low-lying crags. The closer we got to the main peaks the more daunting they appeared. The Diamond Couloir seemed to go on for ever and looked impossibly steep. We had great views over the turquoise Lewis tarn and across onto the Lewis Glacier which stretched away to Pt Thompson and

Pt Lenana. Cpl Thumbi led us at a steady pace up to the Austrian Hut in just over two hours. Built in 1972 to take up to thirty people it was already badly run down. Steadily building clouds threatened a break in the weather so, with the summit of Pt Lenana so close, I decided temporarily to postpone our ice climbing and get it in the bag. We made our way up the left edge of the Lewis Glacier, skirting several crevasses. A fresh covering of snow, the day before, made our approach treacherous. We walked with ice axes and were forced to kick steps. Cpl Thumbi delighted in a succession of morbid stories. For him, every landmark was the site of a previous rescue or disaster.

The final summit ridge is attained by a simple mantleshelf move. The summit cross was only a few feet beyond. Strangely I didn't feel any real sense of achievement. It had been too easy but more than that was the apprehension of tackling the North East Face of Nelion which loomed above us. The route looked very long and had a fair covering of snow. Unfortunately and unavoidably we were between seasons on the mountain. The ice routes weren't in condition and the ice shattered if you hit it with the pick of your axe. However the rock routes were also difficult. At this time of year the weather was often unsettled and the rock prone to be verglassed.

We spent the time practising ice axe arrests, ice screw placement, deadman anchors and snow bollards. Everyone was keen to learn. Somehow in the sunshine Nelion didn't look so imposing and I began to feel that with a good day we could get up it without too many problems.

On the way back to the hut we stopped at the base of the glacier by an ice cave. It had a huge curtain of icicles hanging across the entrance. Inside it was stunning. It was fifty feet across, seventy long and up to twenty high. The ceiling was a variety of shades of blue water ice. Towards the back, bands of red soil and rocks were held frozen into the ice. It was eerie to walk around beneath the glacier.

Back at the hut the other group had just arrived so there was general pandemonium with kit everywhere. Richard Stanford and Mike Baker had already set off towards Pt Lenana, Carolyn was outside sunbathing and the rest were taking it easy. Sgt Duncan accosted me to tell me how much he was enjoying learning the modern climbing techniques. He was literally dancing with pleasure like a small boy and insisted I pass his feelings on to Bongo.

We collected our kit and set off down fast, running the screes. All the way the views of the mountain changed with the different angle of view but it only ever appeared more impressive. In the evening we spent an hour bouldering on some nearby rocks.

Once the second team had rejoined us next day I talked over our plans with Bdr Lawes, Sgt Nundy and Richard Stanford and we came up with a plan. The first attempt would be made by Bdr Lawes and Sgt Ward on the lead rope with Sgt Nundy, Bongo and myself on the second. We would move back up to the Austrian Hut the next day ready to climb the day after. The next attempt would be selected from Richard Stanford, Mike Baker, Sgt Thubron, Gdsm Bell, Cpl Williams, Cpl Winch, Cpl Thumbi and Sgt Duncan. The remainder of the team were going to make a circular tour of the main massif taking three days. I was glad that the decisions over team selection had been made and prayed for good weather.

It took some time to sort out the logistics to support two assault teams based for five days up at the Austrian Hut. Loads had to be packed including personal kit, climbing hardware, rations, cookers and gas cartridges. Despite arranging for the walking group to drop off an extra supply of rations on their way past we set off with very heavy packs.

The first five of us took it slowly up the screes not wanting to be exhausted before starting the climb the next day. Up at the hut each person dealt with the wait in their own way. Bdr Lawes and Sgt Ward spent most of the afternoon with the guidebook staring across the glacier and figuring out every turn of the long, complicated route. Sgt Nundy organised and re-organised his gear. I preferred not to think about it too much and chatted to Bongo. It was certainly going to be the hardest route that I had ever been on. I had two main worries: first that we might get frozen off the route by the cold weather that had moved in and secondly that we might lose the route as it wound its rather convoluted way up the great open rock face.

I heard Bdr Lawes and Sgt Ward getting up and making brews from about 3.30am. We were planning to leave a little after them so as not to have to stand around in the bitter cold at the base of the face whilst they began their climb. I lay in my sleeping bag listening to them pack, trying not to psyche myself out by thinking about the route ahead. They left at 5.45am, clattering off into the darkness. Suddenly I desperately wanted to get going and get on with the climb. Sgt Nundy sensed my impatience and muttered reassurances. We walked down to the foot of the glacier. There was a covering of crisp snow and we could see the other pair already on their third pitch approaching the base of Mackinders Chimney.

On the far side of the glacier we climbed several hundred feet up a steep boulder scree slope to the foot of the rock face. It took us time to get cold fingers warmed up, ropes knotted and ready to go. Sgt Nundy led the first pitch slowly. The climbing was straightforward, more like scrambling, with plenty of protection available although we had to be careful of loose rock. After the first pitch we traversed first left and then back right. Once on the face it wasn't as intimidating as I had expected. We all just concentrated on the next move immediately above us.

Above, the others were having problems at an awkward traverse which avoided Mackinders Chimney called the Rabbit Hole. Sgt Ward had led the pitch but couldn't do it with his rucksack on. He had taken the rucksack off and clipped it halfway across to a bit of old rope. Bdr Lawes then had an hour-long wrestling match to get both rucksacks across. We were moving slower as a rope of three so the others dropped a rope down Mackinders Chimney and belayed us up to avoid the time that it would take for us to negotiate the Rabbit Hole.

We carried on all together. As we climbed the exposure increased with a vertical drop hundreds of feet below our feet. Initially I had been confident that we would make the summit but our progress was painfully slow. In many cases the two ropes were impeding each other and then doubling up on effort and belays, all the while costing us extra time. Several rope-lengths followed until a delicate traverse around a corner revealed Baillie's Bivouac above us. I led the last pitch belaying just by its roof. The Bivouac was no more than a small metal box into which two or three people could just squeeze. It involved a climb to get into it and was precariously perched on a granite block. With no door and an enormous vertical drop below it appeared far from safe or welcoming.

The main south ridge of Nelion was just above us. Beyond lay the crux of the climb, De Graaf's Variation, a sixty foot square-cut corner before regaining the ridge. A further couple of comparatively difficult stages led to the summit of Nelion. Once there we would have to abseil into the Gate of the Mists, cross the small icy groove between the two summits and climb the last couple of pitches to the true summit of Batiaan, 17,050 feet. Then we would have to turn around and descend our entire ascent route.

It was already nearly 3pm and we had some decisions to make. Although we were two-thirds of the way up the route we had completed only half of the estimated climbing time. Ahead we could see that the route was steep and heavily iced in places. We ruled out pushing on for fear of being benighted before reaching Howell's Bivouac on the summit of Nelion. No one really fancied spending the night in the Baillie's Bivouac and anyway we didn't have the gear for the others to sleep out on the face. As I didn't want to split the team we were left with little choice but to all go down again and try again in a couple of days, using the experience that we had gained. It was very disappointing to have to go down having come so far.

The descent was long and difficult with pitch after pitch of abseiling. It was hard to follow the line of ascent due to all the traversing that we had made. To make matters more difficult the ropes kept getting stuck as we pulled them through forcing one of us to climb back up and release them. Bits of old sling and tat marked previous abseiling points but still we found ourselves having to bear a long way across to our right to keep on line. Bdr Lawes had to take his rucksack off to lead one abseil to almost an extreme of arc. Following with a rucksack on was very hairy — one slip would have risked penduluming out under a huge overhang.

The next abseil was no more pleasant. The anchor point was an old piton and a chock. As Sgt Nundy went down I could see the piton bend under his weight. It was getting cold and we only had thirty minutes of light left. The cloud was closing in around the mountain but I could make out five people crossing the glacier towards us. The penultimate abseil took us down one at a time to a tiny ledge just big enough to get one foot on. The final anchor point led down to the top of the scree where Matthew, Sgt Thubron and others were waiting. As Sgt Nundy went down, one side of the doubled rope snagged in a crevice. Unable to release it he went down on just one rope. Tired and eager to be down he thought that he was on the ground before the true bottom and released his grip. He fell the last ten feet. The others rushed to help him. Fortunately he was just dazed and a bit shocked. Higher up, a momentary lapse of concentration like that might have had fatal consequences.

I was very relieved when my feet touched the ground just as darkness fell. Willing hands took my rucksack off me and I was passed a cup of coffee. It felt an age before Sgt Ward, the last man, reached the ground. We made our way slowly back over the glacier and up the moraine to the hut, each of us lost in our own thoughts. The hut was packed with all of the team. Welcoming faces greeted us through a blast of heat. More brews and lots of talk followed. It took a while to calm down and relax enough to eat the curry that they had prepared.

Next morning, once the walking group had left on their circular tour, I held a council of war. We would make another summit attempt the next day by the same route. The team was to be Bdr Lawes and Sgt Ward on the lead rope, Sgt Nundy and Gdsm Bell second with Richard Stanford and Mike Baker third. With an earlier start, lighter equipment, and climbing as three roped pairs, and on a now-familiar route I hoped that they stood a much better chance of success.

Through the day I took each group aside and stressed the importance of putting safety first. In particular I told them that if they were running late they should bivvi out rather than try to descend in the dark. I also pressed home the point that no piece of equipment was worth one of their lives and I didn't mind if they had to leave climbing hardware behind in retreat. It sounded rather melodramatic but I was all too aware that this was a dangerous mountain which had claimed many lives.

The climbers got up at 4.30am, made themselves brews and breakfast and left shortly afterwards. I lay in my sleeping bag praying for their success and safe return. I really hoped that they would make it this time. Another group came into the hut on their way to Pt Lenana so I chatted to them for a while.

Up on the mountain Bdr Lawes and Sgt Ward were making tremendous progress. By 8am they had passed the Rabbit's Hole leaving Richard Stanford and Mike Baker struggling on it. I set off with Matthew Roberts, Cpl Williams, Sgt Thubron, Cpl Winch and Sgt Duncan to climb Pt Thompson from where we wanted to watch and photograph the ascent. As we crossed the glacier we saw the lead pair reach Baillie's Bivouac at 8.40am. They had flown up the route. As they disappeared from view I thought that surely nothing could stop them now.

We continued across to the far side of the glacier taking care to avoid the crevasses which were widening with each day's mild weather. A couple of hundred feet of shattered rock and scree took us to the summit of Pt Thompson. It was the closest point that we could get to from which to observe the climb. I felt slightly better that at least we could have some contact with the climbers. I set up my Nikon camera on a tripod with a 600mm lens and settled down to wait.

One hour passed and then a second. I was now getting very concerned that we hadn't seen the lead pair. They should have broken out onto the Nelion ridge far above us. I began to worry that they had either hit bad ice conditions and were stuck or that they had risked traversing across the south face of Nelion direct to the Gate of the Mists. I kept hoping that they would appear just below the summit. After what seemed like another age Cpl Williams shouted that he could see one of them on the ridge. Looking through the telescopic lens I could see that it was Bdr Lawes. He was on top of Mackinders Gendarme, much lower down than I had hoped.

I yelled across to see if he was all right. He replied that they were OK but totally exhausted and were coming down. The distance between us prevented any more detailed conversation and I was left to assume that the conditions had been too difficult on the other side of the ridge. We watched as Sgt Ward appeared and they both abseiled down the outside of Mackinders Gendarme back to Baillie's Bivouac where the other two pairs were now waiting. I felt terribly disappointed both for them and for the expedition. We made our way, rather dejectedly, back to the hut to wait while they made their descent.

As they neared the bottom, at around 4.30pm, we recrossed the glacier with flasks of coffee to meet them. To my relief they were in fairly good heart. They all looked exhausted but had enjoyed their day. Bdr Lawes said that the conditions above Baillie's Bivouac had been awful. They had taken two hours to crack the crux but then had come to an even more difficult pitch where they hadn't felt that they had the strength to go on.

The ice routes certainly weren't in condition. The glacier now had water flowing freely on it. I was not prepared to mount another assault on the same route. Everyone was tired and most had been stretched towards their technical and physical limits. To go at it again might well tempt individuals to take a risk out of proportion to their experience and thus, as we were intentionally a novice expedition, I decided, regretfully, to retreat from the mountain. Disappointing though it was not to have reached the true summit we had all gained valuable experience of climbing on a long, hard, committing route at altitude and mercifully we hadn't had any accidents so far.

It took two days to carry all of our equipment back down the Teleki Valley through the vertical bog to the Meteorological Station. The other members of the permanent cadre were there to meet us with the vehicles. They had all had a good break. We loaded our kit onto the vehicles and drove down to the Park gate to camp. After a brief sojourn in the cool Aberdare Mountains we set off northwards to explore Kenya's remote Northern Frontier District.

We crossed the Equator at Nanyuki and drove on through the White Highlands. Fields of luxuriant, swaying wheat covered the rolling hillsides. Branching north-west towards Isiolo we dropped down to plains of tinder-dry, coarse grass and flat-topped acacia trees punctuated by steep red hills. This was the classic image of Africa that had drawn me on my first visit to Africa and had stayed with me ever since. As we passed Lewa Downs I gazed longingly at the farm where I had had my first experiences of life in the African bush.

We continued on to the Samburu Reserve. There, we spent two nights on the banks of the Uaso Nyiro River, defending our food and belongings against a troop of exceedingly cheeky Vervet monkeys who stole, with impunity, anything that was left unattended. We were rewarded with many sightings of the wildlife indigenous to the rugged northern landscape: the tightly striped Grevvy's zebra, grey-flanked Beisa oryx with their sweeping horns extending far down their backs, reticulated giraffe with their strong network markings and the elegant, slender-necked Gerenuk placing their front feet at full stretch up into the acacia bushes to reach the succulent buds higher up.

The further north we drove the hotter it became. We passed through Archers Post in a cloud of red dust. A group of rather disinterested tribesmen watched as we went by their single short line of wood and corrugated iron dukas. From this point on it was rare to see tribesmen in anything but their traditional attire. We took a badly corrugated dirt road into a flat, arid, semi-desert plain. A couple of small settlements were based on missions; otherwise the area was devoid of life. Previously, vehicles had to travel in armed convoys through this region for protection against bands of Somali shifta.

After several hours the road rose gradually up to the thickly forested 3,000 foot Marsabit Mountain. The administrative capital of the Northern Frontier District, Marsabit's cool greenness is in stark contrast to the surrounding desert. Although no more than a spartan collection of offices and small stores we were able to stock up with some fresh vegetables, meat and bread before turning north once more. The road out of Marsabit north-westwards dropped rapidly back to arid wasteland.

As we continued north it became even hotter and harsher. What little vegetation there was receded until there was just the sparsest smattering of dry grass and occasional low thorn bushes. Amazingly, in amongst this baking hell, we came upon nomadic Gabbra and Rendille tribesmen. Their huts were a series of blankets and rugs draped over a stick framework all of which could be transported on their camels. Their camels were hobbled outside each small group of huts and then further afield we would find their herds of goats searching for any tiny bit of nourishment. It was a desperately harsh place to eke out an existence.

Once past the outpost of Karachal we entered the true Chalbi Desert. We drove across blindingly bright pans of flat, baked mud. Susceptible to flash flooding in the wet season the only relief from the aridity for the remainder of the year were clumps of palm trees. Groups of ostriches, and lone tribesmen with their camels, appeared through the heat haze. It took a full day's travel, continuing ever northwards, to reach Sibiloi.

Tucked into a pocket on the north-eastern shore of Lake Turkana, running south from the Sudanese border Sibiloi holds, at Koobi Fora, the site of Dr Richard Leakey's discovery of the oldest remains of man. It is an area that is exciting by its very wildness. There is little escape from the relentless sun. Aside from the sites of anthropological interest it is known mainly for its bleak isolation. On the lake shore we saw herds of topi, zebra and Grants gazelle and a huge array of birdlife: flamingos, terns, storks, herons, stilts, geese, ducks, plover, sacred ibis and pelicans to name just the commoner varieties. Inland, nothing moved about the rugged landscape save a passing jackal.

We spent two nights camped near Allia Bay whilst we toured the area before heading south down the side of the lake to the village of Loiyangalani. There, we bought some tilapia off the local fishermen before carrying on slightly further to camp looking out over 'the Jade Sea'. That night a terrific wind blew up quickly reaching gale force. Mosquito nets tore at their strings, plates flew from the table and chairs scattered. The sentries ran around lashing down the tentage and retrieving flying equipment. By 2am it had reached such proportions that the tarpaulins threatened to rip themselves apart so we got up, collapsed camp and spent the rest of the night, each man trying to find some escape from the wind and sand. No one got much sleep. At 6.30am with the wind still howling there was no chance of cooking breakfast so we packed up like refugees from a hurricane and left.

We drove out of the valley climbing as we went over some appallingly rough, rock pavements. Several hours later we dropped down into the secluded village of South Horr. Tribesmen in their full finery squatted chatting in the shade or strolled along the dusty street carrying their fighting sticks and long flat-bladed spears. There were certain distinctive themes that ran through their dress indicating their tribal association. Some had ochre dyed hair, others elaborate decorations with feathers on the back of their heads, yet others had horns of woven beads protruding from holes in the tops of their ears. We carried on through Baragoi, Marti and Marigo to camp that night on the lip of the Losiolo Escarpment looking out over a 2,000 foot drop into a natural amphitheatre. In front lay the full width of the Rift Valley.

Maralal is an original Kenyan frontier town. Little has changed. Broad streets running between wooden dukas are full of Turkana, Pokot, Samburu and Rendille tribespeople. Leaving the others to find what they could in the market I set off in the rather optimistic quest of some postcards. A small boy soon latched on to me and began giving me a guided tour of the town. Its primary attraction according to him was the explorer and author Wilfred Thesiger. Just as he was extolling the virtues of having a resident explorer, there across the street was the man himself. An old man dressed in cavalry twill trousers, tweed jacket, tie, brown brogue shoes and deerstalker hat and leaning on a carved wooden walking cane. A sharp series of tugs on my arm dragged me forward and before I knew it I was being introduced to the great man.

He was very easy to talk to, interested in our exploits and full of his own reminiscences. He talked of having visited South Horr fifteen years before, several times. On one occasion a small boy whom he had befriended got into Thesiger's car, refused to get out and announced that wherever Thesiger was going he was going too. They had been together ever since and now to Thesiger's pride that boy had become Mayor of Maralal.

Thesiger cut an incongruous figure beside the tribesmen in the dusty Maralal street but from the way that they reacted to him they obviously held a lot of affection for him. When we left he was still standing by the side of the road waiting for one of his Africans to come and pick him up in the vehicle that he had bought for them. A most remarkable man.

We drove on along the Rift Valley stopping to camp at Lakes Bogoria and Nakuru where again we enjoyed the prolific birdlife. We later camped at the northern end of the great, rolling Mara plains which stretch away for hundreds of miles into Tanzania and the Serengeti. These vast open plains with their rounded hills and acacia woodlands are the scene of the greatest movement of animals in the world — the annual Migration. Currently the migrating herds were in the western corner of the Serengeti making their way north but even so there was a considerable amount of resident game. We saw large herds of zebra, wildebeest, topi, Grant's and Thompson's gazelle. There were also Masai giraffe with their distinctive cloverleaf markings, elephant with much larger tusks than we had seen elsewhere, bat-eared foxes, hyena, jackals and the large cats. Dark-maned male lions of magnificent physique dominated the plains by their presence. But it was a cheetah that provided the greatest spectacle.

On our second morning we spotted a lone female cheetah by some low acacia bushes. She was stalking along, marking bushes with her scent as she went. A group of impala fled before her and a cheeky Thompson's gazelle bounced along, barking at her, almost mockingly, but the cheetah ignored her. Then she spotted a herd of male impala in front and her mood changed. Her head dropped down and she began to stalk them, very slowly, using the grass and bushes for cover. The gazelle moved into her way so she lay down and waited. For forty minutes she waited whilst they grazed on by.

Suddenly she appeared to have made her mind up. She stood up, took several crouched paces forwards and then shot off towards the gazelle. As they began to flee and she identified a specific victim she dropped even lower and surged forwards in an extraordinary display of sleek power. The gazelle tried to turn out of the way but the cheetah cornered, leaning right over so that we could see her pale underbelly and, with a final burst of speed, took the gazelle by the back of the neck and brought it down. It had taken no more than thirty seconds from the launch of the attack to the kill, a vivid example of nature's cruel selection process but also an awesome demonstration of speed and power.

As we watched, the cheetah began feeding on the haunches of the gazelle and then as the sun grew stronger she dragged her kill off to a nearby bush and lay panting in the shade. When we returned later in the afternoon the cheetah was lying, bloated and sleeping under the bush. The gazelle's carcass had been stripped clean. All that remained were bones and horns. Three vultures sat up in a tree surveying the scene. Further on we saw a pride of three lionesses with their six cubs. The cubs played and fought constantly. They would stalk each other and then charge, finishing with a flying leap and a wrestling match. We spent an hour just watching them. We finished an almost perfect day with the sight of a herd of elephant wallowing in the Mara River.

We managed to locate a new cylinder head for my Land Rover which had been overheating at Cooper Motors in Nairobi who very kindly gave it to us in sponsorship thereby saving us about £1,200. Money was still very tight and it was a constant concern whether we would be able to afford to mount the last phase of the expedition.

CSM Bennett had taken Debbie shopping in Nairobi on the last day before she flew back to England. Whilst they were walking down the street two African youths ran up and ripped the gold chain from around her neck. CSM Bennett, who had been window shopping, heard Debbie scream, looked up, saw her holding her neck, saw the two Africans and dived on the nearest. The youth pulled a knife but had more than met his match and was swiftly disarmed and knocked down. By the time the police arrived he was trussed securely. As Debbie was leaving that day the police took all three straight to the courtroom and using CSM Bennett and Debbie as witnesses the youth was tried, convicted and sentenced to three years hard labour. Justice can be swift in Africa.

Meanwhile word had reached Nairobi that the Migration had just arrived at the Sand River and was expected to cross into the Mara any day. With all of the vehicles back on the road again, we hastily reorganised our plans and raced down to catch the spectacle. Fortuitously I had also learnt that Martin Thompson and Simon Rhodes of Abercrombie and Kent were staying at Kitchwa Tembo, on the far side of the Mara, so I arranged to visit them. Both had been instrumental in helping us. Martin, as Managing Director of Abercrombie and Kent in England had granted their original sponsorship and Simon, as one of their representatives in Zimbabwe had done a lot of work helping plan our forthcoming journey on the River Zambesi.

At Roan Hill we met the vanguard of the Migration — large herds of zebra. To the south, the other side of the Sand River, we could see enormous herds of wildebeest, thousands upon thousands, spread across the plain, edging forward like a living tide. As yet few had crossed the river. When we arrived at Kitchwa Tembo I had a very useful meeting with Simon, tying up our arrangements in Zimbabwe and then we all had a most enjoyable dinner together.

Next day, on our way back across the Mara we saw a huge concentration of wildebeest gathering on the southern bank of the Sand River. Still, few had crossed. We based ourselves near the Sand River bridge. From there we made frequent trips to observe the wildebeests' progress. By the third day they were streaming across the Sand River. Enormous lines, each one thousands of animals long, stretched back from the southern bank. This was only the tip of the iceberg. Once across they still had to cross the much more serious obstacle of the Mara River. Steep-sided, fast flowing and full of crocodiles the Mara River claims many victims. All around prides of lions began converging for the rich pickings.

Unfortunately time was pressing on and with two mountains still to come we had to continue on our way. Once across the Sand River we made our way to the small border post. There we encountered our first example of blatant non-cooperation and deliberate, rude obstruction. This we were to learn was symptomatic of Tanzanian officialdom. Having argued our way through and paid the extortionate park entry fees we set off across the Serengeti. Much larger than the Masai Mara, the Serengeti's terrain changes regularly and dramatically. It began with lush green grass covering rolling hills with a large escarpment to our east. We then passed some impressive rock kopjes before crossing a hot, dry plain of yellowed grass and acacia scrub. Beyond, expansive woodland led to a final billiard table-flat plain. There was no shortage of plains game but we had left the great concentrations of zebra and wildebeest to our west. We stopped briefly at the single 'showpiece' government-run lodge, Seronera. Imaginatively sited high on a central rock kopje, commanding sweeping panoramas, it should have been a magnificent place. Instead it felt worn out and in places looked as if the original plans had never been completed. Bare concrete stood out starkly against the natural rock and mainly wooden construction. Windows were cracked and the furnishings dirty and worn. A sign announced that there was no water in the lodge that day. When asked about the Serengeti the staff proved sullen and uncommunicative.

Driving towards Ngorongoro, next day, we climbed up from the plains into lush pasture lands. We passed several Masai Kraals with the warriors tending their herds. A group of young boys dressed in simple black robes with their faces painted into white masks were undergoing their tuition period prior to their circumcision and recognition of manhood. Finally we reached the highest point of the road and there, before us, lay the Ngorongoro Crater. Despite the haze we could make out the full circle of the crater walls twelve miles away at the furthest point with Lake Magadi 2,000 feet below on the crater floor.

After a night camped on the rim we drove down a steep track that led us to the crater floor. A heavy layer of mist reduced the visibility giving an air of mystery. A copse of tall, yellow-barked Fever Trees gave way to a plain of deep grass surrounding the lake. Four single, thickly tapering horns revealed the presence of four black rhinoceroses lying concealed in the grass. Elsewhere zebra, Coke's hartebeest, Thompson's gazelle, buffalo and elephant all competed for space. As the mist lifted we had fantastic views across the crater. In the foreground flamingos, plover and avocets lined the soda-streaked shore of the lake whilst in the distance cloud was pouring, like dry ice, over the crater rim. We came across several prides of lion, one of over twenty. They were lying beside a small pond, streaked with blood and with distended stomachs from a recent kill. In the rich afternoon light it was a fabulous scene: the tawny yellow gold of the lions' coats contrasting against the red soil, deep blue water and lush green grass with the imposing crater wall as a backdrop. It was amazing to reflect that just seventy years before the farmsteads of two German settlers lay on this crater floor.

On our way out, at a viewpoint on the crater rim, we passed a memorial to all those who had died in the service of wildlife: Dr Grizmyek, who had first studied the Migration before being killed in an aeroplane crash on the Serengeti, and many others shot by poachers.

We drove through undulating country, neatly cultivated with wheat, maize and coffee plantations before cresting a high escarpment. Below lay Lake Manyara. Manyara was somehow special to me having read at school — and several times since — Iain and Oria Douglas-Hamilton's account of their life and studies *Amongst the Elephants*. Even at this distance it was exciting to be able to make out, with binoculars, herds of elephant in the forest. Sadly there are now only 180 of the original 500 elephants at Manyara. I longed to go down and explore but the demands of time and money dictated that our eyes turned eastward where, beyond Arusha, Kilimanjaro lay waiting.

Kilimanjaro, at 19,340 feet, is the highest mountain on the African continent. Seen from the sweeping plains of Kenya its massive dome-shaped summit appears sugar coated and friendly. From the south its visage is rather less amiable. Dense tropical rain forest, coating the lower slopes and ridges, gives way to heather, scrub and then alpine moorland. Above that the steep, heavily glaciated south-west face of Kibo guards the access to the domed summit. We intended to approach using the ill-frequented Umbwe Route and then split at around 13,000 feet into a climbing and a walking group. The former hoped to climb the Heim Glacier, a Grade 3 ice extravaganza, whilst the latter made their way up to the one flaw in the southern defences, The Western Breach and ascend via the crater floor from there.

Any ascent of Kilimanjaro, by whatever route, is expensive. The standard daily rates for Tanzanian game parks apply with extra charges for mountain rescue and mandatory guides. The system is heavily weighted to steer climbers towards flogging up the Normal Route, a vastly over-used and somewhat characterless ascent of the mountain with no technical climbing interest. Avoiding this incurs severe financial penalties through the doubling of guides' and porters' fees and almost trebling camping fees. In an effort to limit the rapidly spiralling cost of our climb we went to Moshi to recruit our guide privately. This wasn't without risk as guides obtained without going through a local company, who in turn imposed their own level of fees, had a nasty habit of doing a runner with all the money entrusted to them for porters' fees.

After a number of meetings with a succession of rather shady characters we were introduced to one Thomas Alois Meela. He produced a guide's ID card and a letter from an American referring to past expeditions and instructing him to arrange a private climbing party for the client. Thomas assured us that he was an experienced guide, had climbed the mountain many times in the past and would do everything that he could to help us. After a hasty conflab with Richard, I decided to take a chance and so we engaged him.

The next day was spent sorting out kit, sharpening crampons, issuing rations and packing rucksacks. I hate the administration period before a climb and always feel very ill at ease until I get onto the mountain and get going. In this instance my disquiet was significantly exacerbated by the notable absence of Thomas who, by mid afternoon, I was convinced had done a bunk with the porters' wages. Fortunately my fears were unfounded and at 5pm he appeared, rather nattily dressed to tell me that all was set for the next day.

The next day the porters engaged by Thomas arrived on time so we loaded everyone onto both Land Rovers and one Bedford and set off to the roadhead. We stopped once again at Moshi to buy food for the porters and then continued up an ever narrowing series of mud tracks through several miles of banana plantation. All was going well until we came across a rather rickety bridge. The Land Rovers had no problem but as the Bedford mounted it, the combined weight of lorry together with its load of chattering porters was too much and to the sound of splintering wood the cross planks shattered leaving the truck bellied on the main support logs with the wheels spinning in free space. We were lucky that the lorry hadn't turned over and fallen into the stream below, the consequences of which didn't bear thinking about. However it was now to cause us a serious delay. By the time that a major recovery operation had been mounted, the Bedford returned to the safety of firm ground through the application of a mechanical Tirfor winch and the bridge rebuilt I was faced by a deputation from the porters.

Led by a shame-faced Thomas, they insisted that it was now too late to start up the mountain. I felt that they were just being idle and trying to get an extra day's pay but no amount of cajoling or offers of cash inducements would move them. It all boiled down to the fact that they weren't prepared to walk in the dark. I suggested that we should walk until it got dark and then stop and camp but they solidly refused. I was furious with them for being so wet and particularly with Thomas for failing to make any attempt to stand up to them. He met all of my questions and accusations with dumb silence. As we had already paid them they had us over a barrel and we had no choice but to camp where we were and start out next day. The worst of it was that we would have to pay for another day's fees which we could ill afford. I sat fuming through sheer frustration.

In the evening the cloud cleared and we got our first clear views of Kibo 13,000 feet above us. The rich evening light made it look warm and distant but we could make out a number of steep sections on the Heim Glacier and we had heard that it was very cold higher up.

In the morning we started up a disused vehicle track that led us deep into a dense, humid forest. The top soil was greasy and although the angle was fairly gentle, traction was difficult and we slipped often. After several miles we branched off onto a narrow twisting path. Dense undergrowth encroached on the track from all directions. Thomas said that we were the first group to come up this way that year. After some time the track steepened noticeably as we began to follow a narrow ridge line. Tall trees towered above us, draped in moss and lichens. Beneath, shrubs competed with lush green ferns. Coral pink orchids provided occasional splashes of colour together with smaller horn-shaped orange flowers trimmed with yellow. It was a refreshing atmosphere which somehow combined the impression of spring mingled with autumn through the vibrant bright flowers and the dead leaves underfoot. It was an interesting if awkward route. The act of clambering up the steeper sections using roots for handholds, or crawling under fallen trees broke your pace. I felt unfit after a month of travelling in the vehicles.

The first section ended at a series of insubstantial rock overhangs to the side of a small, natural bowl in the ground. On the map it was rather extravagantly billed as 'Forest Caves'. We arrived at 3pm, a full two and a half hours before the last of the porters. In the main they were a most unimpressive crew. Several of them hadn't been on this route before and I was strongly beginning to suspect that several of them weren't regular porters but members of Thomas's family.

It was a mild morning, as we packed up and set off on the next stage towards the Barranco Hut. As we climbed out of the bowl and into the sunlight the temperature quickly rose. Within another hour it was baking hot. Several of the team felt weak. We were still only at around 10,000 feet

Bdr Lawes abseiling back down from Mackinders Gendarme as Sgt Ward waits above.

Top: Rendille tribesmen with their camel caravan, Northern Kenya.

Bottom: Mt Kilimanjaro, 19,320 ft.

Sgt Thubron and Sgt Nundy surveying the route from the base of the Heim Glacier, Mt Kilimanjaro.

Top: Camp on the shores of Lake Malawi.

Bottom: Gdsm Humphries practising eskimo rolls.

One of the rafts in the Boiling Pot at the base of the Victoria Falls.

Top: Dropping into a rapid is a lonely and daunting experience.

Bottom: Once committed it was a question of powering forward and fighting one's way through.

Top: Kayaks were engulfed by massive stoppers; Cpl Topps in Rapid Eighteen.

Bottom: Rafters in action.

Top: Not every rapid was negotiated successfully; Gdsm Hutchinson finds himself alone in the raft.

Bottom: Mike Fawcett, Rob Shattock, Richard Gaffney and Cpl Hall inspect the gaping hole left by the second hippo attack

and thus not really high enough to be affected by altitude so I put it down to dehydration and lack of fitness. We left the trees and shrubs behind and entered a large area of head-high tree heather. The sun shone through the beards of lichen casting a rich, yellow glow over everything.

Higher again, we came to alpine meadows with the same dried helichrysum flowers that we had seen in the Ruwenzori. I could feel myself dehydrating so I stopped frequently in the shade and drank as much as possible. Just after midday we crested a ridge and there below us was the Barranco Hut. It was no more than a circular tin shack. Outside were several flattened tent sites which we occupied leaving the hut to the porters. Again they trailed in far behind us.

For the rest of the afternoon we studied the climbing route ahead. From our current vantage point the bottom section of the Heim Glacier looked difficult up to the bivouac on top of Window Buttress. From there the last day to the summit appeared to be a long, gradual pull up the glacier. That evening, together with CSM Bennett, I got hold of Thomas and his two assistant guides to discuss our plans. The climbing and walking parties were to separate at this point, the climbers heading for the Heim Glacier whilst the walkers carried on towards the Western Breach. Most of the porters were to turn back here but I wanted to negotiate for a couple more to carry some of the technical kit and food higher up the mountain.

As soon as I ran over the plan that we had agreed at Marangu Thomas began shaking his head. He said that we should do the climb in two days not three from here and then the walkers and himself would only have to spend one night in the derelict Arrow Glacier Hut. I refused saying that I wasn't prepared to rush the climbers for fear of an accident and that we would stick to the plan. He played dumb and sat shaking his head. When I tried to negotiate for the extra porters he became very agitated and then suddenly announced that he wanted an extra day's pay for every porter. I countered by pointing out that he had produced four less porters than I had paid for and so he was sitting on their wages. In addition this new demand was out of the blue and I didn't agree to it. At this point he exploded, shouting at me that I had insulted him and that when we got down he was going to call the army and I would be led away in chains. I remained seated and determined not to lose my temper. However, no matter how much CSM Bennett and I tried to calm the situation he refused to speak to us. Using one of the assistant guides who spoke good English as an intermediary, the negotiations carried on for three hours around the campfire. By the end the atmosphere had relaxed and we got everything sorted out but my opinion of Tanzanians had reached a new low.

In the morning I discussed a contingency plan with Matthew, who was leading the walking group, in case either of us had a problem. I then set off in pursuit of the climbers. We had to drop down from the hut to the valley floor and then scramble up the steep but straightforward far wall. With the sun fully up it was hot on the dry rock face but we all felt stronger than on the day before. We had a fantastic view back across the valley to a waterfall several hundred feet high that had previously been hidden to us. Above the rock band long, fine scree slopes led us to our intended bivouac site at the base of the glacier.

I began setting up my tent with Gdsm Bell when Richard Stanford came to me to say that I had better go with him quickly. CSM Bennett had been sick several times and was now vomiting blood. I went over straight away. He was very white and was throwing up thick, dark red blood. There was no question — we had to get him down quickly. I called everyone together. Richard and Mike Baker volunteered to escort him down as they were to be his rope partners. I was extremely impressed by the speed and total lack of complaint with which they did this as I knew that both of them would be very disappointed not to make the summit. Sgt Nundy and Gdsm Bell started leading him down immediately whilst I briefed Richard on the plan. He was to drop down to the circuit route 1,000 feet below us and make his way eastward to the Karanga Valley another 1,000 feet lower. They should rest the night there and assess CSM Bennett's condition in the morning. If he had greatly improved they could go up to the Barafu Hut and then, if after another night there, he was fit, they could try for the summit. If he was not fit then they were to take no chances and all go down together via the Normal Route. He left with a wry smile. I watched until they were out of sight.

Once they were gone I turned my attention to the route in front of us. At this close range I was in a much better position to judge the difficulties. The bottom section looked fairly straightforward although there was almost no snow cover and the ice was rock hard. However, above that, large sections of ice had fallen away leaving a very awkward almost overhanging pitch. It was certainly now well above the guidebook grading. I was concerned about our ability to cope with this standard of climbing with such heavy rucksacks. The weight was unavoidable. With several days still to go on the mountain we were carrying food, climbing hardware, ropes, warm clothing, sleeping bags and bivouac gear; a total of about seventy pounds each. Teetering around on front points with that lot on wasn't going to be easy. I chatted to the other five. Bdr Lawes had a severe headache. In view of that and the fact that I didn't want to end up with small groups of the expedition members spread across the mountain I revised the plan. Depending on the condition of the group in the morning we would give this lower technical section our best shot with a cut-off time of 1pm. If we succeeded in breaching it then we would make a decision whether to bivouac at the top of Window Buttress or to carry on and try to bivouac further up the route. The technical section aside I was still concerned with the length of the route remaining to the summit on the second day with the weight of our sacks. If on the other hand we experienced major difficulties then we would descend and follow the others around to the Barafu Route.

As the sun receded, in a spectacular sunset, the temperature quickly dropped. Unacclimatised as we were, I spent one of the coldest nights that I have ever experienced. Despite getting into duvet jacket, sleeping bag, bivvi bag and tent outer I lay awake shivering, longing for morning to come. When it did come it was a long time before the sun crept over the summit to warm our tiny camp. We packed up and moved to the bottom of the ice. The first threesome roped up and started on the bottom pitch. The extreme hardness of the ice made gaining purchase with their crampons difficult and the destabilising effect of such heavy rucksacks quickly made itself apparent. They made their way very slowly upwards. Before long they came to an awkward ice barrier from where they could see the full implications of the harder section ahead. Already a couple of people were having problems. Time seemed to evaporate. We were rapidly approaching our cut-off time having made minimal progress and with the major difficulties still to come. Tempted though I was to throw everything we had at the route to fail would mean that we would have exhausted our supplies and wouldn't be able to reach the summit. In view of that I decided that the summit was our main objective and thus I called Bdr Lawes down from the ice and we set off in pursuit of Richard Stanford's party.

It was roughly five miles to the Barafu Hut. Although the line on our map contoured steadily around the mountain in reality the path dropped into and climbed back out of an endless succession of steep-sided valleys emanating from the main massif. We had to set a stiff pace. My back was protesting painfully at the weight of my pack. We reached the intersection with the Mweka and Barafu route as darkness fell. Turning uphill a final 1,000 feet of ascent lay between us and the hut. Ridge followed ridge offering false hope of the hut before us. We spread out, each pushing on at his own best pace. By the time that I reached the hut I was bumping into boulders in the dark and practically staggering.

Richard Stanford, Mike Baker and CSM Bennett had arrived only shortly before us having taken all day to cover the same route. The latter was feeling better and hoped to go for the summit in the morning although some of the others were now questioning their own intentions. We turned in with little delay.

When it came to it, everyone decided to go for the top. We had just under 5,000 feet to climb. We had a quick brew with the last of our water and then set out. After an hour we reached the first patch of snow where we stopped to brew up and fill our flasks. Several people had felt weak from the previous day's exertions but after a break and several brews most felt a lot better. As the morning wore on we spread out up the screes, rock slabs and ice. I stayed near the front of the group. I always found being at the back totally depressing. Behind me several people were having problems. Bdr Lawes again had bad headaches which were getting worse and CSM Bennett and Mike Baker were moving very slowly in the rear. There was no technical element to this route. From now on it was just a question of individual motivation and willpower.

Richard Stanford and I began to draw ahead of the remainder. By the time that we reached the crater we could only see Sgt Nundy a couple of hundred yards behind us. The last 1,000 feet of ascent along the crater rim took us over an hour including a most frustrating false summit. It became a case of walking ten yards, stopping, resting and steeling ourselves to walk again. As we approached the summit I felt very choked with emotion. We were already higher than either of us had been before. This was it — the Roof of Africa. After all the years of planning and dreaming we had finally made it. It may not have been Everest or K2 but it was every bit as special to me and at that moment I felt a tremendous sense of achievement. I thought back to my time lying in the Spinal Injuries' Unit and that original glimmer of hope. How very far away that all seemed now.

I looked out across the crater. The panorama was stunning. From Uhuru Peak the crater rim stretched away to left and right. Eastward it continued past the point where we had joined it to Gilman's Point, where those climbing the Normal Route gained the rim. Beyond was Leopard Point, site of a leopard's carcass frozen into the ice. To our east the rim continued for a couple of hundred yards and then dropped away into the Western Breach. Below us on the crater floor we could see the walking group's tents — two tiny orange specks on the great white plain around them. Behind those were the stepped tiers of the northern ice cliffs and further east the Reusch Crater and Inner Ash Pit. In the far distance we could make out Mt Meru poking its head above the surrounding plains.

Whilst we were taking all of this in the remainder of the group were slowly making their way along the crater rim to join us. Sgt Thubron and Sgt Ward were next, then Bdr Lawes followed by Sgt Nundy and Gdsm Bell. As we were waiting for the last two, who still hadn't come into view, Matthew's cheerful face appeared from the other direction. Behind him trailed the walking group. They too were shattered. They had started at

5.30am up the steep screes above the Arrow Glacier Hut through the Western Breach and into the crater. They had set up their tents and rested there before Matthew had got them going again. DSgt Coull and Carolyn Ellis looked particularly exhausted. It was great to get both teams to the summit together.

Just as we were about to go down — the climbers back to the Barafu Hut and the walkers to their tents — CSM Bennett and Mike Baker appeared in view on the crater rim. They were moving terribly slowly and with time ticking away I was keen to get everyone down the mountain, but after all their effort and having come so far I didn't have the heart to leave before they made it. CSM Bennett had done particularly well in the face of his earlier altitude problems. There was a rousing cheer as they came up the last slope.

It was now 4.25pm, over two hours since Richard and I had reached the summit. Our descent to the Barafu Hut was likely to take at least three hours. I brought up the rear. I was concerned about CSM Bennett and Mike Baker both of whom were staggering through exhaustion. With a vertical drop of 1,500 feet down to the crater floor on one side this was no time for a slip. I felt tired myself and had to concentrate on placing my crampons. The descent was slow and painful. We reached the hut, carrying supplies of snow to melt for brews, well after dark.

Next day we evacuated the mountain. From the Barafu Hut we had to drop down to the circuit path and traverse eastward around the mountain to join the Normal Route before continuing right down to the Park Gate. The ten miles and 8,000 feet of descent took us nine hours at a forced pace. It was a weary, footsore group that arrived at the bottom. The walking group had an even harder route. They had spent a bitterly cold and uncomfortable night camped at 18,000 feet in the crater. Two of them, Matthew Roberts and Carolyn Ellis had suffered from a somewhat unnerving disrupted breathing pattern known as Cheyne Stokes Breathing which had frightened them quite badly. They had tried various methods to overcome it from altering their lying positions to breathing exercises and massage. As a result no one had had much sleep. In the morning they had packed up their tents and then trudged across the heavily rime-iced crater floor to the far side where they had climbed up the rim to reach Gilman's Point and the start of the Normal Route. To reach this stage had taken them four hours. From this point they had to descend 12,000 feet covering a similar distance to the climbers. I had expected them to stop at one of the huts on the route down for the night and then continue down in the morning. However just in case they did decide to press on I had sent a Land Rover and driver to wait for them at the Park Gate. At around 7pm a totally dishevelled and exhausted group arrived back at the campsite. They had kept going all day with few breaks. Carolyn's feet had been so sore that she hadn't wanted to stop and so forged ahead. With a woman in front none of the men, no matter how tired, would stop and so they had kept on going cursing her as they went. They now looked utterly dead beat. Several of them had terribly sore feet which were deeply blistered by the unfamiliar mountaineering boots. Gdsm James was in the worst condition. His feet were completely disfigured and had grotesque blood-filled blisters. We sat around comparing our experiences over a few beers before retiring for a well earned rest.

I woke up still exhausted after a solid ten hours sleep. Judging by the look of the others as they hobbled around sorting out the kit and loading it into the trucks they felt the same. After a final tea and egg banjo frenzy we boarded the vehicles. For the next three days we drove south. Initially we passed through maize fields, banana plantations and enormous sisal plantations. Further on we entered rough bush land dominated by baobab trees. The countryside became more dramatic as we crossed the Great Ruaha River.

We stopped at Tukuyu, the last town of any size before the border, to do some shopping. The market contained little and a singularly unimpressive collection of rundown shops and tracks surrounded the dirty streets. We had parked beside the local football pitch. Just as we were about to leave, the town's team appeared and began to practise. A few of our guys stopped to watch and before I knew what was happening a gleeful shout went up 'Come on boss, we've got a game'. With that thirteen of us took to the pitch. The excitement of doing something different was obvious.

The match was hysterical. The Africans were skilful and fast, passing the ball between them with deft, accurate passes. We, on the other hand, had almost no one with any form of footballing skills but met them with sheer enthusiasm and dogged persistence. The pitch was extremely slippery, bumpy and covered with a liberal smattering of cow shit. At times our play was like slapstick, with people falling flat on their faces just as the ball came to them. Not altogether surprisingly the sight of thirteen Britons performing like circus clowns in the middle of the town attracted a fair amount of interest and before long the touchline was packed with a crowd of several hundred people. They were fantastic, rooting for us and hurling light-hearted abuse at their own team.

To everyone's amazement we scored first with Sgt Thubron and Cpl Williams charging up the pitch trekking boots flying. The crowd went mad and invaded the pitch chanting 'Roof of Africa'. The Tukuyu team just looked bemused at how, despite all their efforts and far superior skills, they were getting beaten by these clearly mad foreigners. By half-time the score was 1-1 and we were knackered.

We went off to change into shorts, all of us being in the clean clothes we had put on for the border crossing. The second half was even wilder. High kicks, falling bodies and more laughter from all. The referee was permanently doubled up and gave a number of dodgy decisions in our favour. By the final whistle justice was done and Tukuyu won 3-1.

We stopped just out of town to wash and change before driving the remaining hour to the border at Songwe Bridge. The Tanzanian formalities were as painful and protracted as we might have expected. They began with a check of all our medical documents, an act whose relevance escaped me as we were in the process of leaving the country, with the official holding most of the forms upside down to read them. The usual succession of currency declarations, immigration, customs and police all followed with much searching and cross-questioning until two and a half hours later we were allowed through.

As we drove across the bridge and onto Malawian soil the sun was shining for the first time in days. I took it as a good omen. At the check-point on the far side we were greeted by a friendly policeman who was smartly dressed, welcoming and polite. He wanted to check that the girls were wearing skirts not trousers or shorts which were forbidden to them in public in Malawi. The rest of the formalities were conducted swiftly and with the minimum of fuss and we soon found ourselves on our way. The first major town that we came to, Karonga, was bright, gaily painted and well laid out. We camped on a beautiful beach on the north-west shore of Lake Malawi. Dugout canoes lay on the beach beside us and in the background waves crashed onto the shore. We were surrounded by a group of children who all competed to help us set up. Every time we tried to set up a camp bed or hammer in tent pegs little pairs of hands would appear to assist. They were wonderfully friendly people and I had a great sense of well-being.

Lake Malawi forms the eastern border of most of the country. For the next few days we drove south alongside it stopping to camp in a variety of interesting or beautiful places. We drove towards the lakeside town of Nkhata Bay. As we dropped into the town the lake glittered bright blue beneath us with a smattering of brightly coloured fishing boats bobbing at anchor. Dugout canoes poled between them. It was a very tranquil scene. We drove through the small town and over the hill behind to camp on a small beach of white, grainy sand. Surf three to four feet high was pounding the beach. Beyond, the lake stretched away to the horizon. It was great to swim in the fresh water.

We continued south through Nkotakota, Cape Mclear and Zomba to the ex-capital Blantyre. Steep hillsides with sheer rock faces flanked our route through otherwise open bush. In Blantyre the Managing Director of ICI Malawi, Tony Hicks, took us under his wing. He was busy but his attitude was exactly what we needed: 'Help yourselves to the phone, use the fax and yell if there is anything else you need. If not I will meet you for a drink at the Sports Club later'. The rest of the day was spent making contact with the UK, reprovisioning from the market and well stocked shops. Wherever I went I was struck by the friendliness of the Malawian people. Not for nothing is Malawi known as the 'Warm Heart of Africa'.

After a morning of administration and recovering from the after-effects of a heavy night of whisky drinking with DSgt Coull we continued south-west. For thirty-seven miles we passed through lush tea plantations. The orderly, flat-topped tea bushes flashed golden green in the afternoon sun. Teams of pickers moved amongst the bushes with large wicker baskets on their backs.

The Mulanje Sports Club is set on an island of perfectly mown grass amidst the tea plantations at the foot of Mt Mulanje our seventh and final mountain objective. Above, the Lichenya Plateau sits on top of great open rock faces and impossibly steep slopes. Crowning that is the 10,000 foot Sapitwa summit. The club provides a focal point for the small expatriate community of tea and coffee growers. They had kindly given us permission to use their facilities whilst we climbed the mountain.

I packed my kit in a dream, feeling absolutely awful having been sick several times during the night. Some of the team had opted to go rock climbing or try their hand at parapenting so leaving them I set out with the walkers to the Likhabula Forestry Office to book huts and organise porters. What a change it was from the other mountains. There was no Park entry fee, minimal hut fees and helpful staff. The porters were friendly, totally unconcerned by the weight of their loads and their salaries were a pittance. The whole thing was organised and ready to go in just a few minutes. By the time that it came to set off however I felt ghastly. I agonised over whether to go up but I felt so rough that, as I wouldn't have let any other member of the team go up in a similar condition, I took myself off the team. Once I had seen them set off I went to crash out on my camp bed.

By the next day I felt much better and was thoroughly regretting not being on the mountain so I went back to the Forestry Office, arranged a porter and set off in pursuit of the others. We took the Chapaluka path, a pretty route which rose up through cool woods to the Lichenya plateau rim at 5,600 feet. We crossed several streams that poured down into crystal clear pools on their descent to the Likhabula River. We stopped for a rest beside one of these pools. As we shared some chocolate,

Connex, my porter, told me that he was on holiday from boarding school. He hoped to go to college and study to be a primary school teacher.

We started making our way across the plateau initially along the side of a large pine forest and then broke out into rough moorland. Alongside the path there was a great variety of wild flowers: some large, some small, some lush, others desiccated. There were delicate blues, beds of yellows, clusters of orange, pink orchids, several varieties of helichrysum and tiny white stars. I saw no animals but honey bees buzzed around the more exotic flowers and an engaging little vermilion and green sunbird hovered to insert his finely curved beak into the trumpets of the larger blooms. In contrast great white-collared rowans swooped above us, cawing loudly. Austere grey peaks rose up from the plateau in all directions. We stopped for the night at a small, tin shelter.

In the morning I got up stiff from sleeping on the uneven floor of the shelter. After a quick brew we set off, turning away from the main path. We crossed a wide stream and then made our way for a couple of hundred yards through thick bush and boulders. This brought us to the base of a series of slabs receding some 1,800 feet above us. The angle steepened considerably as we scrambled upwards. The slabs supported the odd straggly tree and tuft of grass. It was hot going under a strong sun.

Once above the slabs the route took on totally new dimensions. It twisted and turned frequently doubling back on itself. We clambered over boulders, squeezed around boulders and even crawled under boulders. The path seemed to have a life of its own, leaping from boulder to tussock, through narrow channels in between rocks and dense bush and up several small slabs. Many of the giant, granite boulders were the size of huts. It was impossible to get any sort of rhythm as we ducked and weaved, scrambled and crawled. Even as the summit cross appeared before us we jinked away to approach it from behind. By 10.15am I was sitting on the summit, looking at views disappearing rapidly behind banks of incoming cloud.

My pleasure at having reached the summit of this, our last mountain, was tinged with regret that we hadn't managed to make it on Mt Kenya and complete all seven. However, of more immediate concern was to get back down to the plateau before the cloud came in and without breaking a leg or my neck. Connex jumped nimbly from rock to rock whilst I blundered along behind.

Once down on the plateau we stopped briefly for a drink and had a flapjack and then set off to Thuchila, four miles away across the plateau. We were going across the grain of the country and so had to cross many wooded ravines. Clear streams filled with enormous tadpoles ran through each. The scent of wild flowers hung heavy in the still air. The Thuchila

Hut, set in a clump of cedars, looked out from the far edge of the plateau. That night I settled down to write my diary beside a roaring cedarwood fire.

I heard Connex get up as soon as it was light. I lay in my sleeping bag for a while enjoying the solitude. I had missed the other group who had obviously opted for one of the other huts on the mountain so having packed up I started to make my way down. The path dropped precipitously to the valley 3,000 feet below. As we climbed down I could see waterfalls dropping off several edges of the plateau into the valley and the main river running from pool to pool. It looked most welcoming. At the roadhead Cpl Winch was waiting with a Land Rover to take me back to the camp.

He was full of news. Richard Gaffney had hurt himself parapenting, but not badly. Iraq had invaded Kuwait, Zimbabwe was in uproar, the situation in Zambia was still unsettled and according to a letter from Carolyn's mother Africa was never out of the British news.

Back at the camp Richard looked rather sorry for himself. After our parascending in the Sahara, he and CSM Bennett had been determined to try parapenting, self-launching themselves on a parachute from a hillside. After a successful flight on a small hill they had climbed some way up the side of Mt Mulanje. Richard had launched himself first but there hadn't been enough wind and his chute dumped him before it ever got going. He had dislocated his finger and turned his ankle over quite badly. CSM Bennett had put his finger back in place and he had then had to hobble down the mountainside on an inflamed ankle. Whilst I felt sorry for him I was relieved that nothing more serious had been incurred. At least they both seemed less hellbent on leaping off big mountains and were talking in terms of launching from sand dunes until they had got the hang of it.

The walking group arrived back having all enjoyed their trip and full of praise for their porters. With the last mountain behind us and the phase nearly over we were bound for our next changeover point in Zimbabwe. We drove back north through Blantyre and Lilongwe before entering Zambia. There was a certain amount of trepidation amongst the team as we crossed the border. Zambia had regularly featured on the BBC World Service News as the scene of recent widespread rioting. On the overlanders' net there was much talk of general lawlessness, trigger-happy soldiers, police brutality and travellers being beaten up, raped and killed. I intended to keep a low profile for the team, drive hard and get through the country as quickly as possible.

To my surprise we drove along an excellent tarmac road through rather bland bush. There was almost no agriculture of any form. The villages that we passed looked grey and dingy. Along the route people were noticeable by their scarcity. Somehow the countryside had a used, empty feel about it. At the police checkpoints we came to we were treated politely and waved on with no problem as soon as they had ascertained that we were foreigners. However I was still careful to make sure that we camped well into the bush and out of sight of the road.

On the second day we crossed the Luangwa River. The bridge was heavily guarded by vigilant, AK47-toting soldiers. We were told to drive across one vehicle at a time at no more than twelve miles an hour. If we went too fast we would be shot. This was said politely and even rather matter-of-factly but their intent was obvious.

It wasn't until we reached Lusaka, some 375 miles from the border that we saw any significant number of people. In contrast to its surroundings it is a large bustling city packed with people. We had a certain amount of business to conduct. There was mail to be collected, telephone calls to be made, sponsors to be visited and we had to check in with the British High Commission. At the latter we were advised strongly against camping in the bush or at the campsites in town. Instead they sent us off to stay with an expatriate agricultural adviser living on the edge of the city. I was rather annoyed as it meant driving back the way that we had come and as we had managed to look after ourselves for the last six months I felt that we were quite capable of continuing to do so. However it was later to prove a great blessing.

Paddy Duncan didn't seem at all surprised or put out by the arrival of twenty soldiers, two lorries and two Land Rovers to camp on his lawn. Instead he threw his home open to us. Over the course of the evening and most of a litre bottle of whisky he talked of his extensive travels throughout Africa. He had a seemingly inexhaustible supply of anecdotes with which he regaled us. He was always on the lookout for new adventures and enthused greatly about Zambia saying that there were still many parts of the country that were wild, uninhabited and never visited. His eyes lit up as he described swamps twice the size of Okovango and just as beautiful. I wished that we had more time to explore and left for bed, slightly the worse for wear with my head spinning with ideas for future expeditions.

I awoke with a pounding headache to find Paddy's two golden labradors pissing on my camp bed. We set off early taking the road for Zimbabwe.

Chapter Four
Wild Waters

Phase Four

Captain John Warburton-Lee, Welsh Guards, Expedition leader
Captain Richard Gaffney, Welsh Guards, Expedition Second in Command
Captain Matthew Roberts, Royal Army Medical Corps, Expedition doctor
Company Sergeant Major Alan Bennett, Welsh Guards, Expedition Senior Non Commissioned Officer
Miss Tetta Nicholls, Expedition secretary
Captain Sarah Pipe, Royal Army Educational Corps
Lieutenant Mike Fawcett, Royal Navy
Second Lieutenant Guy Bartle-Jones, Welsh Guards
Lance Sergeant George Ellis, Welsh Guards
Lance Sergeant Jock Williams 38, Welsh Guards
Lance Sergeant Darren Evans 15, Welsh Guards
Corpral Charlie Hall, Royal Army Medical Corps (V) Territorial Army
Lance Corporal Des Topps, Welsh Guards
Lance Corporal Stuart Mayor, Royal Electrical and Mechanical Engineers
Lance Corporal Shaun Galvin, Welsh Guards
Craftsman Dave Jones, Royal Electrical and Mechanical Engineers
Guardsman Jason Hutchinson, Welsh Guards
Guardsman Paul McIlvogue, Welsh Guards
Guardsman 'Frog' Humphries, Welsh Guards
Guardsman Woody Woodward, Welsh Guards
Guardsman Matthew Cobley, Welsh Guards
Paul 'Tosh' Burke, Weston Spirit

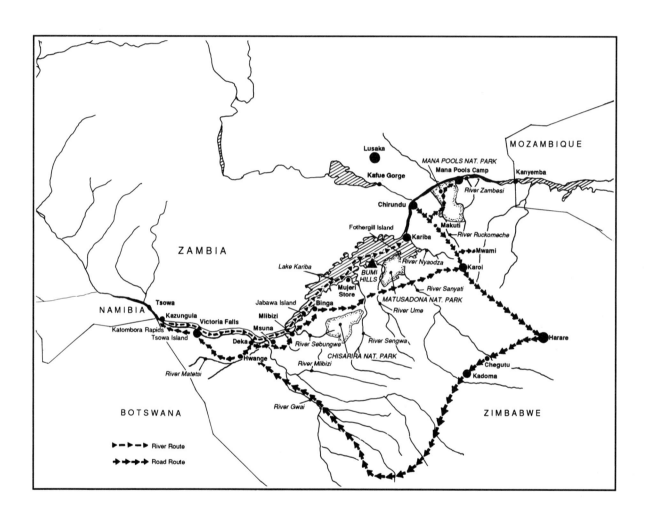

We arrived in Harare with a great deal to do. The vehicles needed a thorough servicing. All of the mountaineering equipment had to be packed up either to be stored in the deepest recesses of the vehicles or freighted back to England with the outgoing team. Tents, cookers, campbeds and all of the other camp paraphernalia had to be cleaned and repaired.

Leaving all of this in CSM Bennett's able hands Richard, Tetta and I set about tackling the usual paper war of reports, thank-you letters, news letters, approaches to sponsors and plans for the next phase of the expedition. To pave the way for the latter 2Lt Rupert Hackwill, a Welsh Guard and native Zimbabwean, had flown out to Zimbabwe ahead of us. Rupert, together with Simon Rhodes of Abercrombie and Kent, had the plans for our descent of the River Zambesi well mapped out. Guides had been booked, equipment hired and clearances to canoe through tribal trust lands secured.

The phase changeovers were always a period of frenzied activity with too much to be done in too little time. We were very lucky that Sir Nicholas Powell, an ex-National Service Welsh Guard who lived just outside Harare had invited us to camp on his land. Nicholas had a piratical air about him. His reputation was of a man who was a hard-working, determined coffee farmer with more than a streak of wildness. He is an avid racing fan and had been one of the leading racehorse owners in Zimbabwe with a keen eye for the fillies. During the Rhodesian War he had held out on his coffee estate which, located close to the Mozambique border, was one of the most dangerous areas in the country. He was inclined to refer to repelling the frequent terrorist attacks with the casualness of an Englishman describing a day's pheasant shooting. His son now farmed the coffee estate whilst Nicholas bred ostriches on his farm and talked of going into business shooting crocodiles in Mozambique.

One of the more memorable moments of our stay was being led by the gallant Sir Nicholas on an expedition to discipline one of his more irascible charges. He drove at high speed up alongside the ostrich, hooked its neck with a shepherd's crook and, whilst avoiding the potentially bone-breaking kicks from its powerful legs, cuffed it soundly about the head before letting it go, suitably chastened. Both Nicholas and his wife Dee overwhelmed us with their kindness and hospitality and we were constantly showered with gifts of vegetables, meat and beer for the whole team and a liberal supply of whisky for those deemed in particular need.

Our intended descent of the entire 450-mile length of the River Zambesi in Zimbabwe attracted a fair amount of interest. We gave press interviews and set up photo calls. Rupert announced with a particularly smug grin that he had arranged for me to be interviewed on Zimbabwe Television's 'Guest of the Week' programme, adding that it was all confirmed, I couldn't back out and he was planning to video it to send back to the regiment. Muttering darkly about Second Lieutenants who exceeded their brief, I was led to the studios at the appointed hour. Although trying hard not to show it I was extremely nervous at the prospect of a one-to-one, half-hour interview and kept running over in my mind my answers to the pre-arranged questions. As I sat under the arc lights I was pouring with sweat and shaking like a leaf. My concentration wasn't helped by my African interviewer who spoke in an extremely heavily accented, husky voice that concealed the fact that she kept straying from the script and wore an extravagantly ruched pink dress which served only to emphasise her enormous bosom and distract me further. Nor was I helped by being able to see Rupert, Richard and Tetta killing themselves with laughter behind the cameras.

Inevitably amongst all of this mayhem something had to go wrong. The Phase Four team had to change planes at Lusaka on their way out. The second aeroplane was considerably smaller than the first and couldn't carry the rafts and canoes that they had brought with them. Despite all of their efforts at persuading the Air Zambian crew to help they arrived empty-handed. Time was by now pressing so I set off towards Bulawayo and then Victoria Falls with the team to marry up with our guides, leaving Richard to sort out the muddle in his inimitable way.

The new team settled in quickly. I knew most of them quite well as they were either Welsh Guards or had taken part in our training camp in North Wales. In Wales the canoeists had conducted their own training. They had formed a good spirited, tightly knit group. They had been training on the white water course at Nottingham just prior to their departure and led by several strong characters they were determined to beat the Zambesi. My sister, Jenny, had also come out for a while. It was great to catch up on news from home and also to have someone totally unrelated to the expedition whom I knew well and could talk to.

The Victoria Falls are as impressive today as when David Livingstone discovered them in 1858. Known locally as 'Mosi-O-Tunya' or 'The Smoke that Thunders' the spray cloud and roar of water, as it plunges 400 feet into the gorge below, can be seen and heard from a considerable distance. The water falls across a 1,650-yard frontage with the centre of the river marking the border between Zambia and Zimbabwe. Due to the constant rain or spray the immediate environs had evolved as an isolated strip of lush rain forest in marked contrast to the surrounding dry thorn brush.

The magnitude and power of the falls is captivating and the onlooker cannot help but gaze in awe. As the force of the water surges, the dizzying drop to the base of the gorge is obliterated by a rising cloud of spray. It is possible to see several rainbows in succession spanning the gorge. For two to three nights at full moon there is an ethereal moonlit rainbow. To anyone who has seen them there is no doubt that the Victoria Falls are truly one of the seven natural wonders of the world.

I made my way down into the gorge just downstream of the main falls to see for myself one of the sets of rapids that we were to face once we reached this part of the river. It was hot work following the near-vertical path into the gorge and then scrambling over the many boulders in the bottom. From afar the rapids looked disappointingly tame but as I got nearer I could see that I had seriously misjudged the incredible volume of water. With little warning the river dropped down a main central chute into a world of foaming whiteness. It seemed to have a life of its own, growling, snarling and spitting. The central chute of water flipped viciously over to its right between two deep black holes, which threatened to hold a canoe for ages, before turning back into a monstrous haystack wave which, as far as I could see, would hurl your canoe straight up into the air. A raft, with its weight, might be able to power through but in that appalling turmoil a canoe would be tossed around like a leaf in a gale.

I sat mesmerised by the power of the water, not a little frightened by what I saw. Doubts began to creep into my mind as to whether we, as a relatively novice team, would ever be able to handle water conditions of this severity. Was I leading them into a challenge for which we were unprepared and with the likelihood of taking serious casualties? I was all too aware of my own limitations as a canoeist and was glad that there were other much more experienced paddlers amongst the group. Fortunately there was fifty miles of upper Zambesi from the Botswana border down to the Falls to be covered before we would reach this point. That held a number of lesser rapids on which we would practice our white water techniques and make the final selection of the canoeing team. If the worst came to the worst we would have to abandon the kayaks and shoot the high grade water in rafts alone but I hoped to avoid that.

Back at the campsite I met up with Paul Connolly, the Managing Director of Shearwater, who was providing guides for the Upper Zambesi and the white water section. Paul was a tough, fit-looking Zimbabwean who was a high class canoeist in his own right and had started the white water rafting operation on the Zambesi. He gave a detailed briefing to the whole group. He held everyone's rapt attention as he spoke of 60,000 crocodiles, aggressive hippos, campsites open to prowling lions and rapids that would chew up rafts and kayaks.

Afterwards the team was buzzing with anticipation, their reaction varied: Cpl Topps felt a lot more confident due to Paul's obvious competence and experience. LSgt Evans very honestly admitted to being afraid but said, interestingly, 'Anyway the whole point of being here is to be frightened'. It was an unusual moment of seriousness from him as he was more familiar in the guise of team joker and morale booster. He and I had joined the Welsh Guards around the same time and having served together often knew each other well. He was a highly amusing man who was inclined to use barefaced cheek or, when that failed, charm to get himself out of the many scrapes into which he had an unerring ability to fall. Cpl Topps I had known for an equally long time. His military career had been even more chequered. He had left the army for a while following a particularly bad spate of disciplinary offences. However he was back in, happily married and a proud father. He had never canoed before our training camp in North Wales but had quickly impressed all of the instructors with his determination and phenomenal strength. These two, although by no means the strongest of the paddlers, tended to be at the centre of whatever the group was doing and held considerable sway over the others. With them onside there was a very strong positive attitude in the team overlaid with a liberal measure of soldierly humour.

I rang Richard in Harare. At last the canoes and rafts had arrived thus saving him having to drive all the way to Lusaka to go and pick them up. However, they were now locked into Zimbabwean customs and he was having a battle to extricate them.

In amongst all of this planning a bolt struck from the blue. Cpl Galvin came running up to me to tell me that the Shearwater office had just been called from England. I was to ring the regiment immediately. Developments in the Middle East had been filling the news and I had been dreading this call. I rang the Adjutant and then waited whilst he took an urgent call from some senior officer. As soon as he came on the line I could hear from his voice that he was under pressure. The regiment had been stood by to go out to Bahrain in reaction to the Iraqi invasion of Kuwait. The Commanding Officer and Operations Officer were due to fly out to recce the situation the next day. Nothing was confirmed but the regiment was gearing itself up to go. It had been decided that we were to continue for the time being but were to be ready to fly home if required.

We discussed the practical implications of getting everyone back to England quickly and various options for dealing with the equipment and then arranged that we would be contactable through the Shearwater office. I put the telephone down with a heavy heart. This expedition had been my dream for so long and I desperately wanted to finish it. On the other hand as a Welsh Guardsman I couldn't bear the thought of the regiment going on active service and of my not being with them.

I went back to the campsite to tell the men what the situation was. Inevitably the news caused a tremendous stir. Every nuance was debated long and hard. By the end of the evening many of the theories had far exceeded the realms of possibility. I tried to impose a level of rationality and calm amidst some of the more alarmist rumours that sprang up around the campfire. Richard arrived late in the evening having talked the equipment out of customs and driven the whole way to Victoria Falls in one day. We were now ready to begin our river journey.

We made an early start in the morning with everyone up at 4.30am and on the road by 5.30am. The sun was rising as we drove forty-four miles to Kazangula, the point at which the Zambesi crossed the Botswanan border into Zimbabwe. We turned off the road just before the border and took a dirt track through the bush to the river's edge. At this point the Zambesi is wide and slow moving. A large herd of waterbuck were browsing on the near bank. A flock of vultures sat on watch up in the trees whilst a variety of jacanas, plover and storks paddled in the reeds. Further out in the river a school of hippos watched us.

For the first stretch of the river down to the Victoria Falls we were using the six new kayaks that we had flown out from England and a number of old fibreglass, two-man kleppers on loan from Shearwater. I started off in one of the kayaks. Having not paddled since the previous October I felt ill-at-ease and unbalanced. As soon as we got onto the water the school of hippos began creating and one or two moved towards us demonstrating and snorting aggressively. Paul Connolly, who was guiding us for the first day, moved us all close into the bank. Two male hippos were known to guard the deep middle channel. We skirted around one, hugging the bank, as he continued to move closer and threaten us. Paul stopped in a small pool and gathered us around his kayak to talk to us.

'Hippos pose the biggest threat to you on the river. Never get between them and deep water, which provides safety for them, or they are likely to attack you. You cannot rely on me to spot them all so each of you must keep a careful watch, warn everyone when you see hippos and stick close to the bank.' No sooner were the words out of his mouth when the water underneath him erupted and he was thrown bodily upwards by a large bull hippo. There was instant pandemonium. Canoes flew in every direction as people shot for the bank. Tosh, the young Weston Spirit member panicked, stood up in the rear of his klepper, dived into the water and struck out for the bank as if all the devils in hell were on his tail.

Paul, taken totally unawares, had been knocked over in his kayak and, feeling the hippo swirl beside him, and fearing another attack, bailed out.

He scrambled on top of his upturned boat and began using his arms to propel himself to the shore. I paddled up to him and, offering him the stern of my kayak, helped tow him to the side. He looked very shocked but got hold of himself, put on an amazingly cool expression and began directing people to safety. He emptied his boat over mine and then we crept slowly along the reeds past the hippo to join the others.

Two boats were still the far side of the hippo and Tosh was marooned on a clump of reeds. Paul took a klepper back on his own, coaxed the terrified Tosh into getting back into the klepper with him and ushered the whole group over to us. There was the usual nervous laughter that fills that rather awkward void after any dangerous incident. Several of the group looked fairly shaken by the experience. There were a lot of jokes at Tosh's expense, but highly excited as he was, the speed of his speech, vocabulary of undiluted slang and expletives, and the strength of his Geordie accent rendered his replies almost totally unintelligible.

It was a very cautious group of paddlers that edged their way on along the river. After six and a quarter miles we came to the Katombora rapids. The first chute led us into a series of standing waves which bounced us all around but claimed no victims. We were all beginning to feel rather cocky until Paul assured us that had only been grade 1 and below the falls grade 5 and 6 rapids were waiting. The Zimbabwean grading system was clearly more rugged than that which we were used to in England where the Thames at Putney would almost qualify as grade 1. With this sobering thought we found our way through a maze of narrow, shallow channels which passed through a myriad of small islands of rocks, trees and papyrus.

We stopped on a sand bar below the rapids to have lunch. Some children poled across to us in dugout canoes from the Zambian bank. The difference in equipment, they with their hollowed-out tree trunks and we with our brightly coloured plastic Pyrhana kayaks, made an amusing visual contrast.

A nine-mile slow moving stretch led towards the next set of rapids. I had swapped into a klepper with Guy Bartle-Jones. Any number of long ignored muscles began to complain at this unexpected exercise. The land on the Zimbabwean bank was part of a hunting concession so we saw little game but on the river there was a panoply of birdlife from jacanas, to reed cormorants, fish eagles, purple herons, darters, skimmers, sacred ibis and a variety of kingfishers. Much more insidious were the many crocodiles which lay basking in the shallows only to disappear sinisterly into the deep water on our approach.

We pulled into camp as the sun sank low over the river behind Tsowa Island. We had completed our first day on the Zambesi. The stories became ever more exaggerated as they were regaled time and again over supper around the campfire. Hoots of laughter penetrated the peace of the African night with each reenactment. For all the hilarity, we had definitely got the message that hippos were to be avoided, that the rapids were big and that 450 miles of the Zambesi was going to be hard earned.

For the next two days we concentrated on the serious business of practising our kayaking techniques. We stopped at each of the rapids whilst the kayakers worked in the white water. At each we shot the rapid first and then paddled back up to practise breaking in and out of the eddies; ferry gliding across the fastest water holding a position in the mainstream; surfing on waves and rolling back up if we capsized. With each successive rapid each individual's skills improved and confidence increased. In that volume of water, a slight lean the wrong way or hesitation with a support stroke and you had capsized before you knew what was happening. It was physically very demanding and required the utmost concentration. It was now that the skill of the more experienced paddlers began to show.

LSgt Ellis had been instructing canoeing for years and had taught most of the team from basics. He was a solid paddler and a good instructor, always watching for safety. On previous trips he had always been the group leader, choosing the line down river and avoiding capsizing whilst all the novices got regular dunkings. As a result a great cheer went up when he was bowled over in the Kandahar Rapids, let go of his paddle and had to swim with his boat. The others were highly delighted and tormented him mercilessly for being old and losing his touch.

Gdsm McIlvogue had instructed canoeing at an Outward Bound school in North Wales prior to joining the army. The best paddler in the group, he was quite at ease even in the largest of the water and made it look infuriatingly easy. Mature for his years and impeccably mannered he instructed with a quiet confidence that in turn inspired confidence in others regardless of their age, position or experience. Mike Fawcett was another very able and stylish paddler, always with an eye for the safety of others. He had been on Navy canoeing expeditions in the past and worked hard at helping everyone else. A quiet man, with a natural, easygoing manner he was well liked on the team by all ranks. His blonde hair had earned him the nickname 'Ice Man' from the men after the character in the film *Top Gun*.

Below these three came two recently qualified instructors. Cpl Galvin was solid, dependable and strong. Although at times surprisingly reticent he fancied himself as something of a ladies' man and carried a certain quiet assurance. Gdsm Humphries on the other hand was more brash. He was a natural canoeist and had an easy style which he tended to exaggerate for effect rolling his wrists at the end of strokes. There was no mistaking his canoeing ability but he set himself up for a fair amount of flak from the others.

From the remainder of the team there were eight others who wanted to try their luck on the high grade white water. Some, like myself, were instructors qualified to lead novices on lower grade water and lacked high grade experience, others were novices. Cpl Topps was learning fast and relied on his substantial strength to get him through. Gdsm Hutchinson was doing well on this section but wasn't that confident about the bigger water later on. LSgt Williams, LSgt Evans, Cpl Hall, Gdsm Woodward and Sarah Pipe were all working hard but getting up towards the upper end of their ability. LSgt Williams was naturally cautious but was going for it. LSgt Evans was happier shooting the rapids than playing in the water and tended to hide behind a mask of humour. Gdsm Woodward had been a total novice at the training camp in Wales and was trying his heart out and Sarah Pipe who had impressed everyone by her gutsy approach in Wales was now finding that she lacked the strength to deal with the high volume of water in the Zambesi.

There was no fixed order of merit. Individuals' relative performances varied from day to day. I came in somewhere around the halfway mark. Selecting the six kayakers to begin the white water wasn't going to be easy. I only hoped that we would be able to cope with the conditions. It was rapidly becoming clear that this was likely to take us closer to our limits than any other part of the expedition.

As we approached the Victoria Falls the river widened noticeably. A herd of elephants crossed a wide side channel up to their shoulders in water making a wonderful sight. A light aircraft spotted us and flew low over our heads along the river waggling its wings as it passed. We could see the passengers' faces pressed against the side windows.

As we paddled the last stretch we hugged the Zimbabwe bank. In front we could see the spray cloud from the falls highlighted by the sun. We passed a small crocodile lying fast asleep along a low branch and then hauled the kayaks and kleppers out of the water.

That night we held a briefing in the campsite for the white water to come. Paul Connolly was going to lead the kayakers for the first day. We had two raft guides, Lawrence and Heath, from Shearwater. Each gave a briefing. I then gave a short pep talk and announced the names of the first six kayakers. LSgt. Ellis, Gdsm McIlvogue, Mike Fawcett, Cpl Galvin and Gdsm Humphries were all obvious choices and I then selected Cpl Topps for his sheer determination and effort. I had decided not to put myself in a kayak to begin with as I wanted to be in a position to watch everyone and change over kayakers and rafters if necessary.

After the briefing most of the team went down to the Victoria Falls

Hotel for a last bit of civilisation and a measure of Dutch courage. Once we were in the gorge it would be bush camping for three weeks. I remained behind to sort out all of the camera gear and write up the film records.

We were up at 5.30am, had breakfast, packed our kit and then headed for the steel girder bridge which spanned the Zambesi gorge linking Zimbabwe with Zambia. To put our boats in right at the base of the falls we had to cross over into Zambia and access the gorge from that side. We looked a very motley crew as we traipsed through both sets of Customs and immigration clad in T-shirts, shorts, buoyancy aids and helmets, and carrying deflated rafts, kayaks, bundles of paddles, pumps and camera gear over our shoulders.

We lugged the boats down a steep uneven path, scrambled over an area of black boulders at the bottom and emerged on a rock platform fifteen feet above the water. There we inflated the rafts with foot pumps, attached the rigging lines and began getting kitted up. The kayakers sat quietly to one side staring at the first rapid, two hundred yards downstream. Even from that distance the roar of the water seemed to penetrate your mind. Some sat and brooded whilst others indulged in rather stilted humour but the air of nervous tension was pervasive.

We lowered the rafts into the water on ropes and then clambered down into them. Just around the corner, upstream, was the Boiling Pot, a bowl formed where the river turns through ninety degrees at the eastern end of the falls. We paddled hard upstream, fighting the current and hopping from eddy to eddy until we reached another lower rock shelf in the Boiling Pot.

In front of us we could see away up the gorge along the line of the falls, on our right a great curtain of water formed the right wall. All around towering cliffs rose vertically, dwarfing us. The constant roar of water drowned out any conversation. Spray surged soaking us. We sat and gazed, drunk on the scale and image of raw power that assailed our senses.

Finally Paul signalled that it was time to go. There was a feeling of going to face the inevitable. I repacked the cameras into their waterproof bottles, ensured that they were strapped in and took my place at the front of the first raft. The rafts were Avon Mark 10 self-bailers. We had seven people in each — three down each side and the raft guide in the centre at the back. Maintaining control of the raft required an instant response to the guide's shouted instructions with strong, well co-ordinated strokes from each of the paddlers. We sat on the outside tube, getting support from the action of our paddles on the water. There was a safety line tightly secured around the outside and across the bottom to assist in righting a raft that had flipped but we were not strapped in or attached to the raft.

The first rapid dropped and then turned sharply right as the river dog-legged. Above the rapid the water became smooth as velvet and there was a sudden calm. The awful sense of anticipation was broken as we lurched downwards dropping into a deep hole. The whole raft leant slowly downstream and then flicked up. I was nearly thrown out and only just managed to regain my balance and get back in. The raft bucked and kicked, twisted and rolled as we careered through the waves. It had been a far more dynamic ride than I had expected and this was one of the smaller rapids. The kayakers came down one at a time. Each disappeared totally from view in the first drop and then burst out through the white water at the base. All stayed upright.

The second, third and fourth rapids were in a straight line down the gorge and overlooked by the steel girder bridge. The second and third were straightforward wave trains but no less exciting for it. Perched precariously on the outside tube of the raft, with no footstraps and leaning out to get maximum purchase with the paddle you presented a perfect target for the great walls of water which broke over the raft, sending the unwary sprawling into the centre of the floor if they were lucky or flying overboard if they were not. CSM Bennett just caught Guy Bartle-Jones as he disappeared over the edge. A couple of kayakers flipped over but each time they rolled back up. Paul was beginning to look impressed.

Rapid Four was the first of the larger ones. There was a long run of huge standing waves each of which was like paddling into a solid barricade. Paul and Gdsm McIlvogue ran it first. Cpl Galvin went next and got knocked straight over. He tried to roll up several times but couldn't fight against the foaming water and came out of his boat. Cpl Topps followed and again didn't get past the second wave. He tried to roll once, twice, three times. He was now over 100 yards downstream and still being buffeted around. I couldn't believe that he had hung on under water for so long. He went back into the roll position and finally way downstream he rolled up to tremendous cheers from everyone else. Mike Fawcett, who was rapidly establishing his pedigree as a very stylish paddler, even having the neck to play in the largest water, also got knocked over. We got through intact but the second raft took a pasting and a couple of people were thrown out.

Once we had swept everyone up and rejoined them with their rafts and paddles we carried on downstream towards Rapid Five. This was the monstrous rapid that I had come down and looked at prior to us starting our river journey. We pulled into the bank just above it so that everyone could get out and look at what they were about to tackle. Whilst the kayakers deliberated over the best line to take and the raft guides briefed their crews on the tactics that they wanted to employ, CSM Bennett and I grabbed all of the camera gear and scrambled down to the base of the falls to set ourselves up in preparation for the action. He loaded a fresh tape into the video and moved back to a position from which he could take in the whole rapid in a single pan whilst I ensured that there were new films in the cameras, motor drives fitted and went forward. I wanted to get close and try to capture the scale.

Paul came down first. Alone in his kayak he looked tiny and vulnerable as he approached the top of the rapid. He took a line following the central vee of smooth water. He plummeted down the initial drop, falling sixteen feet into an enormous standing wave. He was bowled over and then lost to view in a white wilderness of boiling enraged water. He emerged twenty yards further down and rolled back up. The other kayakers went down in turn. It was terrifying to watch as each crashed down into the waves only to be engulfed in the maelstrom. Each was knocked over and each managed to hang on and roll up again. The boys were really flying. They had got over their initial trepidation and were now living on straight adrenalin.

Even the rafts appeared insignificant in this volume of water. The others went first whilst we filmed. As they hit the first standing wave they were spun around out of control and two of the crew were flung out. It was then our turn. We checked that everything was strapped in, tightened our buoyancy jackets and took a firm grip on our paddles. We paddled strongly upstream out of the eddy to position ourselves to take the central tongue of water. As we approached the edge we couldn't see the bottom — just the spume and spray thrown up from below. The top of the rapid was as smooth as glass. Suddenly we picked up speed and then we were swooping down, our stomachs left somewhere behind. We hit the first wave as an out of control train would hit its buffers. We flailed with our paddles to keep the forward momentum. The front two of us were leaning forward, out over the front of the raft to try and keep the raft driving on and stop it tipping over backwards. We were momentarily held by the stopper and then we were tumbling down the far side and into the next haystack wave which knocked us all flying. For several moments the whole world seemed to turn white. The raft reared up on its end and then we were through and plunging on. Trepidation, excitement, adrenalin, relief, anticlimax all coursed through my mind in that order.

After that the next rapid was relatively tame: relatively because in the previous three hours our criteria had changed dramatically. Below we pulled out into an eddy for a welcome lunch break. We tore into breadsticks filled with salad, tomatoes, meat and cheese and then basked in the sun swapping stories. The kayakers looked completely shattered, both physically and mentally, now that they had come down from their high.

There was a notable lack of action when Lawrence called out that it was time to get back on the water. The early afternoon sun was baking hot and we had to throw water over the raft before we could sit on it. We were straight back into the affray. Rapid Seven was another monster, more technical than the others, with such evocatively-named features as Indicator Rock, the Crease and the Land of the Giants, each of which held its own unpleasant surprise for the paddler.

The afternoon continued in similar vein. We finished at an eddy above Rapid Eleven. The rafts and kayaks were hauled up onto the shore, well back from the river, and we then climbed up a steep, dusty track to where the vehicle party had already set up camp on the rim of the gorge 600 feet above. Story vied with counter-story until Hurricane Betsy was just a splash in the bath by comparison. I delivered a short Sunday briefing, gave out the teams for the next day, having changed over the drivers, and then everyone turned in early.

For the first time on the entire expedition no one stirred before reveille. Even CSM Bennett was late getting up and making breakfast. Having packed up camp we donned our kit and walked back down into the gorge. Once we had launched the boats Rapid Eleven presented a fearsome hole and a ragged line of rocks which would chew up anyone who took the wrong line. The kayakers portaged around it.

Rapid Twelve was a series of three big wave trains with a gap between each and Thirteen lay close after. We shot it first in the lead raft. It was a rough run. Gdsm Cobley was knocked overboard and Tosh went flying letting go of his paddle. I was the only person left paddling on my side of the boat. CSM Bennett leapt from rear right to front left of the raft, grabbed hold of Cobley by the shoulders and hauled him back on board. The second raft lost all four people in the front and Lawrence in the back leaving only Jenny, LSgt. Evans and Cpl Hall in the boat. They flew off down river trying to pick up the flotsam of paddles and people. The kayaks came down in a variety of attitudes, cool, smooth, racing, unsteady, panicked and upside down.

Rapid Fourteen was straightforward. Rapid Fifteen was wide with a big drop and an evil-looking stopper in the centre waiting to catch anyone who didn't power forward. For the rafts it was short and sharp with a heart-stopping downward lurch and then they were punching through the stopper. The first couple of kayakers whistled through but Cpl Galvin was stopped in his tracks and pulled slowly back down into the hole. His kayak bucked and kicked and then suddenly reared right up on end. With that he was thrown backwards out of the stopper upside down. He rolled back up with a flourish. The kayakers were certainly getting wild water experience.

Rapid Sixteen was another wave train and the eddy below provided a suitable lunch stop. As we relaxed in the sun, eating and dissecting the morning's events, everyone's minds were on the next two rapids which were reputed to be two of the biggest on the river.

We pulled over above Rapid Seventeen to look for a safe line and so that we could get the cameras in place. It was enormous. When the kayaks came down it was almost too much to watch. As always they approached singly. We could see them in the eddy above paddling around, and waiting for their turn. Each broke out, took up their chosen line and with a great defiant war cry powered forward plunging into the mercy of the water. They were dwarfed by the waves. Having hit the first standing wave they were lost in the seething whiteness, appearing seconds later well downstream. Cpl Topps did another of his spectacular breath-holding exploits. He was taken out fairly early in the rapid and tried time after time to roll up. It was painful to watch. Normally a strong roller, he was obviously tired and weak, but he held on until 200 yards further down. Mike Fawcett got to him and gave him a bow rescue.

At first inspection Rapid Eighteen didn't have the largest drop that we had seen but the river narrowed channelling the water and giving it enormous power. At the base were two huge stoppers in a line, the second of which appeared to swell and then subside approximately every four seconds. Mike Fawcett went first. He got through the first few waves and then hit the big stopper at speed. His boat was thrown into the air and ejected upside down. He rolled up. Gdsm McIlvogue went next. What followed was one of the most awesome and frightening sights that I have seen. Typically he went straight for the biggest water. He was going well until he hit the second stopper which he must have caught as it swelled to its most powerful. He was stopped dead, thrown back into the trough and then cartwheeled end over end, backwards, forwards, and then backwards again. Through the camera lens I could see him fighting to find a way out, leaning first one way and then the other. One moment his boat would be swallowed up into the wall of water and then it would leap back into the trough bow over stern. From the bank we were helpless to do anything but watch and pray. After what seemed like an age he was sucked bodily out of his boat and both body and boat were spat free.

The afternoon finished with a series of smaller rapids leading to Rapid Nineteen. We paddled with CSM Bennett braced against the rear tube of the raft videoing the action. The kayakers showed up as silhouettes against the sparkling, silver water surface. The waning afternoon sun painted the gorge a rich ochre. In places the side walls had eroded leaving tall spires of rock reaching up into the sky. On the top of one, far above us, a Habdim's stork perched on her nest looking down on the tiny human specks that dared to invade her territory.

Once again we camped up on the rim overlooking the gorge. Everyone clamoured to see the video footage which was replayed time after time. When I gave out the teams that night I included myself amongst the kayakers. I was happy with the way that things were running and had plenty of action pictures. It was now time for a bit of leadership by example even if it wasn't likely to be a very good one.

With twenty miles to cover that day we made an early start. As I walked down to the boats carrying my paddle, helmet and buoyancy aid my stomach was in knots of apprehension which bordered on sheer blue funk. I felt a bit better once I was settled in to the Mountain Bat with my foot rest adjusted and the Kober paddle in my hands. It had a comfortable, solid feel to it. Also kayaking for the first time was LSgt Evans.

We were into a rapid within 200 yards of setting off. It was only a mild wave train but I was stiff and awkward, wobbling precariously. We continued through a series of rapids each growing in size. I began to relax and paddle more confidently. The rapids themselves weren't so bad but at the bottom of most were awkward swirls and whirlpools which would catch a kayak and spin it without warning. If you weren't ready either with a support stroke or to lean into the turn you would be knocked over. We went through the last two numbered rapids Twenty and Twenty-One and then into Morning Shave, Morning Shower and Open Season. There were huge standing waves. Low down in the kayak it was hard to pick your line. When you hit the first wave the front of the kayak reared up, water smashed across your helmet and face temporarily blinding you and then you were falling down the far side of the wave and into the next. In some of the wave trains the waves came in alternately from left and right, slewing the kayak to either side.

Whilst the likes of Gdsm McIlvogue and Mike Fawcett glided through the rapids putting in deft strokes as appropriate, I fought my way down paddling at full power and reacting more in the vein of crisis management.

Close Season was split in two by a rock island. We broke out on the right of the river to have a look at it. There, there was a fifteen-foot waterfall with a step in it and a rather evil-looking reversing wave at the bottom. We paddled across to the left bank, ferry gliding against the current. The rapid there descended in a long tongue of smooth water to a white wilderness. If you slightly lost your line and were pushed by the current to the left of the tongue there was an enormous gaping hole that would flip either a raft or a kayak and promised to hold both for a long time. Sitting on the bank, looking at the intimidating void I felt real fear. It would be hard to keep any control in the huge volume of water and getting it wrong didn't bear thinking about.

A raft went first. It was hurled up into the air and just as it was breaking through, it was sucked inexorably backwards. It got through but this only emphasised the terrible power of the stopper. LSgt Ellis went down, the first of the kayakers, got his line wrong and was knocked over but fortunately hit the right edge and was carried through. Gdsm McIlvogue punched through but Mike Fawcett was very nearly dragged back in. They signalled from the bottom that LSgt Evans and I should take the other side. LSgt Evans was angry and wanted to follow the line that the others had taken but I overruled him. These were not conditions for mucking about on a point of pride.

We ferry glided back over to the other side and got out again to check the line. LSgt Evans suggested, in the sort of way that soldiers do when you make them do something that they aren't keen on, that since I was so adamant on this chute wouldn't I like to lead. I settled my boat on line and paddled hard. I hit the centre of the chute and, as I dropped over the edge of the waterfall, leant back and raised my paddle over my head to keep the nose of the boat up. As I hit the water I felt myself stop dead and then began to be sucked back. A couple of strong strokes and I was through, breathing heavily. LSgt Evans wasn't so lucky. As he came down he too was stopped and was then taken back into the stopper and knocked over. He came out of his boat under the water and let go. The boat was spat out but he was held below the surface. To those watching he had vanished. Mike Fawcett, who was standing ready with a throwline, was helpless to assist.

Under the water he was thrown against the rock wall of the waterfall. Jarred and badly frightened he could see the silvery surface above him but as he rose towards it the water took hold of him again and once more dragged him down and threw him into the wall of the fall. By now desperate and out of oxygen, he involuntarily began to breathe water. His body had taken over. He still had the presence of mind to follow the drill that he had been taught and began to strip off his buoyancy jacket, intending to swim down and out under the stopper. He was jolted on the bottom once more and finally thrown clear, bobbing up some fifteen feet downstream. He came to the surface coughing and spluttering for air.

We raced to him in our kayaks and dragged him ashore where he lay heaving up water and shaking from the experience. It had been a nasty incident. He had been held underwater for over twenty-five seconds, and was justifiably shocked by the battering he had been given. It was some time before we were ready to go on.

Below we went into a series of rapids called the Narrows. They varied in size and length, passing between a narrow steep-sided gorge within the main gorge. Black basalt rock walls towered intimidatingly above us on both sides. At the first rapid LSgt Evans capsized again and this time he was taken down by a whirlpool. He reappeared three times, only to be dragged down for up to ten seconds at a time. Still shattered from his previous experience he admitted later to having literally cried with fear as he was under water praying not to be held again. When we got him out of the water and calmed him down he asked to be replaced. LSgt Williams took his first shot in a kayak whilst LSgt Evans gratefully slumped into the relative safety of a raft.

Still in the Narrows we entered another series of three rapids. Fresh into his boat and still unsteady LSgt Williams was taken out at the first. He was being held in a large stopper but LSgt Ellis managed to paddle back upstream to get to him and after a great battle got him out and to the bank. He wasn't long in his boat before being taken out again. After these three came a second area of narrows. I was powering through but was caught in the tail by a whirlpool. My boat was drawn backwards into it. I tried to fight my way out and put in one, two and then three strong slap-support strokes but was taken out.

The last rapid of the morning was Chimumba. As large as anything we had encountered so far, there was a huge chute of water which drove you towards the right rock wall. The wall bent around leftwards. Against the wall was a great, boiling cushion of water. I cannoned into it. I braced my paddle above my head but the blade was still only halfway up the water cushion. I was trashed instantly. I was fairly comfortable upside down in the water and hung in my boat for the buffeting to subside. When it didn't and I couldn't roll I came out cautiously holding on to the boat as I did so. I was still being held in a stopper and had I let go I would probably have been taken down and given a pasting. As it was my boat was thrown free with me clinging to it.

By that time we had been on the water for six and a half hours. It was by far the largest water that I had ever paddled and I was right on the limit of my ability. I felt physically and emotionally shattered and my nerves were in tatters. Looking around, most of the other kayakers looked knackered. I sat in the sun still shaking and slowly began to unwind.

That afternoon we had to negotiate the Upper and Lower Mwemba Falls. The former was a rapid of such power and ferocity that as Mike Fawcett shot it he was launched, still sitting in his canoe, through the air, landing beside one of the other paddlers. The Lower Mwemba Falls had a vertical drop of thirty feet. To have tried to shoot it would have been suicidal. We had to portage the boats around and then lower the rafts on ropes into the water below whilst the kayaks made wild seal launches from a high rock platform. The last rapid, curiously named Somebody's Lunch Box, held yet more surprises. The first raft and most of the kayaks shot it without a problem but the second raft hit a standing wave at the wrong angle and flipped over backwards scattering paddles and bodies in all directions, much to the amusement of everyone else. There was much cheering and a major mopping up operation.

The white water action continued for the next three days, tailing off towards the latter stages. There was no access to vehicles so we carried just the bare essentials for camping strapped into the rafts in waterproof bags and containers. There were still some large rapids to be negotiated. The Ghostrider claimed two victims, Cpl Hall and Sarah Pipe. They were taken out in a massive wave train which had a strong reversing eddy at the bottom. Both came out of their boats which disappeared. We found the boats one mile further down the river, fortunately still serviceable. Another large rapid threw one of the rafts up into the air ejecting all but one of the paddlers. Gdsm Cobley disappeared by the stopper and only came back to the surface fifty yards downstream. He missed the throwline and was swept straight over the next rapid, fortunately not being held.

The gorge became less sheer and both flora and fauna abounded. The banks were lined with African ivory, large-leaved and red-leaved figs, tick berries, paperbark trees, white syringa and ilala palms. High above black eagles and gymnogene watched from their eyries whilst down by the river hammerkops, fish eagles, wagtails, pied kingfishers, water dikkops and flocks of pratincoles flitted about. More concerning were the large numbers of crocodiles we were seeing. The kayakers paddled close together to avoid presenting single targets.

We passed several basic fishermen's huts perched high on sandbanks safe from flood waters. Some had fish-drying racks and small vegetable patches. On one the tell-tale dinner-plate footprints gave away the first signs of hippos this side of Victoria Falls.

We camped beside the river cooking on an open fire and laying our sleeping bags out on the sand under the starry African night.

On the third day we passed a few native fishing settlements and several schools of hippos before we found the vehicle party waiting for us at the Matetsi River mouth. We took the rafts out of the water, de-rigged and deflated them. From now on it was kayaks, kleppers and canoes for the remainder of the river.

Our guide for Lake Kariba and the Lower Zambesi was Rob Shattock. Fiftyish, Rob looked and acted like Zimbabwe's answer to Crocodile Dundee. He had accompanied us on all of the river journey so far and had emerged as an extraordinary character. His knowledge of the bush and all that was in it was encyclopaedic. Paddling in a klepper with him every aspect of the surrounding natural world came alive. He was fascinated by everything from the smallest insect to the most obscure tree. Every bird, animal and plant no matter how insignificant was elevated to celebrity status and took on a character all of its own. He was never happier than when pottering off into the bush revealing its innermost secrets to the uninitiated with an all-embracing enthusiasm. Termite mounds were probed, discarded tortoise shells split and re-married, spoor followed and every species of flora and fauna lovingly identified. He seemed to be able to talk to the animals and understand them. In fact he was a skilled mimic and could imitate most animals' and birds' calls so accurately that they would reply with answering calls thus giving away their position.

We bade farewell to Paul Connolly and the Shearwater guides and set off down river. An hour and a half took us down to the Deka Rapids, the last set on the river. They only claimed Matthew Roberts and Gdsm Woodward, whose klepper had been leaking so badly that they were already half full of water. We paddled on for five miles before stopping for lunch. By this stage the current had dwindled to nothing and we were beginning to experience the headwind which was likely to plague us on the lake. Small waves constantly broke over the front of the boats throwing spray into our faces.

We paddled on for several miles. As we were approaching the Sabankwazi Police Station we saw some hippos in the water on the Zimbabwean side. To avoid them we struck out towards the Zambian bank. I noticed that we had become very spread out. With the wind and spray each person was locked in their own little world, toiling to make progress. As I was trying to make myself heard to stop those in front there came a shout from behind me that Richard Gaffney and Rob Shattock had capsized at the back. I could see two bodies in the water 200 yards behind me. Telling the others to make their way to the shore I raced back with Mike Fawcett and Cpl Hall who were also in kayaks. Our boats were surfing on the waves. We passed Guy and LSgt Evans who said that Rob had waved them away. When we got to them, they were one hundred yards from the shore, their klepper was almost totally submerged and they weren't making any headway. We got each of them to hold on to the back of our boats, attached two lines to the klepper and towed the whole lot to shore, glancing nervously over our shoulders for signs of any further attacks.

On the shore we could see the full extent of the damage. The hippo had come up under the boat in a deliberate attack. Both upper and lower teeth had punctured the bottom of the klepper, the teeth of the powerful lower jaw making a large rent in the thick fibreglass. The klepper had sunk immediately. Thank goodness the hippo hadn't come back for a second go when they were in the water. As we were considering what to do the police launch pulled up to see if we were okay. According to them this section was notorious for hippo attacks. The previous year, they claimed, a boat had been attacked and sunk by a hippo and the occupant had then been attacked by a crocodile as he was swimming towards the shore.

Next day we paddled twenty miles with no current, against strong headwinds to reach Milibizi at the south-western end of Lake Kariba where we were to meet up with Rob's wife Dee and our support boat *The Ark*. We made our way out from Msuna Mouth, along the river for nearly six miles before entering the Devil's Gorge. It was hard, relentless going.

After thirteen miles the Devil's Gorge was not dramatic but was steep-sided enough to prevent either human or any significant animal occupation. Any self-respecting crocodile was keeping his head down in the chill wind. Another couple of hours brought us to a fork in the river and a short distance further on we broke out into the bottom end of the lake. We stopped for lunch on some rather uncomfortable windswept rocks.

At this end the lake is only one and three quarter miles wide but with that broad fetch there were large waves out in the middle. We attacked the last three and a half miles half paddling, half surfing our way across to arrive tired and sore shouldered at Milibizi. There was no sign of Dee and as it was Sunday, in typical African fashion, both the police and the lake navigation service had turned their radios off. The lake has a reputation for sudden, vicious storms so Rob was worried.

Lake Kariba was formed when the Zambesi valley was dammed in a joint Rhodesian-Zambian hydro-electric scheme at Kariba in 1956. The resulting lake is two hundred miles long and up to twenty-five miles wide. It is one of the most beautiful places in Africa. Many islands were formed where the water failed to cover hills and all around the edge petrified trees rise up from the water. For the Sunday briefing that night we got out all of the 1:100,000 maps of the lake. At the scale of 1km:1cm our route covered two-thirds of the side of my Land Rover. The size of the task in hand couldn't have been displayed more graphically.

Rob remained with the vehicle party in the morning to try and raise Dee on the radio. I set off with seven kleppers and three kayaks. We were late getting away but made good headway for the first half-hour. The wind then sprang up and with it the waves. The next couple of hours became a bit of a battle. The petrified trees forced us away from the shoreline out into the larger waves. I was paddling with Guy. We worked well as a team, paddling steadily in a fixed rhythm but the heavy klepper wasn't designed for surfing. Map reading from a canoe wasn't easy. We were so low down

Sunset on Lake Kariba; Sgt Evans and Sgt Ellis.

Top: Hippos, ever watchful, Lower Zambesi.

Bottom: A tusker wades between grass islands on the Lower Zambesi.

Top: The Skeleton Coast, Namibia.

Bottom: Male ostrich and offspring; Botswana.

Left: CSM Bennett parascending from a dune at Sossusvlei.

Below: Yet another breakdown; Cpl Phillips, Cpl Peake, Cpl Saxon and Sgt Smith, Namib Desert.

Top left: Trees were brought down by violent storms blocking our route; Southern Zaire.

Top right: Crossing the basic log bridges required careful guiding and a steady nerve for the driver.

Bottom: Mud and more mud.

Top: Alasdair Johnstone and Gdsm Harris prepare dinner after a long day of vehicle recoveries in jungle, Zaire.

Bottom: A jungle ferry.

that it was difficult to make out the shape of the shore. At a couple of miles' distance everything appeared to lose its relief.

We paddled past Kamawendwe Island and then took a line by guestimate across to the Sebungwe Narrows. Fortunately we got it right and made good progress until we met up with the vehicles at Jabawa Island. Rob had been in touch with lake navigation. There had been a storm two days ago and all of the boats had been ordered into safety for thirty-six hours. *The Ark* was now steaming south towards us. We spent the late afternoon patching up the kleppers and cutting old inner tubes into strips to try and reinforce the seal on our spraydecks.

Next day we paddled on up the shoreline, crossing Siankumi Cove to reach Binga. Most people had now paired off with a regular paddling partner. We were all growing stronger and were keeping up a brisk pace of just under four miles per hour.

Finally, once we were settled in at Binga *The Ark* hove into sight. Rob looked happy and relieved to see Dee and Brenda, his thirteen-year-old step-daughter, safe and sound. They were tired, having had a long, rough journey. *The Ark* is a 35-foot, steel hulled, twin engine cruiser with quite a history. When the dam had first been built and the waters rose, slowly flooding the Zambesi Valley, many thousands of animals had been left stranded on steadily receding islands. A group of committed expatriates led by Rupert Fothergill had mounted a massive rescue operation to catch up as many as possible and save them from drowning. *The Ark* had been Fothergill's flagship.

We developed a routine for the next eight days: we got up early, packed up our simple camp and got on to the water around 6am. We then paddled for two to three hours with *The Ark* steaming either ahead or alongside of us depending on the conditions. By the time that we stopped Dee would have an enormous breakfast of eggs, sausages, bacon, tomatoes, toast and pots of tea and coffee. After an hour's break we would paddle for two to three more hours until we stopped for a lunch of meat-filled rolls and salad. We would take a siesta through the hottest part of the afternoon before paddling a final two to three hours into the sunset. In the evening we set up camp near *The Ark* and enjoyed another of Dee's culinary extravaganzas. By 8pm most people had slunk away to their campbeds exhausted. We saw the vehicle party every couple of days when they could get to us.

I held a briefing each night to discuss our progress and describe the next day's route. As an average we had to cover twenty miles per day. Despite that it was hard to get volunteers to go with the vehicles. It was great to have everyone so enthusiastic.

I woke several times during the night due to strong winds. Looking through binoculars I could see white horses out on the lake. We delayed our start in the morning hoping for it to calm down. When we set off we were in the lee of the land but as soon as we came around the headland we were exposed to the full force of the wind. Waves five feet high were coming at us head on, tossing the kleppers around all over the place. We quickly began to take on water through our inadequate spraydecks. Every stroke had to be made accurately and powerfully. A moment's lapse and you found yourself surfing uncontrollably backwards. The lumbering kleppers were hard to control in these conditions. It became obvious fairly quickly that Richard and Tetta couldn't cope with the conditions. It was no reflection on them but Tetta just wasn't strong enough. I called The Ark over to lift them out of the water. Even at twenty yards' distance I had to yell to make myself heard above the waves.

For the rest of the team I was worried in case the kleppers should become swamped. They would sink quickly, we were a long way from shore and a rescue operation would have been both difficult and hazardous in that swell. I kept shouting at everyone to stay close together. The men, as usual, were totally unconcerned for their own safety and whooped with delight as each wave picked them up and dropped them down with a thwack into the trough. They revelled in the action. We fought our way forwards for two hours. We seemed to make no appreciable gain in distance but each wave that broke over us deposited yet more water inside the kleppers setting them lower and lower in the water. This extra water, which was now halfway up our legs in the kleppers, greatly added to the weight of the boats and made the paddling hard graft. Finally we made it to a small rocky island where we dragged the boats out of the water and collapsed on the beach, for a brew and a rest.

For the remainder of the day we had to hop from island to island using whatever channels and lee shores we could to gain the most protected route. We stopped in a sheltered cove on Mubende Island. The wind died and it was a glorious evening. The moon rose early, a perfect pale red orb casting a shaft of amber light across the lake.

Gradually we made our way up the lake. A difficult start with strong cross winds kept the rear paddler in each klepper continually making strong sweep strokes to keep on course but everyone felt strong so we kept pushing on. That afternoon Kariba showed itself off in all of its full glory. The water was like glass and the afternoon light rich. We gave a wide berth to a lone hippo guarding a narrow channel and then came across the fabulous sight of a herd of elephants wallowing in the shallows and throwing cool wet sand over themselves. It was quite beautiful but it was a very tired team that paddled the last mile or so as the sun was setting over the distant Zambian hills. We had paddled over twenty-five miles that day — no mean distance in the heavy kleppers. Muscles ached and faces glowed as we settled in to camp.

Next day we had problems with a strong wind but then it died as suddenly as it had sprung up and we paddled on along the shore. A fabulous array of birdlife lined the meadow that stretched back from the water's edge. We pulled into the harbour at Mujeri Store. The vehicle party had been game viewing in Chisarira Park and were full of their news. We took on a resupply of food, changed over teams and, after a night's rest, bade them farewell for another three days.

A short day's paddle took us to Paradise Island. From the top of the hill the sunset was spectacular. A capenta fishing boat, far out on the lake, broke the receding sun's golden trail.

We woke up to a wonderfully calm morning. Rob had heard a leopard coughing on the island during the night. Needless to say I had heard nothing. With all of the exercise that we were taking I slept the sleep of the dead. As we carried on past Namagwaba and Namambere Islands we began to see large herds of game. Waterbuck, impala, zebra and the elegant sable antelope all competed for space. A tortoise the size of a pudding bowl swam under my canoe. We stopped for a late breakfast having already covered twelve miles. After another of Dee's feasts we carried on reluctantly. The small, heavily vegetated rock outcrop of Suche Island was reflected perfectly in the mirrored lake surface.

It was baking hot as we followed the shoreline, avoiding several schools of hippos and watching the grazing herds. Our intended night stop at Katete Harbour was so shallow that we couldn't get *The Ark* into it. Added to that it was teeming with hippos. We carried on beneath Bumi Hills. Sheer slopes descended to a belt of flat-topped acacia trees and then an open grassy plain leading down to the water. We watched as a baby elephant practised his charge against a nearby impala, swinging his rubbery trunk and racing forward trumpeting shrilly. Families of warthogs ran unconcernedly amongst mixed herds of waterbuck, zebra, elephant and buffalo.

We camped in Bumi Harbour. At some point during the night a large herd of buffalo grazed their way peacefully through the camp.

As we crossed the Ume River we entered the Matusadona National Park. Thick bush flanked the lake making game viewing difficult but we caught glimpses of the rich red coats and dappled flanks of browsing bushbuck and some unusually large waterbuck. In the middle of the day when all of the other animals were sheltering from the sun the shy kudu came down to a series of lagoons to drink. We had hoped to catch sight of the Chura bull, a massive tusker reputed to have ivory weighing 150lb on either side, but he remained elusive.

It was a calm day and the group spread out as we paddled on past Tashinga towards King's Fishing Camp. *The Ark* motored on ahead and anchored in a secluded bay surrounded by a herd of buffalo several hundred strong. The kleppers pulled in with the sun setting behind them. The wind picked up and flocks of red-winged pratincoles flew in to the lee shores. It looked as though we were in for a big blow.

The wind got up as expected in the night. I had secured my mosquito net to two camp chairs which gave in to the strengthening gusts and came crashing down on my head. Feeling not a little stupid I took off the mosquito net and lay watching the half-moon edge its way across the sky. Going to bed so early made for long nights and we were ready to get up by 5.30am when it began to get light. By morning the wind had died down again and the lake was as still as a mill pond. The heat of the sun beating down on us and the reflection back off the water bore into you. Any energy was sapped away and my brain felt as if it was being slowly addled. We paddled gently on, game viewing and taking photographs. We reached Fothergill Island to find the vehicle party already ensconced. They had had a busy three days with a long drive inland to cross the Ume River. Our tyres had worn almost threadbare and they were constantly plagued by punctures on the bush tracks. It was imperative that we should get some new tyres.

Our last day on the lake required us to paddle fifteen miles across to Kariba town with just one island on the way. I decided to make a very early start to try and take advantage of the morning calm. We were up at 4.30am and ready to go by 5am. We wore head torches so that we wouldn't lose each other in the dark. We set a fast pace paddling hard towards Long Island. The soldiers sang and joked through the darkness. Yet again they revelled in difficult conditions. The sun rose gradually bathing the lake in golden light. We reached Long Island after an hour and a half and stopped for a brew and to empty out any water that had found its way through the spraydecks.

After Long Island it was a long hard flog. Setting off into such an enormous expanse of open water, with the far shore barely visible above the horizon was fairly daunting. We dropped into a steady rhythm. Everyone fell silent, concentrating on maintaining the pace. Two-thirds of the way across, we stopped and tied our kleppers to *The Ark* for breakfast. Whilst the others sat bobbing up and down in their kleppers, swigging from cups of tea and munching egg banjos I got on the radio.

We had arranged to meet Liz Whittaker, a trustee of the 'Save the Rhino Campaign', on her boat. Liz had seen our vehicles in Harare and had approached us to ask if she could use our name to raise money for her campaign. I had agreed readily. Since then she had been approaching

Zimbabwean companies to sponsor our descent of the Zambesi. So far she had raised Z$8,500 to go towards a translocation programme and sanctuaries for rhinos. Poaching still posed a critical threat to the survival of the rhinos and without these protected havens there was a grave danger of the rhinoceros becoming extinct.

Instead of Liz I got hold of her son James who was on board with a couple of the fundraisers and a group of friends. They had harboured overnight not far away and so said that they would motor over to see us. We relaxed and swam whilst we waited.

Their boat was aptly named *Utopia*. We watched an, extremely comfortable gin palace steaming towards us. As they got nearer we could see a number of scantily clad girls draped along the upper deck. With a great cheer all of our crew leapt into the water, swam over to *Utopia* and scrambled aboard. Although it was only ten o'clock in the morning, beers, gin punch and Pimms appeared. After about an hour of drinking, chatting and basking in this unexpected paradise I decided that we had better leave before we drank their boat dry. Twenty soldiers can get through a prodigious quantity of drink especially if they have been out in the bush for a while. No one wanted to leave but as I passed the word around the boys were great and leapt back overboard with ever more extravagant dives.

The next hour was close to farcical. We climbed back into the kleppers to complete the lake crossing. A strong tail wind made the kleppers surge uncontrollably. The men were in high spirits and sang and laughed as they whizzed all over the place. After a while, with the shore well in view, Guy announced that he couldn't hold on any longer and had to have a pee. He stood up, tilting the klepper precariously from side to side. He tried sitting on one side of the canoe nearly tipping us over and then compromised by kneeling. As he began to relieve himself he got the giggles and just leant further and further over. I yelled at him and lunged with a support stroke but he just carried on leaning and peeing until we capsized. We were quickly surrounded by other kleppers. The men were in hysterics, mobbed Guy mercilessly and sang a medley of songs from 'Yellow Submarine' to 'I am sinking' and 'Why was he born so beautiful'. Having paddled 200 miles over twelve days, survived large waves and night paddling it was the ultimate ignominy to capsize within a mile of the end.

It was a fairly short paddle to the Kariba town shoreline. We took the boats out of the water, bade farewell to *The Ark* and established camp in the grounds of the Carribea Bay Hotel. *Utopia* sailed back in later in the day to restock their depleted drink supply. We partied hard that night.

The next day was spent sorting out the arrangements for the last stage of our Zambesi journey and relaxing. I woke at 5.45am feeling surprisingly bright and breezy, got up, washed and showered and began writing up my diary. As the sun came up I began to go into decline and a fairly fearsome hangover set in. Later on we loaded the kleppers onto a ferry going back up the lake. I went in to the hotel to ring the UK. Rumours were rife in the team about the regiment going to the Gulf. Several of the men had spoken to their wives who had seen an article in the *Daily Mail* saying that the Welsh Guards were being sent out. When I got through to the Adjutant all was calm. The rumours were unfounded. Indeed the reverse was true: the regiment had been stood down and an armoured brigade based in Germany was preparing to fly out.

By the time that we got up next day I was looking forward to getting back onto the river. We were away from the campsite by 6am and drove to a drop-off point close to the base of the Kariba Dam wall. For the last section of the river we had elected to use two-man open canoes. They would be perfectly capable of dealing with the milder water conditions and more comfortable in the intense heat of the lower Zambesi Valley. We carried the canoes for a mile down a dusty footpath to the river's edge.

I planned to paddle the rest of the river with Rob so that I could concentrate on photography. We managed to rig a tripod together with camera and 300mm lens into the front of the canoe. By the time that we had finished it resembled a floating machine gun platform.

The current was strong and swept us swiftly down river into a steep heavily vegetated gorge. There was little animal life save for the occasional bushbuck or troop of baboons.

We stopped for lunch and a siesta at the mouth of the Chimwa River. I felt restless and swam up the creek into a beautiful little lagoon, whose access Rob had assured me was too shallow for crocodiles. The water entered by pouring over a rockfall. At this time of year it was dry and the rocks burning hot to the touch. I scrambled up and then followed the shaded river bed above, surprising a small group of bushbuck who skittered away barking out their alarm. It was a wonderful secluded spot.

Two and a half miles further downstream we broke out of the gorge. The scenery changed quickly and dramatically. The river broadened and the cliffs receded leaving open grass flats on the Zambian side and a vertical sand wall forming the Zimbabwean bank. Immediately we began to see large schools of hippos and scores of crocodiles. Sometimes the crocodiles would leave it so late before diving for the security of the water that we were splashed by the whiplash of their powerful tails. Plovers, storks, greenshanks, ruffs, egrets and herons of all descriptions populated the banks.

We camped on a flat shelf of sand at the water's edge. As it grew dark we could hear lions roaring nearby. Later on the chorus was taken up by elephants trumpeting as they came down to drink. The bass line was provided by hippos guffawing in the water.

We woke to find fresh lion pug marks close behind the shelf of sand. It was a fearfully hot day. When the wind blows up the Zambesi Valley it does so with the intensity of a giant hairdryer. We had a reasonably short paddle to Chirundu. Along the river banks were a great variety of flora in vibrant greens and flaming reds: knob thorns, sausage trees, vegetable ivory, mangoes, wild figs, tamarinds and mahogany as well as the ever present acacias.

We passed the rotting carcass of a hippopotamus that had recently been poached. All around basked bloated crocodiles, so overladen by the carrion that they had eaten, that they could barely flop into the water as we approached.

At midday the breeze dropped. The heat was choking. We stopped on a sand bar to swim and cool off. Below the metal suspension bridge, which forms one of the two road links between Zambia and Zimbabwe a young bull elephant was throwing mud over himself. One mile beyond we came to Rob's camp. It was a wonderful Heath Robinson tree house. Three storeys high it was built of mud, local wood and thatch around an old acacia tree. Outside an enamelled bath had been sunk into the earth and screened with a rush palisade leaving it open to the river. You could sit and bathe, watching the hippos cavort in the water, whilst the sun slid down the sky to set in front of you. There wasn't a single straight line anywhere in the construction of the treehouse but it was the perfect complement to such an idyllic spot. In many ways it was a reflection of Rob's character.

Tosh rushed up to me, beside himself with excitement. He had watched a small olive bush snake catch a waxbill. It had then proceeded to dislocate its jaw to devour the tiny bird. He greatly enjoyed the wildlife and trained by CSM Bennett he could recognise more of the birdlife than most other members of the team. He had changed greatly since coming on the expedition team. When he first appeared he was a small, uncouth, ball of energy. Beneath an unruly mop of curls lay a determined character. He may have been small in stature but was not afraid to square up to the soldiers if he felt that he was being taken advantage of. He had had to leave the training camp early to return to face an Actual Bodily Harm charge — aged sixteen and a half. In Africa he had annoyed some of the team initially with his constant foul-mouthedness and cheek. However he had latched on to CSM Bennett and despite receiving several clips around the ear for his troubles stuck with him all the time. It later transpired that he had never known his father. His mother had brought him up the best way she could in the hardest area of Newcastle. Naturally fairly wild, he had played truant from school and subsequently, barring a short period on the Youth Training Scheme from which he had removed himself, he had been unemployed. He was involved with a number of street gangs and, I suspected, on the verge of serious crime. Shortly before coming on the expedition he had been recruited by Weston Spirit where he found a number of kindred souls. He openly expressed his enjoyment of the expedition and all that he was seeing. Most satisfying of all he emerged as a polite, constructive member of the team albeit requiring strong guidance at times to curb the 'bandit' side of his nature. Later in the evening we had a barbecue to thank Dee for all of her hard work, looking after us on Kariba.

Before setting off in the morning I said goodbye to Jenny. She had to go back to Harare to catch her plane home. It had been great fun for me having her with us. She had got on really well with the soldiers and mucked in well with all of the chores. The wildlife, scenery and simple way of life in the bush was certainly far removed from her life as an interior decorator in London.

Every day we saw new species of birds: little bee eaters, white-fronted bee eaters, goliath, greenbacked and rufus bellied herons, or African skimmers scooping the surface of the water with their prominent orange beaks. It was an ornithologist's dream. Towards the end of the day we came across a magnificent lone bull elephant wading the river.

The vehicle party were waiting for us with the news that Tetta was ill. Matthew thought that it was either a virus or malaria but hopefully not the latter. Fortunately as we had broken the back of the distance we could afford to take it easy for a couple of days.

By morning Tetta was worse. Leaving Matthew to look after her and take some tests, the remainder of us split into small groups to explore the park. Mana is one of the few parks where you can walk freely. I went with four others. We headed through some thick jesse bush back from the river. As the sun came up there were herds of impala, eland and elephants all around us. We came to a narrow stream which we followed to a line of pools. It was an attractive shaded trail through country which epitomised classic Africa. Zebra and waterbuck wandered around as vervet monkeys chattered in the background.

The first pool was home to a flotilla of crocodiles who slid off the mud verge as we approached. Black-winged stilts, hammerkop and saddle-billed storks stood sentinel in the shallows. Overhead red-billed hornbills swooped awkwardly under the weight of their comically outsized bills. A kite flew low overhead and stooped to take a fish.

An overwhelming stench wafted towards us from the last of the pools. A hippo, stiff and bloated in death, lay face down in the water. Open scars on its back, now thick with large blue flies were evidence of a lost fight. The nostrils of a second hippo protruded from the water in the middle of the pool. We looped back towards camp through bush that was alive with the sights, sounds and earthy smells of the wild.

The group that had gone with Rob were buzzing with excitement. He had taken them to within twenty yards of a lion.

Matthew's face was of concern. Having studied slides of Tetta's blood under the microscope he was now as confident as he could be that she had got malaria. She was feverish with a headache and aching joints. He began to treat her with a course of nivaquine but warned me that if she got any worse we would have to get her to a hospital.

After another night's rest Tetta was showing signs of improving. I went for a walk with Rob and a few of the others. In the pleasant pre-dawn coolness the animal kingdom was beginning to come alive. We walked downstream, along the river bank, for a while passing herds of elephant and impala. A lone bull elephant was having a sand bath. We were able to approach to within twenty feet, where from behind the safety of a large termite mound we could make out every detail of his body from the distinguishing rents and tears of his tattered ears to his long, delicate eyelashes.

Walking with Rob each spoor was read, each bird's nesting habit discussed and everything from buffalo to banded mongoose was stalked. He explained the traditional uses to which the Africans put the natural assets: sausage trees for curing skin cancer, thorny palm fronds for trapping fish, resin from the rope lianas to entrap birds and that of the umbrella tree for heart disease. He introduced us to a host of new characters from the bird world: palm swifts, Melba finches, Kyrrachaim thrushes, bateleur eagles, scimitar-billed wood hoopoe, white-faced whistling duck, to name just a few. Exotic names for exotic creatures. I had never met a man so at one with his environment or who took such obvious delight in sharing it with others.

Beyond Mana Pools we passed through the Sapi Hunting Reserve. Immediately we noticed the scarcity and shyness of game. It took a reasonably hard paddle to complete the day's mileage and reach the rendezvous with the vehicles. The light was fading when we finally saw them parked on a shelf of sand overlooking the Chewore river.

A strong wind blew all night. Anything not tied down had to be secured by those on sentry. There was a lot of ragging next morning at breakfast. LSgt Evans had been on sentry in the middle of the night when he had seen a torch go on. When he went over to see what was the matter he found Rob sitting up in bed peering into the darkness having heard a noise. Rob gave him the torch and sent him to see what was out there warning him that if he saw a pair of blue eyes it was a leopard of which there were many in the area. LSgt Evans had ventured off timorously and then shot back gabbling that he had walked into six leopards. When they both went to verify this unlikely tale they found themselves looking into the enquiring eyes of a small herd of impala. He wasn't going to live it down quickly.

The wind kept up all day giving us a rough passage through the Mupata Gorge. At lunchtime instead of hiding from the sun as normal we took cover behind rocks and shivered in our thin jerseys. There was little evidence of game save for isolated klipspringers who darted nervously away on their agile, pointed hooves and a pair of purple crested lowries who flashed from tree to tree in a blur of scarlet, green and purple.

We stopped for the last time on the river to make camp at the Tunsa River Mouth. Having completed the familiar routine of dragging the boats away from the water's edge, setting up camp beds and mosquito nets and helping erect our field kitchen I wandered back down to the river. As I stripped off and washed in the shallows I was sorry that our river journey had to end. I had really enjoyed the simple physical way of life: getting up early; paddling all day; game viewing and going to bed physically shattered to sleep under the stars. I felt fit, strong and well. This team had established a great camaraderie. We sat around the camp fire for a long time after supper swapping stories in an effort to recapture the journey and draw out our last night beside the Zambesi.

Heavy, dark clouds and strong head winds conspired to put a twist into the tail of the final section. We were soon battling with some fairly large waves which although not on the scale of those that we had encountered on Lake Kariba posed a significant problem to us in our open canoes. Rob and I tried to hug the lee shore as much as possible to try and protect the camera equipment from too bad a soaking but there was little that we could do to prevent the spray flying up from our stern or the water slopping over the gunwales. Our progress was slow. We were now entering the head waters of Lake Cabora Bassa and the current had all but died away. We paddled on, stopping frequently to sponge out the water that we had taken on board.

When we finally arrived at the Mozambique border it was something of an anticlimax. Kanyemba turned out to be a collection of scruffy, dirty houses. It seemed all wrong to be stopping with more river still in front of us just because we had reached an invisible boundary that someone had once placed on the map. I wished that we could have paddled from the source in Zambia, through Angola, Botswana, Zimbabwe and Mozambique to the mouth at the Indian Ocean. It was easy to have such thoughts as we clambered out of our boats for the last time. In reality it would be an enormous undertaking with a journey of more than 1,250 miles including a second lake, Cabora Bassa, over ninety miles longer than Kariba. Politically it wasn't possible to enter Angola or Mozambique and even if we could have it would have taken a great deal more time than we could afford.

As it was we had taken twenty-nine days to paddle 450 miles of the Zambesi on its course through Zimbabwe. Not bad for a bunch of novices.

Chapter Five
Mud and More Mud

Phase Five

Captain John Warburton-Lee, Welsh Guards, Expedition leader
Captain Richard Gaffney, Welsh Guards, Expedition Second in Command
Captain Matthew Roberts, Royal Army Medical Corps, Expedition doctor
Company Sergeant Major Alan Bennett, Welsh Guards
Miss Tetta Nicholls, Expedition secretary
Captain Alasdair Johnstone, Welsh Guards
Lieutenant Richard Weekes, Royal Army Medical Corps.
Second Lieutenant Linda Orr, Royal Army Medical Corps
Sergeant 'Smudge' Smith, Royal Electrical and Mechanical Engineers
Corporal Willy Phillips, Royal Electrical and Mechanical Engineers
Corporal Martin Saxon, Royal Electrical and Mechanical Engineers
Lance Corporal Les Peake, Welsh Guards
Lance Corporal 'Mo' Morris, Welsh Guards
Guardsman Jason Harris, Welsh Guards
Guardsman Neil Evans, Welsh Guards
Guardsman Steve Jones 42, Welsh Guards
Guardsman 'Spider' Webb, Welsh Guards
Gunner Mike Reid, Royal Artillery
Gunner Colin Searl, Royal Artillery
Maurice Miller, Weston Spirit

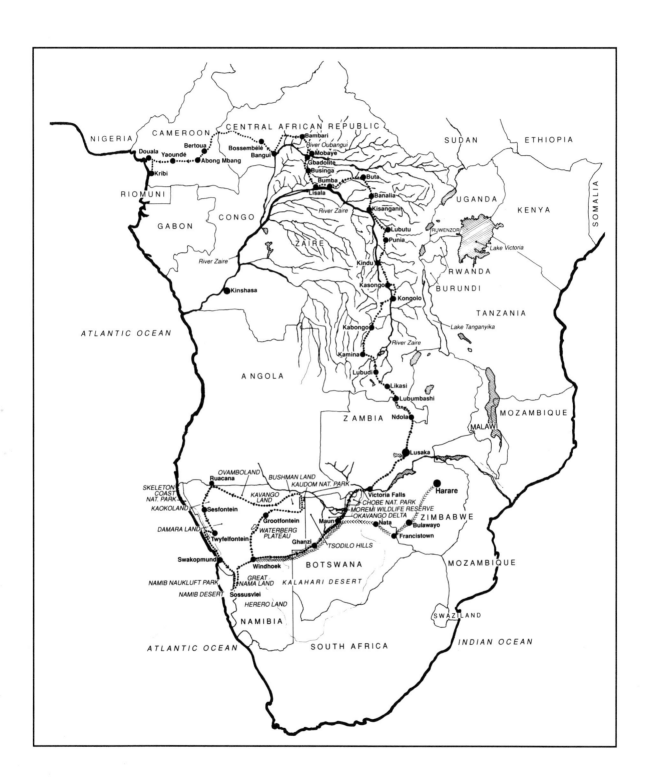

A beaming Alasdair Johnstone led the Phase Five team through the Jan Strijdom Airport customs. They cut a comical image struggling with trolleys laden down under Bedford tyres, Land Rover tyres, main leaf springs, propshafts, windscreens and turbo units in addition to their own baggage. Alistair looked as if he had achieved the feat of a lifetime by getting them there. When I learned that he had got all of these desperately needed spares, over twice their weight allocation, out to Namibia for the cost of a bottle of champagne I was inclined to agree.

The last two weeks of Phase Four had proved harsh on the vehicles. From Kanyemba we had driven to the Whittakers' coffee farm at Karoi. We had spent a couple of days there relaxing and enjoying their wonderful hospitality. Our Commanding Officer, LtCol Reddy Watt had flown out to see us and was already installed with the Whittakers when we arrived. It was great to exchange news, show him the video footage of the Zambesi and discuss contingency plans should our return journey not go according to plan. He took his usual robust line, supporting whatever decisions we had to take at the time but suggesting certain options should we not be able to get through Zaire on our intended route.

We had driven to Harare for an administrative stop and then carried on via Bulawayo to cross into Botswana at Plumtree. The road to Francistown and Nata was excellent and covered with tar but there it ran out. Beyond, deep soft sand tracks, interspersed with sections of savage potholes, led away into the Kalahari. Unlike the classic image of a desert, the Kalahari is characterised by thick thorn scrub on a base of fine white sand. Almost immediately we began to experience problems with the vehicles. All of the tyres were worn virtually threadbare and so we were plagued by frequent punctures. A fuel pump gave out requiring temporary repairs as we reached Baines Boababs on our second night. By the time we reached Maun we were forced to negotiate the best deal that we could for two new lorry tyres. The law of supply and demand halfway across the Kalahari put the advantage firmly on the side of the supplier, in this case a very shady Greek. With no alternative available we had no choice but to pay his grossly inflated price of US$1,000 for the two tyres.

We had turned north at Toteng and continued for 125 miles through the featureless thornbush until we reached the Tsodilo Hills. Highly acclaimed as the spiritual home of the Bushmen people, the Tsodilo Hills are visible as two rounded rock knolls, from quite some distance away. Up close they rose steeply above us in a series of sheer pink rock faces and overhangs broken up by vegetated boulderous slopes. We camped for a couple of nights between them. In the daytime we scoured the rock for traces of the Bushmen's paintings. There were crude images of hand prints, animals including giraffe, antelope and rhinoceros, and other indistinguishable shapes. A group of Bushmen hunters were clearly depicted with their characteristic permanently erect penis grossly exaggerated in size. Interestingly we found pictures of whales and what looked like a penguin. With over 550 miles to the nearest point of the ocean the inspiration for these images raised many questions. The two main hills are known as Man and Woman. On the second evening I climbed to the summit of Woman and sat alone absorbing the remoteness whilst watching the sun set over the distant plains.

Having regained the main Maun to Ghantsi road we turned west finding ourselves encountering deeply channelled sand tracks which were often heavily corrugated. The front leaf springs on both Bedfords had gradually surrendered to the constant pounding of off-route driving and were now inverted. As a result each time the lorries struck one of the partially concealed bumps the chassis came up, undamped by the action of the springs and smashed the oil filters. This happened several times until we modified the filters by cutting them down to half their normal size. By the time that we crossed the Namibian border all of the vehicles had been subjected to a rivet-shearing pummelling for over 400 miles. They urgently needed a complete overhaul and each had major components which required replacement.

We had established ourselves in a campsite in the small Daan Viljoen Reserve just outside Windhoek. It was there that we took the new team to spend their first night. They looked slightly aghast at the state of the vehicles but after a night's rest the mechanics set to with a will, servicing and fitting the most pressing major assemblies whilst everyone else changed every tyre that we had.

The challenge for the phase was to make a south to north crossing of the Zaire jungle. Little was known of the route except that it had long since fallen into disuse and was reported to be anything between extremely difficult and impassable. Prior to that we intended to conduct a vehicle mobility exercise around some of the wildest parts of Namibia to see something of the country and practise our driving and recovery skills for the route ahead. With a journey of around 8,000 miles still to go and most of that expected to be through extremely hostile terrain our vehicles were now our most important assets. Our slender stock of spares had to be husbanded carefully.

Whilst I continued with the paper war Richard and CSM Bennett led forays into Windhoek in search of last minute items of equipment and food. Windhoek was quite unlike any other town that we had encountered in Africa. Its character and architecture was an unusual blend of its German colonial origins with the trappings of a modern, civilised city. On the one hand there were Lutheran churches, German-style civic buildings, cafés offering *apfelstrudel* and *kuchen* linked by streets full of *bratwurst* stalls with names such as Kaiser Street, Bismarck Street and Rehebotherweg. On the other hand there were modern, well-stocked shopping malls, banks operating state of the art computer systems and tourist orientated high-rise hotels. There is an air of affluence. People of all colours and creeds appear to enjoy a high standard of living. All walks of life are well dressed and look healthy. Unlike anywhere else in black Africa it is commonplace to see white people performing menial jobs.

Having completed our business in Windhoek, obtained clearances, prepared the vehicles to the best of our ability and packed up camp for the first time with the new group we set off towards the north-east corner of the country and the Kaudom National Park. We drove due north initially through flat thorn scrubland dominated by impressive rock kopjes. We camped the first night at the foot of some cliffs leading up to the table top plateau that formed the Waterberg mountain. Forked lightning arced across the sky momentarily transposing night into day. We put up the tarpaulins for the first time in two months. I hoped it didn't signal the onset of the short rains. Access to many of Namibia's wilderness regions is extremely tightly controlled by the Afrikaner-dominated Department of Nature Conservation and any rain could seriously thwart our plans.

Next day we drove on under a mantle of cumulus. Good dirt roads let us travel at speed, albeit well spread out to avoid the clouds of dust, through conventional and game farming areas. The latter were rearing giraffe, blesbok, gemsbok, steenbok and duiker. We had to stop for two hours to replace a water pump on Matthew's Land Rover. Again, at the end of the day, whilst driving the last section by headlight to reach Kaudom, we had to stop when acrid smoke began pouring out of the dashboard of my vehicle and all of the wiring burnt out. Sgt Smith headed up an experienced REME team including Cpl Phillips and Cpl Saxon. The three of them were ably assisted by Cpl Peake who oversaw all of the routine driver maintenance and tyre repairs.

Based on the past sands of the Kalahari, Kaudom had large areas of old dunes which although now flat, produced tracks of deep loose sand. Either side dense thornbush was interspersed with sections of wild teak, seringa and bastard mopane woodland. Animal spoor and frequent worn game tracks indicated a large wildlife presence but driving through the thick bush we saw little save the odd hare and a couple of steenbok. The first of the two rivers that crossed the park, the Nhoma River, was bone dry. Where herds of gemsbok, roan and kudu would come down to drink in the wet season the only occupants were a bateleur eagle and a long-tailed shrike.

We ground our way on via a series of boreholes spaced every twelve to twenty miles. These provided the only readily accessible surface water for the game in the dry season. At the Dussi bore a herd of fifty elephants were indulging in their daily routine. Some were drinking, others throwing water over themselves, more competed for salt whilst on the edges of the herd others fed on the mopane trees or wallowed in a dust bath. A large bull kept pushing one of the cows away from the herd and then pursued her to the accompaniment of much squealing until he caught and mounted her. The remainder of the herd gathered around to watch this awesome conjugation.

From Kaudom we made our way across the north of the country westwards through Ovamboland. This region, now the powerbase of the country, was increasingly arid and devoid of vegetation. There was little to identify it as a powerbase. The population was sparse and the few towns along the route were little more than scruffy collections of dilapidated concrete buildings flanked by tin shanties. Positioned just across the border from Angola, Ovamboland had been the scene of much fighting between South African security forces, SWAPO and the Angolan MPLA during the struggle for independence.

Our next goal was the Ruacana Falls, a reputedly dramatic waterfall on the Kunene River looking directly into Angola. As we entered eastern Kaokoland the scenery changed dramatically. The arid plains gave way to heavily vegetated hills and we began to encounter groups of Himba tribesmen. The Himba still maintain a traditional pastoral life, eking out an existence with their herds in the harsh Kaokoveld. Both men and women went bare breasted, clad only in brief leather loin cloths. The women wore their hair plaited in crude styles and their bodies were coated in butterfat and powdered oxides to protect their skin from the hostile climate.

The falls were somewhat disappointing, mainly because there wasn't so much as a trickle of water pouring down the tiered rock. We stopped for the night overlooking the canyon and staring into Angola. I had noticed a small military camp on our approach but having been advised in Windhoek that we could camp by the falls I didn't give it another thought. It seemed perfectly natural for there to be a Namibian army post watching the border. We had just finished setting up and were preparing the vegetables for our evening meal when one of the men said that he thought he could see people moving in the bushes. Imagining that the Namibians had come down to take a look at us I told everyone to ignore them and carry on. A few minutes later two African soldiers stepped out of the bushes and advanced towards us bearing AK47s. When they started talking in Portuguese I began to get the feeling that there was something decidedly wrong. They managed to communicate that they wanted the boss to go with them to their camp to see their Captain. Deciding that discretion was the better part of valour I took CSM Bennett, as the largest member of the team, with me for moral support — disappearing alone into the darkness with AK47-toting Angolan soldiers certainly wasn't my idea of a party. We were escorted into the camp where we were taken to a small reed and thatch hut and told to wait.

Eventually two officers came in with an interpreter. A long, awkward and somewhat simplistic conversation ensued whilst they ascertained who we were and what we were doing. They remained perfectly polite but made it equally clear that we were to pack up and leave immediately, drive back the twelve miles to Ruacana to camp and return in the morning to see the falls if we so desired. We were then escorted, giggling nervously like a pair of chastised schoolboys, to our vehicles. Camp was collapsed in record time under the watchful gaze of several more soldiers and we headed off quickly. I had no intention either of returning to the falls or stopping in Ruacana and so pressed on well beyond into the bush all the while hoping that I hadn't just caused a diplomatic incident.

A spider's web of rough dirt roads led us deeper into the rolling wilds of Kaokoland. Parched hillsides scattered with low coarse scrub were divided by wide valleys carpeted in waves of billowing yellow grass. Infrequent groups of abandoned beehive huts gave away the only trace of Himba families.

One hundred miles further south the small oasis at Sesfontein revealed an old German fort built at the turn of the century to control the spread of rinderpest in the cattle. We continued on to Palmwag.

Friday 19 October was my twenty-seventh birthday. I opened a present from my father and Jenny of several novels to last me on the long drive home. We continued south to Twyfelfontein. On the side of a huge broken rockface we found an enormous array of rock paintings and engravings, far more numerous and stylistically diverse than anything that we had seen elsewhere. Images, dating from the Stone Age, of geometric shapes, spoor, animals and highly stylised humans have been attributed to the Damara people.

We turned west through country that found grandeur in its barrenness. Bare hillsides glowed red, flanking plains swathed in a rich yellow carpet of grass which undulated in the constant wind. In stark contrast lone trees stood sculpted by the same wind into frozen, statuesque postures. As we went on even the grassland disappeared leaving a land devoid of life. A layer of black lichen coated the stony ground adding to the atmosphere of austerity. Finally this bleak, featureless land led us to the sand dunes of the Skeleton Coast.

I was excited by the thought of seeing the sea after so long. Far from the burning hot coastland of my imagination the Skeleton Coast was swept by a persistent chill wind which bit deep into our jerseys and fibrepile jackets. Huge Atlantic rollers crashed down onto the beach. Having come so far we had to go for it so we stripped off and ran into the water. The initial impact of freezing water took your breath away. I dived through the first couple of waves and was then picked up by a third, knocked off my feet and carried somersaulting uncontrollably to be dumped unceremoniously back on the beach. Shivering, I scuttled back to the warmth of my clothes.

The beach divulged its own story. It was strewn with seal skeletons and general flotsam. We found the spoor of hyena but sadly no sign of the few lion that were reputed to have adapted to living off seabirds and seals along the coast. Further along we came to the first of a line of wrecks from which the coastline had got its name and reputation. It was an old wooden-hulled fishing boat, now half buried in the sand. Much of the wood had rotted away exposing a convoluted mass of rusting engine components.

Continuing down the coast we passed out of the confines of the national park and into an unrestricted area. Sea fishermen were gathered at favoured spots, with their large beachcaster rods, hoping to catch steenbras, galjoen and cob. The broken hull of another wreck, *The Winston*, stuck up out of the water a short distance from the shore. Cormorants perched on the few protruding spars. The whole ship was wreathed in spray as successive waves crashed down upon it.

On our way south to Swakopmund we stopped at the seal colony at Cape Cross. It was hard to know where to focus on the colony of upwards of one hundred thousand seals. Wherever you looked every rock was covered by sleeping, basking, grooming or fighting seals. The sea was flecked black with yet more seals either fishing or just enjoying surfing on the waves. The sound was overwhelming: tens of thousands of voices were coughing, barking and bleating like sheep. The smell was similarly overpowering. Carcasses lay amongst the living whilst mangy-looking jackals prowled nearby. Wide-eyed pups, still suckling at their mothers' breasts took cover before bulls weighing up to 300lb. It appeared as a living carpet on land.

At Swakopmund we installed ourselves in a large campsite and took a day off from driving before continuing into the Namib desert. To our south towards Walvis Bay we could make out an area of large dunes. We headed east across endless plains of bare grey gravel, the only vegetation limited to infrequent patches of coarse grass or isolated welwitschia plants. The latter appeared to the uninitiated horticulturist like myself to be rather uninspiring, wilting broad leaved cacti but were held locally in great esteem as a fascinating example of plants deriving moisture solely from the sea fog that spread inland. Periodically we spotted small herds of springbok bouncing away from us or the black and white plumage of male ostrich striding across the waste. Later on, large rock hills rose straight up out of the desert, dominating the sweeping panorama. It was strangely beautiful in a wild, empty way.

The plains ended dramatically at the Kuiseb Canyon. Over millions of years the Kuiseb River had gouged its way down through the gravel over 500 feet deep in places and over half a mile wide. This huge fault concertinaed its way between shale and limestone terraces leaving the dry river bed, a green tree-studded ribbon, far below. The magnificent view complemented the surrounding desert. The Kuiseb River prevented the advance of the enormous sand sea that extended 155 miles to the south. We camped under the shade of some large camelthorn trees at the side of the river bed.

Access to the heart of the Namib is restricted not only by the conservation-minded authorities but also by the total absence of any practicable routes through the sand sea. However, by skirting around to the east, it was possible to continue to the south-east from where we could follow the Tsauchab River 37 miles into the desert to the clay pan of Sossusvlei.

We approached early in the morning following a wide flat plain between low pastel pink dunes. As we drove on the dunes rose in height beside us. The sun was still low enough to accentuate the sweeping curves and snaking ridge lines that climbed up to the star-shaped crests.

Currently dry, the pan consisted of a flat basin of baked clay ringed by camelthorn trees and dominated by massive star dunes on all sides. A scattered herd of noble gemsbok grazed the tussocky dune grass.

It was a wonderfully beautiful place — a fitting location for the southernmost point of the expedition. It had taken us ten months to get here and we now had just under seven weeks to get back to Cameroon. It was time to turn north and tackle the last challenge.

We returned to Windhoek to make some final administrative arrangements. I faxed all of our passport details to the British High Commission in Lusaka with a request for their assistance in obtaining Zaire visas for us. I then rang Pirbright to report our progress. Richard Stanford, who was covering for Alasdair, told me that the Welsh Guards doctor had been sent to Saudi Arabia and that Matthew might have to stand in for the battalion's exercise in Kenya during January. When I passed this on Matthew was less than impressed. He had left behind a fiancée to come on the expedition and was very eager to get married as soon as we got home. I knew that their separation preyed on his mind.

We replaced a windscreen in one of the Land Rovers and then spent the rest of the day in the familiar routine of restocking food, fuel and essential vehicle spares. I laid in some essential supplies for myself: a copy of *Time* magazine to catch up with world affairs, a new pair of shorts, a bottle of whisky and some biltong. In the evening most of the team went out to have dinner or drink in one of the livelier bars.

The men drifted back into camp well into the small hours. One of the guardsmen reappeared at 6am, out of breath, having spent the night making new Welsh Guardsmen to populate Windhoek. Once under way we made good progress to the border crossing at Buitepos only to find to my horror that it was closed. With the alternative a detour of several hundred miles through the Caprivi strip, ghastly thoughts of public holidays or diplomatic disputes leapt into my mind. In the event the cause was rather less dramatic; they had closed for lunch. Only in Africa could they shut an international border for lunch.

We pressed on, retracing our original route back towards Maun. Just before Kalkfontein we came upon a lorry that had rolled, shedding its load of grain and humans. Dazed Africans sat by the roadside nursing their injuries. One man had been killed, others had sustained broken arms and legs and several had serious flesh wounds. I was impressed by the calmness and authority with which Matthew went into action, moving around the casualties swiftly, assessing the priorities and issuing instructions to the two student doctors that we had on the team, Linda Orr and Richard Weekes. Although the nearest hospital was over sixty miles away, one man with a badly broken leg was laid out in the back of a pick-up truck whilst others clambered aboard with all of their luggage, seemingly mindless of his suffering. Another vehicle arrived with a simple metal coffin. It all served to emphasise just how cheaply life is regarded and the fatalistic acceptance with which death and injuries are met.

We left them having done all that we could and drove on until sunset. My Land Rover had developed another problem. This time the tappet adjuster had sheared so the mechanics had to fashion a new one.

The drive from Ghantsi to Maun was unremarkable but took all day bouncing along heavily corrugated roads through clouds of fine choking dust. The only interest was provided by a pair of adult ostriches leading their brood along the track. They refused to move over and ran hell for leather up the track until each chick in turn reached exhaustion and lay pretending to be dead. The chicks were no more than a foot tall and covered in mottled brown bristles. One got stuck in a bush so Tetta jumped out to rescue it. The mother, seeing this, fanned out her feathers and ran off trying to draw us away from her offspring. We managed to herd them all back together except for the adult male who resolutely refused to budge and was running further and further from his family. In the end I put my foot down. He was matching us at 40mph when he finally veered away.

At Maun we linked up as arranged with Liz and Bud Whittaker. It was great to see them again. They were escorting a British artist who had come to do some paintings to raise money for 'Save the Rhino'. Their vehicle was fairly shaky and they wanted to travel under our safety umbrella on the off-route sections back to Zimbabwe. They had so much kit with them that the vehicle looked almost certain to break down.

We planned to skirt the Okovango Delta eastwards taking three days to drive through the Moremi and Chobe game reserves and cross into Zimbabwe at Kanyemba. The first day took us up a bewildering diversity of narrow tracks into Moremi. We camped in a near perfect setting in the shade of a small wood overlooking a deep grassy flood plain which led down to two small waterholes. The wood was alive with the song of grey lowries, fork-tailed drongos and brightly coloured Meyer's parrots. The plains were covered with herds of impala, tsessebe, hartebeest and red lechwe. At the waterhole herons, egrets, plover and spoonbills all paddled out of range of the crocodiles. The Whittakers' party provided great amusement by being totally disorganised and taking ages to sort themselves out. They had every conceivable camping luxury from mattresses to a portable shower but they were always buried under the mound of other equipment when required. As I went to bed a large herd of elephants passed close by in a long line of looming grey shadows.

On the edge of the flood plain we passed a single Cape hunting dog feeding on its kill, a lechwe. We left the lush greenness of the plain and went back into the hot, dry thorn scrub. Several hours driving on some fairly horrific sandtracks brought us to the entrance to Chobe National Park. Still in the dry season and suffering from the ravages of an extended regional drought Chobe was oppressively arid and colourless. Most of the wildlife had migrated north to the Zambesi. We saw almost nothing for twenty-five miles until we reached the first major water source at Savuti Marsh. In comparison to the bare scrubland that we had driven through, Savuti was a mini paradise. Hornbills and doves flitted between green acacia trees and patches of succulent grass. Herds of elephant, tsessebe, impala, hartebeest and wildebeest were grazing in the immediate vicinity. We continued past one more waterhole near the park gate before camping in the thick bush out of the park just beyond the Goha Hills.

The next day's drive to the Zimbabwe border and on to Victoria Falls was unremarkable. The Whittakers opted to take a longer route through the park, following along the side of the Zambesi and were rewarded with the sight of a herd of over a thousand zebra together with many elephants, hippos and plains game.

We stopped at Victoria Falls for one day to give this team a chance to experience a short section of white water rafting. I joined up with one of the Zimbabwean raft guides and put a team together including Richard Gaffney, Matthew, Alasdair, Gnr Reid and Gnr Searl to take on the biggest water available. It was great to get back on to the water.

We set out from Victoria Falls on Thursday 1 November. I went ahead in my Land Rover in an attempt to get to Lusaka in time to start the visa application process. We arrived at the British Embassy just as it was closing. We did however catch the Post Office in time. I had two letters. One from Jenny saying that all was well at home and one from Paddy Fleming saying that we were welcome to camp in his garden again.

As soon as the lorries arrived we drove in convoy out to Paddy's house where we set up camp. I went in to see him and exchange our news. He was in typically excellent form and full of enquiries about our exploits. As we began to chat through our future plans, together with his two partners, Grahame and Susie, the seriousness of our undertaking began to emerge. They had all been asking around on our behalf but no one had any information about our intended route or any idea which roads were passable and which were not. The short rains had started in Northern Zaire and were making their way south. If the rivers were in flood, the ferries wouldn't be working and if any bridges were down we certainly wouldn't be able to ford the rivers. In either instance the infrequency of tracks meant that we would have to retrace our route and make a detour of, potentially, hundreds of miles. Different theories were passed around over a bottle of whisky. I had planned on a central route taking a fairly direct line north from Lubumbashi to Kisangani. Paddy favoured a more easterly route staying on the watershed away from the big rivers. The theory behind his argument was good but none of us knew of anyone having got through that way. Grahame suggested an intermediate line maintaining the option of escape in either direction if we came to an impassable problem.

To add to the problem of route finding there was now a chronic fuel shortage throughout Zaire and northern Zambia due to the Gulf Crisis. The railways had already stopped running, and the mining companies were so desperate that they were freighting fuel overland from Dar es Salaam and Durban. What little fuel there was in Zaire was being reserved to keep the mines going. Aside from that they had heard that diesel was being sold on the blackmarket in litre Coca-Cola bottles and paid for in gold dust — not a commodity readily available on the Roof of Africa Expedition. In many of the remoter parts of the country that we would be passing through Paddy said that there was little use for money and all acquisitions were bartered for. It was virtually certain that these outposts wouldn't have been resupplied with fuel for some time.

This presented me with a major logistical problem. It was approximately two thousand miles to Kisangani and our fuel carrying capacity was sufficient for approximately twelve hundred miles on bad roads. I got Richard Gaffney, CSM Bennett and Richard Weekes, who was running the fuel account, together to do some sums and work out our options. Paddy kept passing the whisky bottle around, roaring with laughter and exclaiming over and over again with great glee: 'Shit, you are going to have some problems'. The long and short of it was that we needed to cut the weight that the vehicles had to carry down to an absolute minimum, sell or trade any equipment that we didn't need and buy enough 45-gallon drums to carry the requisite amount of fuel. The next day was going to be hectic. We needed to get visas, buy drums and extra fuel, make some vehicle repairs, replace a windscreen, resupply food, visit Poste Restante and try to find out which of the red lines on our map bore any relation to usable roads in the jungle.

I went to bed with a myriad of thoughts and ideas whirling inside my head. The implications of not getting through were far from straightforward. The escape route to the west via Kinshasa meant passing through the Congo for which we didn't have political clearance. To the east we were hemmed in initially by Lake Tanganyika, then by Burundi for which we didn't have clearance. Rwanda was in the midst of an emergency with the Hutu and Tutsi engaged in civil war and north of that was Uganda from where the rebel Tutsi army had mounted their attack and for which we also didn't have clearance to enter. Added to all of that and assuming that we did get through there was no guarantee that we would be able to get sufficient fuel in Kisangani to take us the final two thousand miles to Douala. It was beginning to look increasingly likely that we would finish late but I was determined that somehow we would get through.

First thing in the morning I held a team briefing to explain our situation and the problems facing us. They took it all well and set about making the preparations. I then went to Paddy's office which temporarily became the Roof of Africa Office. Richard and Alasdair took off on the visa trail. CSM Bennett went off with one of Paddy's drivers to go and find fuel drums and vehicle spares and I went to see a contact of Paddy and Grahame's at the Belgian Embassy.

The Belgians had been the colonial power in Zaire and up until recently had had a major influence in the running of the country. However, with the exception of their main embassy in Kinshasa they had withdrawn all diplomatic representation following a row over an alleged massacre of students in Lubumbashi by Mobutu's Presidential Guard earlier in the year. Mr Vyter Haegan shook his head when he heard our plans with a look of sympathy bordering on pity. He advised us to go to Lubumbashi and seek further advice from the American and French consulates there and the White Fathers Mission Headquarters. The latter was an organisation of missionaries spread throughout the deepest, darkest areas of jungle with a reputation for fairly hard drinking. They had a radio network between Missions and were most likely to know which routes were passable. Adding finally that we should be aware that the areas around some of the gold mines were closed to foreigners he wished us *'bonne chance'*.

Richard had been given a letter of recommendation by the British High Commission who had been very helpful and rung the Zairean Embassy stressing their support and the need for haste. At the Zaire Embassy despite having to re-do all of the forms and chase around getting more passport photographs all went well. He was told to return at 3pm to pick up the visas.

Back at the office I found CSM Bennett had been having a hard time in the markets. There was a shortage of fuel drums, no fuel in most of the pumps and although he had received a lot of interest in some of the kit that he was trying to offload no one was producing any hard cash. I rang Pirbright to appraise them of our situation.

At this stage everything started to go wrong. Richard came rushing back from the embassy highly agitated. The Zaireans were now refusing to issue the visas without authorisation from Kinshasa. He had been told to come back on Monday. He had pleaded with them and then lost his temper but all to no avail. I went back to try a more conciliatory line. I saw the Deputy Ambassador and despite my most placatory tone in my best French he remained polite but adamant. They had signalled for advice from Kinshasa but didn't expect an answer before Monday. If they didn't get a reply then, the Ambassador would make the decision whether to issue us with visas or not. There was nothing for it but to go back to the office. We could ill afford any delays. I telephoned Pirbright again with the news.

Back at the campsite I found CSM Bennett in a muck sweat. After a whole day flogging around the back streets he had managed to buy only one fuel drum. Paddy then played his joker and set up a meeting the next day with Laurie Davis, the managing director of BP Zambia. The mechanics had done an excellent job on the Bedford front springs. By cannibalising a spare they had fitted an additional leaf to each to help take the weight of the extra fuel. Various of Paddy's neighbours had come over and there was wheeling and dealing over equipment going on wherever I looked.

On Saturday I went to see Laurie Davis who very kindly said that BP could give us six drums so long as we picked them up from one of their depots at Kitwe or Ndola on our way north. We would also be able to buy sufficient fuel to fill the drums there.

Meanwhile the mechanics had found further problems with the vehicles. CSM Bennett disappeared back to the markets to hunt for a matching fan and waterpump. The clutch bearings had gone on Matthew's Land Rover. To fix them meant lifting out the entire engine, replacing the bearings and plate and then refitting the engine. Using the Bedfords, both straightbars, a pulley and one of the tirfor winches they rigged up an ingenious hoist. It worked perfectly albeit nearly at the cost of Alasdair's fingers. The bearings had burnt out completely. They also changed the starter motor which was on the way out. Getting the engine back in was more difficult. It took over an hour of sweating, cursing, pushing and pulling to ease it back onto its mountings. I began to question whether the vehicles were going to stand up to the route ahead. All of the major components appeared to be worn out.

Next day I woke up late at 8.15am with the sun already well up and the day hot. The mechanics were working on the Land Rover to complete refitting the engine. I spent the day cleaning the cameras, sorting out odd paperwork and rescuing kit from the termites which had come up through the earth and were busily eating their way through anything on the ground.

On Monday morning we packed up camp. I was waiting at the Zaire Embassy as it opened to pick up the visas. I was told that they would be issued but to process the passports would take all morning and I should return at 2pm. My protestations fell on deaf ears and I was shown out. I went back to Paddy's office where I sat watching the clock and distracting them from doing any work.

At 2pm the Zaireans pretended that it had all been a big mistake and I should return at 3pm. I realised that this was just another stalling tactic and rushed round to the British High Commission to try and elicit their help. The Deputy Consul rang the Zaire Embassy only to be told that they were still waiting to hear from Kinshasa and wouldn't issue the visas until they had. After some consultation they then upped the ante by sending a letter from the High Commissioner to the Zairean Ambassador requesting his assistance to resolve the matter quickly.

I waited a short while to give the letter time to be delivered and read, and then followed it. This time I was shown in to see the Ambassador's private secretary who apologised profusely but said that the Ambassador had just gone home and nothing could be done until morning, however a decision would definitely be taken then. It smacked horribly of another stalling tactic and I wasn't hopeful of getting the visas unless the required authority arrived in time. Presumably the Ambassador had only reached his exalted rank by never taking any decisions. I drove back to the others, practically weeping with frustration.

First thing in the morning I returned to the breach once more. This time I was confronted by the crotchety old matriarch on the front desk who told me to go away and come back at 2pm. No reason was given. I wasn't going to be fobbed off this time. I asked why we must wait but got no reply. I asked to see the Private Secretary. No. Had a message come from Kinshasa? Yes. Would we now get the visas? No reply. Where was the Ambassador? Busy. When it became obvious that I wasn't going to move she made another telephone call. Shortly afterwards the Private Secretary appeared with a very smart gentleman who turned out to be none other than the Ambassador himself. He didn't speak much English so we talked in French. He still hadn't received word from Kinshasa and feared that it would take several more days. At this my heart lurched. As a result he had now made the decision to issue the visas and if I returned at 11am I could pick them up — but of course I should be prepared for it to take a little longer. I thanked him profusely and left on the assumption that if he had wanted to stall longer he wouldn't have seen me in person.

True to his word when we went back at 11am the visas were ready, however not without a problem. The central team, all of whom had a previous Zaire visa in their passports, had been granted two-month visas but the remainder had only been given thirty days. This added a further potential problem if we dropped behind time. The thought of going through the entire charade again to renew them was less than inviting.

After hurried goodbyes and grateful thanks for all their assistance to Paddy, Grahame and Sue we set off northwards at last. There was a surprising amount of traffic as we drove up to the Copper Belt. We arrived at Ndola as it was getting dark and following Laurie Davis's directions went in search of the BP refinery. The approach road to the refinery was guarded by an army checkpoint. The soldiers were fairly aggressive, demanding to know who we were, what we were doing there and searching the vehicles. When they came to Maurice, the Weston Spirit member on this phase they started talking to him in their local dialect. When he couldn't reply to their questions they started getting angry and I had to quickly intervene. We had experienced minor problems like this before. Maurice was an extremely streetwise eighteen-year-old Jamaican who now lived with his family in Cardiff. Wherever he went he was treated with great curiosity and sometimes suspicion by the Africans. Some didn't expect anyone from Britain to be black and others couldn't understand why he was travelling overland with a group of white people. Paddy's cook had told him that he thought that we were very well organised bringing our servant all the way from England. The rest of the men were delighted with this idea but not altogether surprisingly Maurice wasn't. On another occasion in Namibia there was a very awkward atmosphere when he walked into a bar with us that was full of Afrikaners.

The soldiers kept asking him questions and when I explained that he was English one replied 'But he is black like me', inferring that it wasn't possible for someone in Britain to be black. I felt sorry for Maurice who was clearly uncomfortable. Despite his happy-go-lucky exterior he was finding much of what he saw of the Africans and the way that they lived, to which by reason of his ancestry he had a strong affinity, both alien and perplexing.

We talked our way through the checkpoint and found the depot manager waiting for us. He had five drums for us. We topped up every available tank and drum to the brim and then turned north again.

We crossed into Zaire with no problems and carried straight on to Lubumbashi, the capital of Shaba province. There we tracked down the British Honorary Consul in search of any route information that he could give us. To my total horror he insisted that I should make a courtesy call on the Vice Governor of Shaba District to obtain a *laissez-passer*. He explained that the political situation was very fragile due to the imposition of tight military control in the wake of the student riots. In view of this less than ideal situation I felt compelled to take the Consul's advice. Deciding on a new tactic I went with him dressed to impress in hastily pressed and dusted down shirt, tie, trousers and Guards' boating jacket. Two days later after yet another session of stonewalling, prevarication and being pushed around from pillar to post I decided that we couldn't wait any longer and would have to take our chances. I changed gratefully back into my well-worn T-shirt and shorts and having collected the team we slipped quietly out of town.

We made the best speed possible. The next town of any consequence, Likasi, was seventy-five miles away. Until we were past there I was worried that a radio message from Lubumbashi might get us stopped and turned back. Driving through the town a shiver went down my spine as I looked nervously for any military checkpoints. Once we were through I was fairly confident that barring a major incident with the police our problems lay with the route itself.

We turned north at Guba, away from the main Kolwezi road, through lush, verdant bush that made a pleasant change from the dusty aridness of the Kalahari and southern Zambia. Open plains gave way to rolling hills and steep escarpments. Rain swept the hillsides to our east. On the road puddles and patches of dark mud indicated previous downpours. We camped just beyond Lubudi beneath a heavily clouded sky, lit by frequent lightning flashes. We had covered 230 miles which made up for some of the time that we had lost. With a month to go to our sailing date, Douala was approximately 3,000 miles of mainly rough jungle tracks away. We needed every available moment of driving time to maintain an average of 100 miles per day. I brought reveille forward to 5am so that we could be on the road by 6am each day as it became light.

Twenty miles of almost continuous tight hairpin bends took us through a steep mountainous area until we rejoined the main Kolwezi to Kamina track. Excellent graded dirt roads either side of the mining project at Luena quickly degenerated back into narrow potholed tracks. We passed many simple villages. Around each of the mud brick and grass roofed huts the beaten earth was kept spotlessly clean. The children waved and cheered as we passed. It was amusing to watch the new members of the team who hadn't experienced this before waving back manically. In my Land Rover we had little time to appreciate this as Gnr Read was driving as though he was taking part in a demolition derby. Despite several pointed comments about the importance of vehicle husbandry he seemed unable to read the road and soundly clobbered almost every one of the frequent potholes.

We drove into Kabongo the next morning to the sound of pealing bells calling the congregation to the Mission Church. At home it was Remembrance Sunday. In Kabongo it was also market day so we fought our way through the throng to stock up with bread, pineapples, avocados, bananas, tomatoes and peanuts. We drew the line at the local delicacy of mounds of writhing termites. The women grinned with ghoulish delight at our disgust.

We took the new route to Boudi avoiding a section of *trés mauvais piste.* Storm clouds had been amassing all morning and as we stopped for lunch a major storm passed to the west of us. Beyond Boudi the track was blighted with huge potholes and deep pools of water. It suddenly became very dark. A cannonade of thunder cracked overhead preceding bolts of forked lightning and torrential rain. Our windscreen wipers could barely cope with the deluge and visibility was reduced to just a few yards. Within moments the track had turned into a stream with water coursing towards us. The volume of surface water was such that it concealed all but the largest holes. You had to try and read the water like a river, looking for the tell-tale swirls to give away submerged rocks or holes.

At times the Land Rovers plunged into water up to their doors but we managed to keep going until we came across a fallen tree blocking the route. It had only just come down. Donning Goretex jackets and trekking boots we leapt out into the elements and began clearing the obstruction. When machetes, axes and brute force couldn't cope we used the electric Warn winches on the Land Rovers to haul the tree out of the way. As we continued we found several more trees and large branches across the track. With each bolt of lightning I feared the crack of a tree overhead coming down on top of one of the vehicles.

The Bedfords were having a hard time of the conditions. On three occasions one or other bogged down to its axles having slid off the centre of the track into the ditch. I was pleased to see how slick the teams were at the winch recovery operations. However we had slowed up considerably and I feared that this was only a taste of what was to come.

We woke to a dank, dark morning. Thick mist enveloped the wood that we had camped in. Above us the crescent-shaped moon was still visible surrounded by a circle of opalescent light. An otherwise good night's sleep had been spoiled by a rather refined torture; after several heavy showers, water had dripped through the canopy landing on my head in great fat droplets every thirty seconds. I had tried to ignore it for as long as I could but eventually it got too much. I had wriggled and fought my way into my bivvi bag and lain congratulating myself that I was immune to outside influences and could now go to sleep when reveille was given.

North of Nyasa the road became much better. I was amazed to find almost perfectly smooth dirt road with very few potholes. We passed Ebombo and turned east towards Kongolo and the Zaire River. Driving conditions were near perfect, although I could see cumulus clouds building up to our north. I was driving the front vehicle and consciously cut the convoy speed slightly, not wanting to get carried away with the need for speed. At the end of the first hour's driving in the afternoon I stopped to let the Bedfords catch up. Whilst we waited I read Richard's diary of the stretch between Yaounde and Kisangani. It read rather worse than I remembered with several comments like 'very deep potholes today. We made it through but I would hate to have to do it in the wet season'. I wondered if I had underestimated that part of the route.

As I was reading I hadn't noticed the time passing until Gdsm Harris commented that the other Land Rover was taking a surprisingly long time to catch up. I imagined that they had stopped to repair a puncture or buy some fruit in one of the villages. At that point a Bedford pulled up and Cpl Saxon jumped out. The Land Rover was several miles further back and upside down in the ditch, no one was badly hurt but would I come. As I turned around and made my way back to the scene I dreaded what I might find. I recalled the initial planning meetings all that time ago in Pirbright. When discussing various emergency scenarios we had always said that the worst case possible would be a vehicle accident involving multiple injuries or worse in the Zaire jungle where there were no communications and help would be hundreds if not thousands of miles away.

As I pulled up, the second Bedford was across the road blocking any oncoming vehicles. CSM Bennett came forward to brief me. Matthew had been driving. He had swerved to avoid a pothole and gone into a skid. I could imagine with the Land Rover's very soft suspension how it must have swayed. He had fought to regain control but they had clipped the verge and rolled, ending upside down in the middle of the road. Matthew and Richard Weekes, who were in the front, had smashed into the windscreen which shattered but fortunately neither of them had gone through it. Both had blood on their chests and faces. Matthew had a bandage on his elbow and Richard had the fingers of his right hand bound together. Sitting in the back Tetta had fared worse. She was now sitting in a chair beside the road being comforted and tended by Linda. She was covered in grazes and cuts and there were smears of blood and dirt all over her body. A bandage around her mouth concealed a deep cut through her top lip. She was shocked and a little tearful but basically okay. Somehow Linda had got away unscathed.

Looking at the vehicle they had been incredibly lucky not to sustain worse injuries. The front right wing had taken the brunt of the impact and was badly buckled. The entire left side had been bashed in and fittings such as mirrors and doorhandles ripped off. The bonnet was folded and torn. Glass from the windscreen was everywhere. The window frame was ripped and buckled. The roof had caved in at the front and the roof rack had been torn from its mountings. Kit was strewn all over the road. Most of the diesel from both tanks had leaked out giving them a nasty moment when they had come to their senses stuck in the upturned vehicle. They had scrambled out through the windows.

By the time that I had arrived the vehicle had been righted and the mechanics were busy checking it over. Amazingly the damage was mainly limited to the bodywork. The chassis, axles, wheels and engine appeared undamaged. They set up a tirfor winch to pull out the worst of the damage to the front end. After a bit more hammering and having removed all of the dangerous bits of jagged metal and glass Sgt Smith passed it fit to be driven a short distance until they could start making full repairs. Again we were lucky. It would have been nigh on impossible to drag a useless vehicle for the next 2,000 miles.

Those who had been in the accident had fortified themselves with several whiskies whilst we were waiting for the mechanics' verdict. Matthew seemed remarkably unaffected by the accident and well in control. He said that they hadn't been going at all fast and in fact had commented on how slowly we were going in front. Having gone into the skid he hadn't had room on the narrow track to control it and over they went. We decided to go on to Kongolo to see if we could get any help from a large agricultural company there.

We limped along slowly. The boss of the agricultural company was away and his deputy was neither friendly nor welcoming. Instead he pointed us in the direction of a hospital in the small town. We didn't need medical attention or equipment; just a clean place with water where Matthew could get to work and stitch up the various injuries. We were shown into a very sombre building by a doctor. He took us to a bare room with a desk and folding couch. There was no light and cold water was provided in buckets.

I managed to persuade Matthew to take off his T-shirt, which closely resembled an oily rag. He began cleaning first himself and then Tetta with cetriclens. The cut on her lip was deep but straight. He injected her with a local anaesthetic and then put in two stitches. He seemed confident that she wouldn't scar badly. Linda took over the cleaning of all the cuts and grazes on her back and arms and then mummified her with bandages. Matthew turned his attention to Richard Weekes, cleaning up his fingers and covering them with plasters. They then all changed roles and Linda fixed steristrips across a deep cut on the inside of Matthew's elbow. It made a strange sight to see doctor treating doctor but rubbed in the folly of having all the medics travelling in the same vehicle. As before I was impressed with the calm authoritative way that Matthew ran the operation. He might be innately idle when faced with the mundane tasks involved in camp routine but he was certainly a useful bloke to have around in a crisis.

Outside the hospital a large crowd had gathered around the vehicles. Foreigners were an extreme rarity in Kongolo. Leaving the others where they were I went back to the agricultural company to see if the boss had returned. He hadn't, so I gave it up as a bad job. When I got back to the hospital the other vehicles had disappeared. I drove around until I found them outside the Town Commissaire's office looking rather stressed. They had been waiting for me to return when two soldiers had approached and ordered Cpl Saxon to accompany them with all of the vehicles. To emphasise the point they had cocked their AK47s and pointed them at him. Various members of the team had been subjected to some fairly aggressive questioning. I went in to see the Commissaire and find out what the problem was. It transpired that they were expecting a VIP visit by the Prime Minister and six other ministers the next day. It was no wonder that the security forces were jumpy. They were as keen as we were to see us on our way and so having taken our passport and vehicle details they let us go, warning us to stay clear of the area. We left town by a railway bridge over the Zaire River. We checked carefully to ensure that no train was coming and then drove along the rails. There was one large hole in the middle but we found a metal sheet to cover it.

We carried on slowly for about five miles until we found a quarry beside a small village where we could pull off the track. I went to find the village head man. Having got his agreement we set up camp and began sorting out the day's events. The mechanics set to work on the rolled Land Rover. They began by putting a high-lift jack inside the driver's door and jacking the roof back up. Then they cut out the windscreen surround and took it off to knock it back into shape and rivet on new strengthening sections of metal. Fortunately we still had the remainder of the perspex that we had bought in Bangui so they began to cut it to shape.

Tetta was beginning to stiffen up, and, as the anaesthetic wore off, she became quite uncomfortable. We finished late. It had been a long day for everyone. When I got up for stag at 3am the mechanics were still at work. They had fitted the windscreen into its frame and were bolting it back into place. The perspex was cracked in a couple of places but they had patched it up with a second piece. They finished just after 4am.

After a late reveille at 7am we continued to sort ourselves out. The mechanics went on panel beating the Land Rover. They cut off the front of the roof rack to prevent any weight being placed on the damaged windscreen frame. The rest of us emptied all of the vehicles, laid out mounds of wet, muddy clothing to dry and cleaned whatever possible.

We were back on the road at 9.30am just as a storm broke over us. Road conditions became appalling. We were no longer on sand but thick greasy mud. The vehicles spun all over the place. After a couple of miles the damaged Land Rover slipped off the track onto its side in the ditch. A simple winch operation with the electric winch on my vehicle extricated it.

We continued on at little more than a crawl, slithering and sliding our way between deep potholes. On one occasion we drove into a long puddle only to plunge into water that came over the bonnet. We just managed to power through in low gear without stalling. In the first hour we covered seven miles. There was nothing that we could do to speed up our progress, we just had to carry on the best way that we could.

After another hour we came to a gaping trench that had been eroded diagonally across the track extending for about forty yards. In the Land Rovers we were able to squeeze past it but we then had to wait for almost an hour before the Bedfords caught up. One had bogged in. When they arrived Richard suggested to Cpl Peake, the driver of the front Bedford, that he get out and recce the problem with a view to preparing a route to the left. Instead he decided to go straight for it straddling the trench. He made it almost to the top when the trench wall collapsed and the lorry sank in up to its rear axle. We tried anchoring one of the Land Rovers with tirfor plates and pins and Scotch plates, and then winching the lorry out on a 2:1 pull from the rear Bedford, but the anchor plates lifted straight out of the soft ground and the Land Rover slithered forward. The second Bedford then tried to drive past the bogged vehicle to get in a position to tow it out but in the attempt became stuck itself. Over the next few hours we tried everything to get the two vehicles out. Winch systems were employed in a variety of configurations, sand ladders laid and three trees cut into logs to fill the main trench. As various options were tried and failed the frustration increased and tempers frayed. I stood back and tried to act as mediator. In the end we winched the second Bedford out backwards, filled in the trench, reconfigured the winch from the front of the vehicle and half drove half winched it past the first truck. Having anchored it securely with all of the chocks and plates that we could muster, backed up by cables to the Land Rovers, we winched the other Bedford forwards and out of the ditch.

In front the route was no better. Before we had covered another mile we all had to stop and use sand ladders to negotiate an awkward slant in the track. A couple of miles further on a Bedford bogged in and was extricated by a simple tow out. Two more miles and the front Bedford slipped off the road and ended up in the ditch leaning on a tree. By the end of the day we had covered just twenty miles.

We stopped at the first village that we came to, about a mile further on. A large crowd clustered around us as we set up camp on the only available flat patch of ground. Everyone was exhausted. It had been hard physical graft all the way. Cpl Phillips found out from the locals that we could expect similar conditions for at least the next 100 miles, until we reached Kasongo. Having been brought up in Tanzania he could talk to them in fluent Swahili which worked better in these remote areas than my basic French.

We had to push start both Land Rovers in the morning. After a mainly dry night the road conditions were marginally better than they had been although the top layer was still very greasy. Setting off cautiously, we covered seven miles in the first hour and two miles in the second, having dug the Bedford out a couple of times. Further on conditions got worse again. Frequent deep channels had been carved across the track by storm run-off. At best negotiating these involved careful recces, preparation with sand ladders and logs and accurate driving in low ratio, at worst we became involved in more winch rescues. We reached a long Bailey bridge over the Luama River with badly rotted planking. We sent the vehicles over one at a time using sand ladders in relays to cover the gaps.

At Lusangi the mud gave way to sand. We started making better progess along a straight narrow road through huge stands of overhanging bamboo until the Bedfords began bogging into the sand. Three times they dug themselves out before the winch Bedford sank in to its axles. No amount of digging or laying sand ladders would shift it. We rigged the heavy pulley to a tree. When Cpl Saxon tried to engage the winch there was the scream of a slipping ratchet and clouds of thick oily smoke but no pull. After an hour it still couldn't be coaxed into action. This was potentially extremely serious. Without the powerful Bedford winch, with its 50 yard cable, it would be almost impossible to recover the lorries if they became badly bogged. Even with our full selection of winches and twenty of us working flat out digging, pushing and heaving it was proving hard.

With darkness approaching I sent Matthew on ahead to find a campsite and try and collect some fresh water. We dug in relays until we had cleared the sand away from the front and rear differentials and inserted sand ladders as far under the wheels as we could get them. After what seemed like an age of banging, grinding and revving, grimy-faced grins from the mechanics indicated that they had got the winch back into action. It was 7pm by the time that the vehicle winched itself free. We reached the next village in the pitch dark. There was still a lot of work to do before people could turn in. The duty team set up camp and prepared the evening meal whilst the mechanics worked on the winch and the clutch in my Land Rover and all the others helped change tyres and fix wires onto Matthew's Land Rover to protect the windscreen from foliage sticking out across the track. We broke open a crate of beer that we had been saving to celebrate Gdsm Harris' twentieth birthday.

I woke up twice during the night to the sound of heavy rain. By the time that we got up at 5am the campsite was a quagmire and the track had turned into a mud slide. Outside the village the road was impossibly narrow with deep, soft-walled ditches either side. As soon as the Bedford wheels caught in channels or old vehicle ruts their momentum carried them uncontrollably forward until they slipped into the ditch. We had gone less than a mile when the winch Bedford bogged in. For the rest of the morning we winched, dug and dragged our way along. After five hours we had covered seven miles. At this rate it could take another three days to reach Kasongo and if the route beyond wasn't any better we hadn't a hope of making it to Douala in time to catch the ship. I began working through various options, one of which was to see if we could put the Bedfords on a riverboat to Lisala and drive on with the Land Rovers. It wasn't something that I wanted to do but without the Bedfords we could make much better time and still complete our intended route. Not only were the Land Rovers faster but they bogged in far less often and when they did they were so light that they were relatively easy to extricate.

Fortunately, bar one short shower, the sun shone all morning. We had lunch in a small village schoolhouse after the umpteenth recovery of the day. By now recoveries were a familiar routine. The mechanics made their plan and controlled the winching whilst the rest of us dug, sledge-hammered in anchor spikes, pushed and generally wallowed in the mud at their direction. Although individuals had off-days the team was generally working well.

After a morning of drying the road improved noticeably. Although rarely getting above second gear we began to make consistent progress, slowly covering twenty miles to Maas. We were driving across the grain of the country and thus were frequently dropping into valleys and climbing out the far side. In the valley bottoms shoulder-high grass filled the open spaces between giant palm fronds and bamboo archways. The worst potential hazard were the many crude bridges which rarely consisted of more than tree trunks laid side by side across an obstacle. If a vehicle was to slip on these and drop a wheel into any of the gaps or rotten sections we risked shattering axles, differential locks or steering linkage. Each vehicle crept over carefully guided by a man in front.

Maas was grey and cheerless, an unwelcome change from the clean jungle villages with their friendly inhabitants and cheering children. We passed through without stopping. A better road took us on towards Kasongo. I had just decided to stop for the night at the next village that we came to when the rear Bedford lost traction on a downhill slope and careered into the ditch. Sgt Smith said that he had lost all steering and sure enough when he looked under the vehicle the steering rod had snapped. Luckily we carried a spare which didn't take long to fit despite the lorry's awkward position. However the recovery took a lot longer. The vehicle couldn't be driven out and a 1:1 winch failed to pull it free. In the absence of any convenient trees we ended up fixing anchor plates. Swinging the heavy sledgehammers onto hand-held spikes in the dark was fairly hazardous. Once again it was after 7pm by the time that we had set up camp. The days were long and physically demanding and with stags every other night on top of the routine chores, everyone was getting increasingly tired.

Kasongo was a large sprawling town based on the usual grid system of boulevards. It was even more decayed than the other Zairean towns that we had seen and appeared as almost a mockery of its peeling colonial facade. The walls of buildings were cracked and bare, the roads broken by trenches and potholes and there was a general feeling of squalor. Most of the market stalls were either empty or offering a motley selection of flyblown fruit, water was rationed and diesel was on offer in rusty cans at a black market rate equivalent to £10 per gallon.

There was a popular vote to clear out of town as quickly as possible. It was strange to have striven so hard for four days to get there only to rush away. We stopped in a village a few miles further on to get some water. Most of the villages collected their water from springs a short distance into the jungle. A guide led us out of the back of the village along a well beaten footpath and down to a small clearing in the jungle. We caused quite a commotion by surprising several semi-naked girls washing. They covered themselves quickly, giggling to each other, and then became quite coquettish as they helped us fill our jerricans. The water source was so low that we had to fill up the girls' cooking pots and then empty them into our cans. It was a slow process with lots of spillage but I didn't mind as it was the first really clear water that I had seen for days. Several people had been suffering from diarrhoea and vomiting which had certainly been caused by bad water.

We drove on taking advantage of the dry conditions to make up as much ground as possible. At dusk we hit a really bad patch. I fervently hoped that we weren't going to have a repetition of the previous night and my heart went into my mouth when the rear Bedford went into a broadside slide but we got away with it and stopped in a small mud courtyard surrounded by a square of huts.

A half-day's driving, negotiating more rotten log bridges, took us to Kindu. The main part of the town was on the other side of the Zaire River so Matthew took a party across by pirogue to do the shopping. Those of us that remained behind fended off a multitude of requests from aeroplane tickets to our addresses at home. The mechanics took the rare opportunity of a daylight stop to check over the vehicles. The brake pads on my vehicle had to be changed together with the panhard bushes on the other Land Rover. Cpl Peake saw a man with withered legs peddling himself along by hand on a tricycle with a flat tyre. He made a fuss of the man, settling him in comfort while he mended the puncture for him. It was sad to see his disappointment when the African showed no gratitude for this kindness. It was by no means unusual and more a difference in custom than an expression of true sentiment.

Once Matthew had returned laden with fresh vegetables and bread we sped north along a good stretch of road until we turned off onto the track towards Punia and Kisangani. We had heard very mixed reports of this route which one local had described as 'catastrophic'. We carried on for about seven more miles until we came to a small village with a cleared football pitch. There was a festival in progress. Many of the children were covered in flour and most of the adults had clearly been drinking. The head man kindly allowed us to camp on the football pitch. A large crowd turned out to watch us set up. You could instantly feel the difference between these people and those in the town. Here, they were far more friendly and less grasping.

The head man came to see me with some of the village elders bringing with him a present of an egg. We pulled up camp stools and served them tea. He had noticed the ICI Pharmaceuticals logo on the vehicles and asked if we had any medicines so we arranged to sort some out for him to collect in the morning. The crowd stayed whilst we carried out our camp chores and had supper. I noticed several of the expedition members giving their food away to the children. They weren't the first people, and certainly wouldn't be the last, to fall under the spell of the African children. They were genuine, warm and friendly and loved to laugh. As we lay in our campbeds the air reverberated with the sound of drums and singing from the village. It was a wonderful rich sound, both rhythmic and harmonious, that stirred primeval emotions across the breadth of the continent.

We gave the head man a supply of nivaquine and then set off on a first class dirt road for the next fifty miles. Having made excellent progress we were slowed up considerably by an area of deep water-filled potholes. We managed to grind our way through each until we were confronted by an absolute monster. The walls of the pothole were the height of our lorries and there was two to three feet of water and glutinous mud in the bottom. I dropped into four wheel drive, low ratio and engaged the differential lock hoping to grind my way through. I bogged straight in to my axles. Matthew seeing this went, equally impetuously, for the main hole. The entry ramp was so steep that the front of his vehicle rammed the bottom and stuck fast. Both of the Land Rovers were now hopelessly bogged side by side.

When the Bedfords arrived they were highly amused to see the Land Rovers stuck for a change. There was always a healthy rivalry between the crews of the two types of vehicle. By the time that we were all on the north side it had taken four hours of digging, hammering, cutting and screaming winches. Everyone was soaking wet and plastered in mud.

The remainder of the day was a succession of deeply rutted holes and bad bridges. I put the Bedfords into the lead, to their vocal delight. I travelled as passenger in the front lorry chatting to Cpl Peake. Richard crashed out in the back of our Land Rover. For the last forty-eight hours he had been suffering from chronic headaches. Matthew wasn't sure what the problem was but thought that it might be a form of malaria. The medical side of life was fairly busy. Several people had got cuts on their arms and legs that wouldn't heal and were turning septic. In the evening Tetta had her stitches removed leaving a small scar.

It took two more days to reach Kisangani. I kept the Bedfords in front for most of the way. It gave me the chance to talk to some members of the team who never came in the Land Rovers. I had noticed that Cpl Saxon had been subdued and even depressed at times during the expedition. He told me, as he drove, that whilst he was enjoying the challenge of keeping the vehicles going and the off-route driving, he missed his young family terribly and was basically homesick. I knew that several of the married men had been worried that we mightn't make it back home for Christmas. The pessimism of some of the route reports that we had received initially had undermined their confidence in our ability to get through and I was aware that one or two would have opted to have taken an easier route.

A solid green wall of jungle bordered our route to Punia and on to Yumbi. There we crossed a wide tributary of the Zaire River on an old ferry piloted by a hysterical character with a captain's hat and a wall-eye.

Kisangani hadn't changed since April and it was a relief when, after a day's rest, we got away. We drove into a storm that filled up the potholes and brought down a number of bamboo stands across the narrow road. For most of the way from now on we would be retracing the route we had taken on Phase 2. We made it to the Banalia Ferry at dusk and just caught the last crossing. As previously we paid for our crossing with a bucket of diesel. Constant flashes of lightning lit up the night sky.

Next day, two hours, after setting out we came across a Guerba Overland truck. They had taken ten days to get this far from Bangui. They said that the roads around Dulia, Aketi and Bumba were all bad but they had been hampered by a broken rear differential and were operating on front wheel drive only. Their other news was considerably more earth shattering. They had heard on the BBC World Service the previous night that Mrs Thatcher had resigned as leader of the Conservative Party. They had also heard that another fourteen thousand troops were to be sent to the Gulf. It felt strange to be so isolated that we were totally unaware of such momentous world events.

My musing was rudely interrupted when one of the team came up to tell me that the front Bedford was stuck a mile back. I found the lorry half off the right hand side of the road and bogged well in. They had been crossing a built-up culvert when it had collapsed under the weight of the vehicle. We set up a 2:1 pull with the winch rope running forward from the rear Bedford, via a pulley attached to anchor plates and back to the front Bedford. As soon as the tension was taken up by the winch the anchor pins lifted out of the sand and the stricken vehicle remained fast.

This heralded the beginning of what became a six-hour recovery. We were hindered by extremely soft sand that offered no purchase or support to the vehicle and a total absence of any trees substantial enough to be used as anchors. We tried using the Guerba lorry as an anchor but the towing hook that we had attached our winch rope to simply straightened under the strain and the cable flew free with a resounding crack. After that we tried every conceivable combination of tirfor and vehicle winch configurations. Our anchors repeatedly ripped out. Each time we did manage to move the stricken Bedford the situation became worse with the culvert collapsing further and the vehicle sinking deeper into the soft sand at the verge. Before long it was teetering on its point of balance and we were trying to dig anchor plates for a tirfor winch into the left-hand bank of the road to prevent the Bedford falling off the road.

Whilst we were engrossed with the recovery African vehicles had begun to arrive either side of the culvert. We completely blocked the route. Initially they were patient but became increasingly restless. After five hours with the end still not in sight some began to be openly hostile. Led by a couple of vociferous truck drivers they surrounded the Bedford and started shouting at us to move out of the way. I moved around the team telling everyone to do their best to ignore the crowd and carry on. This continued for a while until a couple of them made a half-hearted attempt at pulling up the tirfor anchor. The men bridled and began to finger pick-helves, sledgehammers and anchor pins. The atmosphere worsened quickly and I realised that if we didn't do something fairly quickly it could turn into an ugly brawl. By this stage the crowd were all shouting and the soldiers were beginning to face up to individuals. I yelled at them to stick together, stop anyone touching the lorry or the winches and went to confront the ringleaders. They shouted angrily that we should take down the tirfor winch and let them pass or else they would push the lorry off the road. After some negotiation I agreed that we would let small vehicles past but not lorries.

We gingerly released the tension on the tirfor. To my relief the Bedford didn't slip any further down the embankment. Several vehicles drove past, revving like mad, oblivious to the security of the precariously balanced Bedford. Some lorries then tried to make a dash for it as I had known they would. Fortunately the lead lorry bogged in before it reached us. Eventually we did manage to pull the Bedford back onto the road leaving a totally destroyed culvert and a massive hole in the embankment behind us. It had been a fraught situation on several counts and I was glad to have got clear, when all was said and done, with no major drama.

It rained during the night and continued throughout most of the day. The canopies hadn't held back the torrents of water all that well and several people had found themselves lying in pools of water. The road had pothole after pothole all of which were full of water. Several times we drove in over the bonnets of the Land Rovers. In many places we had to cut our way through bamboo that had been brought down across the track. The worst section was between Buta and Dulia but even after that conditions didn't improve significantly. The front Bedford smashed a rear brake liner when it hit a submerged log in one particularly large hole. I took little part in the day's proceedings. I had woken with a bad headache, sore throat and feeling generally weak. As the day wore on I got worse until by the time we stopped to camp I had a high temperature and was experiencing hot and cold flushes. I sat weak and shivering as the others set up camp and then crawled into my sleeping bag and lay dripping with sweat in the grip of a fever. Matthew wasn't sure if it was a virus or malaria.

I woke after a fitful night with a throbbing headache and painfully sore throat. The fever had subsided and although my temperature was still up I felt slightly better. We made slow progress all day reaching Bumba just as it was getting dark.

I gave the usual Sunday brief. With two weeks left we still had 1,200 miles to cover. The next section was reported to be bad. People were feeling the effects of continual exposure to the unhealthy jungle environment. Linda had been ill the previous night but looked a bit better. Cpl Peake was recovering from a suspected bout of malaria but looked very pale with great bags under his eyes and still complained of feeling weak. Several people had cuts that wouldn't heal and festered, constantly seeping pus. Dressings had to be changed twice per day.

Looking at the local population there were plenty of cases of malnutrition, polio, malaria and scabies. Food was scarce and the markets were empty. Much of the water was suspect. Beside the road stagnant swamps harboured all manner of diseases. Even routine illness flourished in the permanent humidity. I was also concerned about the vehicles. The mechanics were doing a great job keeping them going but I wondered how long they could continue to do so given the pasting that they were receiving. There wasn't much slack in the schedule if we hit any major problems.

We had crossed a time zone the day before and the clocks went back an hour so it was now light when we got up at 5am. We slipped away quietly, managing to avoid the immigration officials who had caused such hassle last time. Richard was driving my Land Rover and complained of a lack of power. Suddenly the engine cut out and refused to restart. The mechanics dived under the bonnet and reappeared with long faces. The timing belt had snapped. We had a spare but to fit it they needed to remove the entire front end of the engine. There was nothing for it but to push the vehicle off the road and get to work. Sgt Smith asked that everyone else left his team alone to get on with it unhindered. There was always a temptation for over- enthusiastic would-be-helpers to interfere. I sent Matthew on to Lisala with his vehicle and all of the empty jerry cans to go and get some water and any supplies he could find.

It was a fearfully hot day. With no shade the mechanics poured with sweat as they worked. We kept them supplied with drinks and otherwise stayed out of their way. By midday they had got to the root of the problem. The timing belt had snapped but much more seriously in doing so it had knocked the timing out and all the push rods had been bent into S-bends in the cylinders. Even with my limited mechanical awareness I winced as I watched Sgt Smith lay each of them along the bumper, hammer them straight, and then put them back in. There was no guarantee either that they would hold up or that worse damage hadn't been caused inside the engine.

Cpl Saxon had felt faint and semi-collapsed through dehydration. Cpl Phillips looked hot and tired and had a glaze over his eyes. Sgt Smith kept working on with a knotted handkerchief on his head, scarlet in the face, occasionally mopping his brow with an oily rag and making ever more obscene jokes. It was 3pm by the time that they had refitted everything and sorted out a coolant leak. We had lost most of the day but at least we were back on the road again, for the time being. We motored gently on, nursing the Land Rover along.

We met the others in a quarry a few miles before Lisala. They had found empty markets and no drinking water. The town was waiting for a river barge to bring fresh water to them. There had been major changes to the town. Paved roads flanked by modern street lighting led up to Mobutu's new palace. Perched overlooking the Zaire River, it was totally incongruous, a great pink villa with lines of Roman columns.

We drove slowly through in convoy hoping to spot a wrecked Land Rover from which to salvage a set of push rods, but to no avail.

Next day we limped on to Liboko and then Businga. There the route split. We had the choice of taking the shorter route to Bangui via Zongo or going by Mobaye which, although twice the distance, was reputed to be on much better roads. I put it to the mechanics. They opted for the latter. We carried on for another twenty-five miles and then stopped to camp in a roadside quarry. My fever came back so I went to bed early to sweat it out.

The roads improved steadily as we continued. We had been travelling for a couple of hours when the lead Bedford started flashing its lights repeatedly. We stopped to see what the matter was to be told that Cpl

Phillips had been taken ill all of a sudden. When he was led to Matthew's Land Rover he was barely able to walk. He moved in a drunken stagger, with sweat pouring off him and agony written all over his face. He looked seriously unwell to me but I hung back to give Matthew some space. After a while he came over to brief me. He had diagnosed a stomach ulcer but wasn't able to say how bad it was at that stage. However, if the ulcer started bleeding or burst we would have to effect a very speedy medical evacuation. With that in mind the further we continued the better the chance was of getting him to a reasonable hospital or airstrip should we need to. I offered a silent prayer of thanks that we weren't still stuck in the mud a thousand miles back. We stretched him out in the back of Matthew's Land Rover in an attempt to give him the most comfortable ride possible and where he could be kept under observation.

The jungle thinned out as we drove gently on to Gbadolite. Shortly before entering the town the track changed to perfect tarmac. Inside the town appeared as a mirage; brand new buildings, office blocks, street lights, well kept verges and ornamental flower beds, serviced by a large airport. It was quite unlike any other Zairean town that we had seen, not through any commercial reason but by virtue of being the President's birthplace. There was another large palace and an obscenely ostentatious graveyard for the Mobutu family. It was so hypocritical, sadly typical of an African dictator, with so much poverty and hardship in the country to squander funds in such unnecessary over-indulgence.

Just beyond the town we came to the border post on the southern bank of the Oubangui River. We cleared Customs and Immigration after the standard session of form filling, vehicle searches and cadeaux-seeking. A flat-bottomed ferry shuttled the vehicles across the river below a small hydro- electric dam. On the northern bank the Central African Republic formalities started in all too familiar fashion. Having ascertained that we didn't have any whisky for him the immigration official relegated us to the go-slow queue until I remembered that we still had a bottle of Malawi Gin which the distillers had given us in Lilongwe. We had to produce every conceivable piece of paperwork but they were given only the most cursory of glances. We left the official standing beside his ramshackle mud office happily clutching the bottle of gin.

We sped on our way, glad to get away from the bureaucracy — or so we thought. Seven miles down the road we were stopped at a police checkpoint. The policeman went through all of our papers again and then refused to accept our letter certifying insurance cover. Whilst I knew it was part fabrication, he certainly couldn't have so I protested vigorously. The more I argued the more adamant he became. He insisted that we send a vehicle back to the border post and get the Commissioner of

Police's authority to proceed. I sent Richard back, not trusting myself not to blow up in the face of any more obstruction. Eventually we got permission and carried on. Officialdom aside, entering CAR was very refreshing. We had left the claustrophobic jungle behind and were now able to look at rolling hills, open spaces and distant views. By comparison to Zaire it felt light and airy. Everyone perked up including Cpl Phillips who looked much better by the evening.

We packed up and got away very quickly in the morning. It was amazing how easily everything was done if there was sufficient incentive. We were stopped at a police checkpoint in Bambari but this time they gave us no problems and after a couple of Bic pens and some Joe's Basement badges had changed hands we carried on. Mile after mile slipped by. We pulled up at the Customs post on the edge of Bangui in the late afternoon. Having got all of our passports stamped we drove into the centre of town.

I despatched Matthew to stock up with fresh food and to get whatever luxuries he could and went straight to the Post Office to ring Pirbright for the first time since leaving Lusaka. They were amazed to hear where we were. I asked Richard Stanford what had happened to the mail that we should have received in Kisangani and now in Bangui. He replied that he hadn't forwarded it as the Foreign Office had said that we wouldn't get through. When I passed this gem of information on to the men outside a ragged cheer went up. He confirmed that the vehicles were to leave Douala on board the *Yolande Delmas* on 15 December. Our flights were booked for the 11th. Lastly he told me that someone called John Major had taken over as Prime Minister.

I collected everyone together and we drove out towards the campsite. The road through the market at Kilometre Five thronged with a writhing mass of humanity. We nudged our way between tradesmen plying everything from bundles of firewood, vehicle spares, ironmongery and household commodities to joints of beef, live chickens, monkeys, smoked bats and goodness knew what else. In the dusk an orange, dusty haze hung overhead.

The campsite was packed. We were beseiged by people asking us about the conditions of the roads, availability of fuel and food and advice as to which route to take. We learnt that there had just been a week of general strikes and rioting in the city that had only been broken up by troops using tear gas and rifles. Having settled in we gorged ourselves on enormous steaks of stewed beef in a red wine sauce with fresh potatoes and vegetables. It was so good to eat fresh meat. We spent the evening chatting to other people in the campsite and enjoying a few beers.

After a day of sorting out our equipment, vehicles and bodies and a fairly unbroken eating programme we left the city early on 1 December.

It was the national Independence Day holiday and we had been warned that the people were going to take to the streets and march to protest at the collapse of the economy. Extra security forces had been drafted in to deal with any rioting. We had seen them strolling around town with loaded rifles and machine guns and carrying grenades. I didn't want to be anywhere near when they started dispensing their version of crowd control. I felt certain that it wouldn't be based on our guiding principle of minimum force. At 5.30am the streets were empty save for a few bread vendors and people brushing the dirt pavement outside their homes.

We passed through the formalities with the minimum of fuss. We drove all day on good dirt roads and we ended up between Bouar and Baboua, fifty miles short of the border, having covered 330 miles in the day. We encountered several more checkpoints. At one or two of these the CAR police lived up to their reputation and gave us a hard time checking windscreen washers and even demanding to see fire extinguishers!

As we continued towards the border there was an increased Muslim influence. A significant proportion of the population had light complexions and fine-boned Arabic features. The men wore the long robes and pill box hats of the Muslim faith.

Four mind-numbing hours of belligerent bureaucracy saw us across the border and into Cameroon. Instantly the re-emergence of deep potholes, ruts and sharp bumps took our speed back down to a more familiar 20mph. The increasingly open country revealed a great proliferation of birdlife. Brightly coloured bishops, pin-tailed whydahs, hornbills, swifts, lowries and kites all perched at intervals in favoured thickets or trees alongside the road. We bounced along all afternoon through increasingly Muslim dominated villages. At the evening briefing I pointed out our progress on the map. The red line marking the route we had taken indicated 1,100 miles covered this week and 7,200 miles for the phase so far.

We drove all the next morning through dense savannah. There were wild flowers in plenty and more prolific birdlife. Having only ever seen them singly or in pairs we came upon the most unusual sight of a flight of black kites in a small copse, up to fifteen birds to a tree. At Bertoua we were advised to turn off towards Abong Mbang. The route took us back into jungle. We drove through Abong Mbang fending off the local police and on to Ayos. There we followed a raised causeway across a wide flood plain. Much of the surrounding jungle was growing out of a swamp. The villages were poor and in bad repair with mud walls crumbling away from the houses. The locals hunted to bolster their meagre subsistence. Monkeys and duiker of different sorts hung up for sale.

We stopped in an old quarry with eighty-five miles to go to Yaoundé. It seemed right that our last night out in the bush should be spent in the jungle. I found it hard to get to grips with the reality that the expedition was nearly over. The whole idea of returning to civilisation felt suddenly alien and unwelcome. Most of the men were beginning to savour the feeling of success at having nearly made it. Those of us on the permanent team became more retrospective. With the end in sight we had drawn closer together than at almost any other time on the expedition. It was an unspoken emotion reflected through our reminiscing. I was very aware of my surroundings as though trying to capture the moment. The heavy night air was alive with the chorus of crickets, frogs and the distant shrieks of monkeys.

We packed up camp and drove on towards Yaoundé doing our best to avoid the maniacal Cameroonian drivers. The local buses tore along the narrow dirt road with no regard for either their own safety or that of anyone in their way. We reached the outskirts by mid morning and then fought our way through the traffic, crowds and general madness to the British Embassy. I went in to see LtCol Simon Fordham who welcomed us effusively and then directed us to his house. There Suzy was waiting with crates of beer and Coca-Cola. Having finally made it everyone sat around looking rather shell-shocked and at a loss as to what to do.

We had a fairly lethargic picnic lunch on the lawn. Looking around at the team the cumulative effects of the journey showed in the lines of tiredness etched into haggard faces. Against the bright cleanliness of the Fordham's home I noticed just how grime-encrusted our clothes and bodies were. We got everyone settled into their accommodation with either the Fordhams or the equally long suffering BASTOS staff. As everyone else began pouring themselves into showers I phoned the Commanding Officer in Pirbright to tell him that, with the exception of the last short drive to Douala, we had completed the journey. He congratulated the team for having made it across the jungle on time. He asked whether the last phase had been worthwhile. He had expressed his concern, when we met in Zimbabwe, that it might just be a long, boring drive. I assured him that it had been quite challenging and adventurous enough.

The last few days passed in a blur of cleaning and packing kit, servicing vehicles, making arrangements for embarking the vehicles and writing endless reports, letters and newsletters. The Fordhams very kindly threw a party for us to thank all of the people from the Embassy and BASTOS who had helped us. We drove down to Kribi on the Atlantic coast for the weekend. A long, palm-lined, white sand beach with small rollers and fabulously warm water provided a pleasant contrast to the Atlantic off the Skeleton Coast. We swam, sunbathed and relaxed.

I gave a central debrief on the phase. This team had had to work as hard, if not harder, than any other on the expedition. They had pulled together and kept going through consistently uncomfortable conditions. They hadn't let the uncertainty of whether we were going to get through deter them and had coped well with the long hours of work.

Afterwards I went through individual's reports with them. Most had performed well. One or two had displayed some difficult character traits under pressure but that was all part of the experience. Linda rather took me by surprise by standing up and kissing me on the cheek once I had read out hers. It wasn't exactly the standard reaction that I was used to on delivering a military report. In the evening we barbecued some delicious white fish that we had bought off a passing pirogue.

Next morning we drove slowly to Douala. We had fitted our last sets of Panhard bushes to the Land Rovers some time ago and both vehicles were suffering from disconcertingly severe wheel wobble. As we entered the grey CAMATRANS container yard our milometers registered just under 49,000 miles of driving on African roads. We unloaded all of the equipment into a container and left the stripped vehicles parked alongside to await loading.

Colonel Simon came to see us off at the airport. Our flight had been delayed due to a combination of snowstorms throughout Europe and a strike by the French air traffic controllers. Obviously nothing had changed during the year that we had been away. Colonel Simon and I shook hands and I thanked him profusely for all that he had done for us.

On the plane I had some time to think. It was going to take a long time to digest the events of the last eleven months. I was greatly relieved that we had accomplished our aims without sustaining any serious casualties. It felt good to have achieved the things that so many people had said we couldn't. Surprisingly, I felt more empty than glad. Suddenly the challenge was over leaving a hollow anticlimax. At that moment all I could think of was starting again, planning another expedition and getting going once more. Latterly I had been running through ideas for future expeditions in my mind. North and South America offered endless possibilities and would be a logical sequel. I wondered if the army would ever sanction me to mount a Roof of the Americas expedition.

We flew back over the Sahara. Looking out through the aircraft window I could see lines of dunes bathed red in the late afternoon light. I longed to be down amongst them.

Index